THE YORK PATROL

THE
YORK
PATROL

THE REAL STORY OF ALVIN YORK AND THE
UNSUNG HEROES WHO MADE HIM
WORLD WAR I's MOST FAMOUS SOLDIER

JAMES CARL NELSON

_wm_
WILLIAM MORROW
An Imprint of HarperCollins_Publishers_

FIRST EDITION

Designed by Bonni Leon-Berman
Maps by Springer Cartographics LLC © 2020

Library of Congress Cataloging-in-Publication Data has been applied for.

ISBN 978-0-06-297588-1

21 22 23 24 25 LSC 10 9 8 7 6 5 4 3 2 1

CONTENTS

AUTHOR'S NOTE IX

MAPS XI

CHAPTER 1: THE DAY 1

CHAPTER 2: THE MAN 7

CHAPTER 3: THE PATHS OF RIGHTEOUSNESS 15

CHAPTER 4: THE SALT OF THE EARTH 25

CHAPTER 5: A TIME FOR WAR 37

CHAPTER 6: FROM PARADISE TO BATTLE 51

CHAPTER 7: TOWARD THE UNKNOWN 63

CHAPTER 8: LOST BOYS 71

CHAPTER 9: TO KINGDOM COME 83

CHAPTER 10: DAY OF DAYS, PART ONE 93

CHAPTER 11: DAY OF DAYS, PART TWO 105

CHAPTER 12: AN EPOCHAL EXPLOIT 111

CHAPTER 13: WHAT WOULD YORK DO 125

CHAPTER 14: A TIME FOR PEACE 135

CHAPTER 15: WAITING FOR THE HERO 149

CHAPTER 16: A CLEAR CONSCIENCE 161

CHAPTER 17: THE SPOILS OF WAR 169

CHAPTER 18: A ONE-MAN ARMY? 183

CHAPTER 19: HIS WAR DIARY 201

CHAPTER 20: HOW A HILLBILLY GOT A FARM 211

CHAPTER 21: AN IMITATION OF WAR 221

CHAPTER 22: OLD SOLDIERS 233

ACKNOWLEDGMENTS 247

SOURCES 249

BIBLIOGRAPHY 257

INDEX 261

AUTHOR'S NOTE

The author has retained the original spellings and punctuation in all quoted material.

My grandfather, PFC John Nelson, served in the First Division in the Great War, was severely wounded on July 19, 1918, at Soissons, and spent the next nearly nine months recuperating in a series of hospitals in France and across the United States. On April 1, 1919, he was handed $60 and his discharge papers and moved on, like most doughboys, to a fairly anonymous life devoid both of cheering parades and much appreciation for what he had done, and what had been done to him, Over There.

Still, it could have been worse; he could have returned a hero.

This book is about one doughboy who did return as a hero—as *the* hero—of the American Expeditionary Forces, and the men who were with him on October 8, 1918, in France's Argonne Forest when he performed a deed that would cause the public at large to regard him as a one-man army.

During the forty-five years between Alvin Cullum York's return to the United States and his death he was lionized, written about, and fussed over—and he did not glory in the attention so much as endure it; he endured, too, whispers and allegations that sought to spread some of his glory to those who were with him on that day when his world, and his life, changed.

The York Patrol is York's story, but it's also *their* story, and hopefully gives the best and most detailed account of what actually happened that day in the Argonne—and of how heroes are made and legends created, for better or worse.

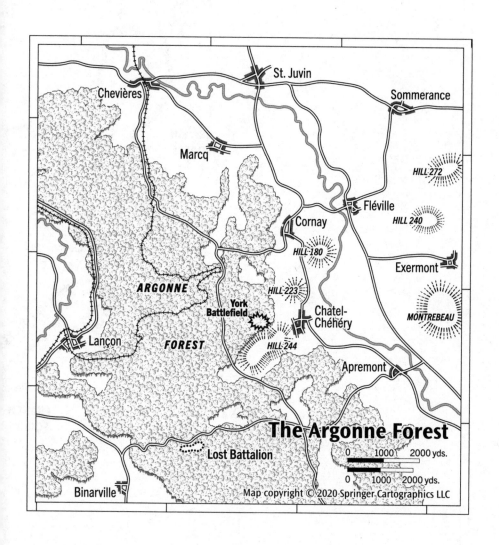

Chevières

St. Juvin

Sommerance

Marcq

HILL 272

Fléville

HILL 240

Cornay

HILL 180

Exermont

ARGONNE

HILL 223

MONTREBEAU

York
Battlefield

Chatel-
Chéhéry

Lançon

FOREST

HILL 244

Apremont

The Argonne Forest

Lost Battalion

0   1000   2000 yds.

0   1000   2000 yds.

Binarville

Map copyright © 2020 Springer Cartographics LLC

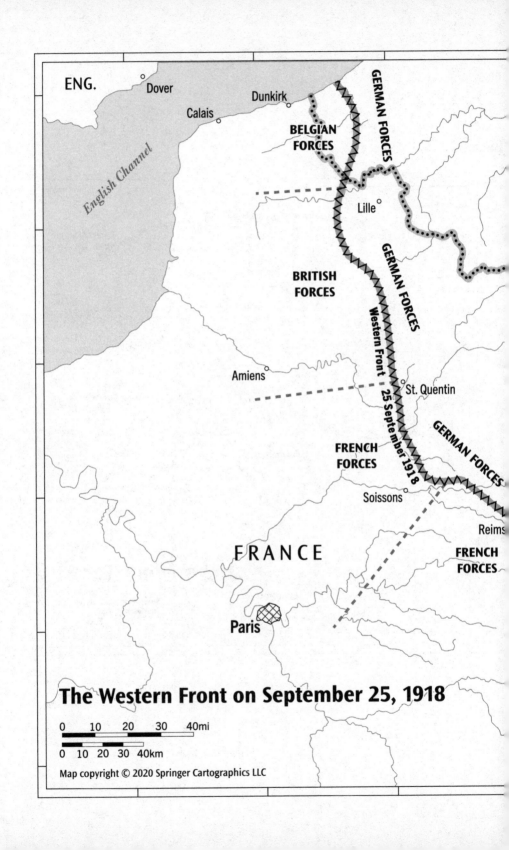

The Western Front on September 25, 1918

1

THE DAY

Thick mist clung to the wet brush, grass, and mud across the front that morning, covering the ground like soggy cotton as men woke and stirred and prepared themselves for another day of slogging, another day of battle, from the Bois de Consenvoye along the Meuse River to the village of St. Étienne, west of the Argonne Forest and east of Reims on the high ground of Champagne.

One of them was Pvt. Henry G. Costin, of Company H, 115th Infantry Regiment, Twenty-Ninth Division. When the advance of his platoon though the woods was held up by intense enemy fire, Costin, just twenty years old, gathered his automatic-rifle team and led it forward through a hail of machine-gun and mortar fire. Costin's brave act would lead to the surrender of some one hundred Germans, plus several machine guns. But he himself would not live out the rest of October 8, 1918.

Near St. Étienne, below the Aisne River and at the plain above Blanc Mont, taken in early October by the Second Division, Sgt. Samuel M. Sampler and Cpl. Harold L. Turner, both with the Second Battalion, 142nd Infantry Regiment, Thirty-Sixth Division, also advanced with their companies that morning, only to be stopped by savage German fire. Sampler, twenty-three, would later remember that of the 178 men of his company who went over the top that morning, more than one hundred were killed or wounded within minutes. The survivors dug in, while Lt. Emil Hornke rose to scout out the German line. He fell almost immediately, a bullet through his heart.

Sampler then rose, grabbed three German hand grenades that he had picked up during the advance, and stepped out and rushed toward the machine gun that had caused such damage. His first two grenades missed the nest. The last found its mark, killing two gunners. Twenty-eight others quickly surrendered to him.

Twenty-year-old Harold Turner, not far away, was also advancing under intense fire. The second-in-command of his platoon, he encouraged his men and kept them moving until only four of his original fifty-odd men were unharmed. As they went to ground, Turner noticed the German gun nest had shifted its sights for a moment, and he raced forward across twenty-five yards over open ground, at fixed bayonet. In a moment, fifty surprised, war-hardened Germans surrendered themselves and four machine guns to Turner.

Back in the Bois de Consenvoye, another Twenty-Ninth Division American hero was being made. Lt. Patrick Regan, thirty-six, led his platoon of the 115th Infantry Regiment forward into the fray, where they, like almost everyone along the line that day, were stymied by hot machine-gun fire.

With an automatic-rifle team of three, the squad made a full-frontal assault on the German machine-gun nest that was holding up the advance. Two of his men fell dead, while Regan and the other soldier were severely wounded. Undeterred, Regan pulled out his empty pistol and dashed forward right into the nest, and effected the surrender of forty Austrian soldiers and their four machine guns.

Regan, despite his wounds, continued to lead the remainder of his platoon that morning before being ordered back by his company commander.

Not far away, Sgt. Johannes S. Anderson and Company B of the 132nd Infantry Regiment, Thirty-Third Division, also faced murderous fire from the German machine guns and from their front and artillery farther ahead. The thirty-two-year-old Finnish immigrant hardly hesitated before he volunteered to reduce a gaggle of German gunners doing much of the damage.

Striking out alone, he came under severe and constant fire as he worked his way across open ground. Before long, Anderson single-handedly silenced the gun and captured it and twenty-three of the enemy.

There were other American heroes performing great deeds that day on the Meuse-Argonne front: Lt. James C. Dozier; Sgts. Gary Evans Foster, Earl D. Gregory, Thomas Lee Hall, and James E. Karnes; and Pvts. Clayton K. Slack and Calvin John Ward. Each would be awarded Medals of Honor for their exploits, two of them—Henry Costin and Thomas Lee Hall—posthumously. In all, thirteen M.O.H.s would be awarded for the day's work.

Those mentioned above account for twelve of the medals.

The thirteenth would be awarded to the one man who would emerge from a ravine near Chatel-Chéhéry as the greatest single American hero of the Great War.

HIS NAME WAS Alvin Cullum York, late of Pall Mall, Tennessee, acting corporal with Company G, 328th Infantry Regiment, Eighty-Second Division.

Though Gen. John Pershing, commander of the American Expeditionary Forces, would single out another man, Lt. Sam Woodfill of the Fifth Division, as the A.E.F.'s greatest soldier—and Woodfill would certainly get his share of accolades for single-handedly killing more than twenty-five Germans near Cunel, in the central Argonne—his acclaim would be dwarfed by the attention paid to Alvin C. York.

In postwar lore, York would be celebrated as a one-man army for his exploits near Chatel-Chéhéry on October 8, 1918, where, it was said, he single-handedly killed two dozen Germans, captured 132 more, and nabbed thirty-five machine guns to boot. When he paraded them to the American line, the story went, one American officer exclaimed in wonder, "York, I hear you captured the whole damn German army."

Magazine articles were written about York, and he was feted across the United States. Twenty-three years after the fact *Sergeant York*, a movie starring Gary Cooper in the title role, would flood movie screens around the country, further burnishing the man, the legend, and his remarkable bravery.

Released in the early fall of 1941, *Sergeant York* was a primo piece of propaganda for a nation that would find itself at war with Germany and Japan before the year was out, and it helped fuel enlistments and a nation's pride in American uniqueness, American bravery.

Like myriad westerns that graced the silver screen for twenty-five years, the movie celebrated the image of a lone hero subduing the enemy in the name of progress and democracy. It celebrated the iconic American who took matters into his own hands and, without protest or whining, single-handedly faced the nation's enemies and carried the day.

In fact, though, York was not alone that day.

He wasn't even in charge.

Seventeen American soldiers were sent to patrol behind the German lines on the morning of October 8, 1918. Only eleven came back alive. And only one returned a hero.

Wills. Donohue. Muzzi. Beardsley. Early. Konotski. Swanson. Cutting. Weiler. Sok. Johnson. Dymowski. Sacina. Wine. Savage. Wareing.

York.

This is the full story of the York Patrol, and of the seventeen men who encountered a superior force of Germans in the woods west of Chatel-Chéhéry, on the eastern edge of the Argonne Forest. Together, they subdued and captured much of that force, allowing the advance of the 328th Infantry Regiment to continue.

While taking nothing away from York and his exploits, the complete story will reveal exactly what happened that day, and track the actions not only of York but the actions of those other young doughboys who were there with him. It will also show how a deeply religious, onetime conscientious objector—a barely literate backwoodsman from a remote Tennessee valley—became, to some degree to his own dismay, an enduring national hero.

2

THE MAN

He would remember the sound of the big guns, mainly, the big guns and the rain and the rumble of aircraft slicing the dark sky overhead, and the flashes and the explosions all around and the screams of the dying as he and the others in Company G, 328th Infantry Regiment pressed their noses deep into the muddy funk holes they'd dug on the side of the Varennes-Fléville road and prayed.

"Oh, my!" he would recall. "The dead were all along the road and their mouths were open and their eyes, too, but they couldn't see nothing no more nohow. And it was wet and cold and damp. And it all made me think of the Bible and the story of the anti-Christ and Armageddon."

The scene, the sights, the sounds on that night of October 7–8, 1918, also caused Alvin York to think of home, and the roughhewn log cabin he'd grown up in in northeastern Tennessee. He remembered, too, the bucolic country that surrounded it, the Valley of the Three Forks of the Wolf River.

Amid the carnage, amid the noise, amid the smells and sounds of a world war, the valley seemed "a long, long way off," he would say.

Alvin Cullum York, who would on October 8, 1918, lead ten Americans and 132 captured Germans from those woods west of Chatel-Chéhéry, was born in Pall Mall, Tennessee. His family had lived in the Valley of the Three Forks of the Wolf River since at least the early 1800s, when York's great-great-grandfather, Conrad "Coonrod" Pile, became the first to settle in the area, having drifted in from North Carolina with several companions who continued west while Coonrod took up residence in a cave and went to work on building a cabin.

Indians still roamed the area at that time. So did bears, panthers, and a myriad of other wild creatures. The valley and its surrounding mountains and woods also in time saw their share of other tough, wild men like York's great-great-grandfather—among them Davy Crockett, who, York would say, roamed the valley on occasion and once hunted raccoons with Coonrod.

Coonrod had taken a wife, Mary Catherine Rich, while still in North Carolina, and five out of their first six children (they would eventually count twelve) were born Tarheels. While the family remained behind, Coonrod left for Tennessee to become the only white man in the Valley of the Three Forks, and he chopped and sawed and hammered and "jes went right ahead and built him a home and put in his crops," his great-great-grandson would say.

Before too long Coonrod owned much of the valley, and owned as well a general store, a blacksmith shop, and some slaves. More children came along, as did other settlers, who bought corn and whiskey from the taciturn pioneer, who by the time of his death at the age of eighty-three in 1849 had assembled quite the fortune.

But there was not always peace in the valley. A dozen years after Coonrod's death, the people in the area who lived in what came to be called Pall Mall, were divided in their sympathies between the Union and the Confederacy. As troops crisscrossed the valley, both sides pursuing each other, two groups of guerilla "bushwhackers" emerged, and soldiers on both sides—and their sympathizers— became targets for murderous reprisals.

It was during this time of bloody discord that Alvin York's great-uncle Jeff Pile was murdered by a northern bushwhacker named

Pres Huff. Jeff Pile had shown no preference for either side, but still became a target.

The killings continued even after the end of the Civil War in 1865. Not too long after its end, a former Union soldier from Michigan named Will Brooks settled in the valley, and before long he had taken up with Jeff Pile's sister Nancy, who was living on Pile ancestral land.

They soon married, and though Brooks had not even known his would-be brother-in-law Jeff Pile, he took umbrage at Pres Huff's murder of Jeff. Brooks and Huff "was always quarreling," York would say—and one day the quarreling descended into threats, as Huff told Brooks that the next time he saw him, he would kill him.

Not long after, Pres Huff was found dead by the side of a road.

Will Brooks and Nancy, who had given birth to a daughter, took off for Michigan. Unfortunately for them, a letter sent to a valley resident was intercepted by allies of Huff, and a posse made its way to Michigan and brought Brooks back to Jamestown, Tennessee, where he was put in jail.

Not for long, though. A lynch mob grabbed him from prison and tied his feet to a horse. Brooks was dragged through the streets of Jamestown and then riddled with bullets.

Will Brooks was Alvin York's grandfather and the father of Mary Brooks, York's mother.

Alvin York's paternal grandfather fared little better. Uriah York, originally from North Carolina but in later life a resident of the Wolf River valley, as a soldier had stormed the walls at Chapultepec in Mexico City in 1847, during the war with Mexico, and subsequently fought for the Union in the War Between the States.

Taking sick while with his regiment, he returned home to the valley. But the southern bushwhackers soon came for him, and he slipped out and took refuge in a canebrake. Already sick with the measles, he soon developed pneumonia and died.

"So you see that both my grandfathers lost their lives as a result of the Civil War," York would say.

Mary Brooks grew up and married Uriah York's son, William York. They lived together in the ramshackle one-room cabin in the valley, where Alvin was born on December 13, 1887, the third of the eventual eleven children they would have.

Their education was slim, and hard work was plentiful. Alvin's father set up a blacksmith shop in the same cave in which Coonrod Pile had lived while building his cabin, and Alvin helped with the blacksmithing and with farming the scratchy seventy-five acres that was but a vestige of the real estate empire Coonrod had built.

All told, Alvin's book learning amounted to two and a half months of school each year for five years. The 1900 federal census, taken when Alvin was twelve years old, listed his occupation as "farm & day labor." His older brothers, Henry and Joseph, plied the same trade. Alvin would later say he didn't read his first book until he was twenty years old.

And the Yorks were indeed poor, as were most of the residents of the valley at the turn of the century. His mother performed chores for other farmers at the rate of a quarter a day, and his father never made more than fifty cents a day. Alvin, from the age of six, pumped the bellows in the blacksmith shop, or hoed and chopped out in the fields. He did this barefoot; he didn't get a pair of store-bought shoes until he was sixteen years old, and even then was only allowed to wear them to church on Sundays.

All in all, though, Alvin had few complaints; he knew nothing else. He would say he and his siblings grew up "like a lot of little pigs"—they were sent outdoors and roamed the hills and valley, playing and hunting. "We was sort of brung up by the hair of the head," he would say.

By the time he was sixteen, York was six feet tall and weighed 160 pounds—a gangly but sinewy youth, his muscles forged from hard work in the fields and blacksmith shop and from roaming the valley in search of something to hunt. His father was an avid hunter who often neglected his work in the shop to head out to the hills and look for prey; Alvin tagged along, a muzzle-loader in hand, as they went after foxes and skunks by day and possums and coons at night.

William York, it seems, was a hard taskmaster whether in the smithy shop or on the trail of game.

"My father often threatened to muss me up right smart if I failed to bring a squirrel down with the first shot or hit a turkey in the body instead of taking its head off," York would remember. It was a lesson that would serve him well on a different continent some years later.

In 1911, however, William York died of typhus, leaving Mary York with eleven mouths to feed—and Alvin with a new responsibility to help support his mother and eight younger siblings.

He was left with the additional burden of grief over his father's passing. They had had a particularly strong bond, developed during their years of roaming the surrounding hills and the valley in search of game.

Twenty-three when William York died, Alvin "sorter went to pieces for a few years," he would remember. He took to drinking and cussing and brawling in the "blind tigers"—shacks that straddled the Kentucky border with dry Tennessee—where a man could find a drink and a fight and perhaps a woman, if one was so inclined.

The ad hoc bars were illegal, and so the proprietors painted a line on the wooden floor that carved the shack in half and left one-half in Tennessee and the other in Kentucky. If John Law showed up the boozers would simply move to the Kentucky side, and so avoid arrest. York would later compare the wild goings-on within those shacks to Sodom and Gomorrah; besides fights with hands and knives there were out-and-out murders, gambling, and encounters with women who "used to sorter drift in."

Traveling in a pack with some buddies and a few of his brothers, York before long was able to handle a full quart of moonshine—the preferred and abundant booze—a night. "We used to think it was right smart to drink each other down," he would say. "I was hog-wild."

The wild times brought the notice of the local authorities, and on one occasion Alvin and his mates had to cross into Kentucky to evade a grand jury that wanted to bring them in for questioning.

Another time, a very drunk future national hero was riding his mule when he saw a flock of turkeys fence-sitting a long way off. He took out his pistol and fired at them, and six toms were soon laid out, dead. Nabbed by the authorities, he went to court on the charge of destroying another man's property but paid for the damage and went on his way.

When he returned to that one-room shack of a cabin after a night of carousing, his mother, Mary, would be there waiting, having sat up all night worrying that he would be harmed or even killed during his drinking bouts.

Mary, who had read but one book during her life—the Bible—would gently remind her wild son that his revered father had never drunk or gambled or run with a bad crowd. And she told him he was wasting not only this good life but any chance of going to Heaven.

Alvin took at least some of this to heart, and he was beginning to question himself, and his path in life, when a preacher rode into Wolf Valley to do a little sermonizing. The Reverend H. H. Russell spoke, and Alvin listened; the good reverend spoke some more and before long Alvin was praying to God for forgiveness for his wild ways, and on January 1, 1915, he gave up drinking, and smoking, and "gambling, cussing, and brawling."

"I went bad," York said many years later. "Sowed a plenty of wild oats. I gambled and drank moonshine and rough-housed. But it never got me. I got it. I knowed deep down in my heart that it wasn't worthwhile. I was missing the finer things."

He also joined the church—the Church of Christ in the Christian Union, which had just one creed: the acceptance of the word of the Bible as written. The members were fundamentalists, to be sure, and though they in their piety and certain faith in the Good Book stood out among the more liberal Methodists that populated the valley and even Alvin York's own family, they weren't wild-eyed snake handlers or speakers in tongues. Alvin York took to their beliefs like a man deprived too long of water, and he allowed himself to be washed in the Word.

The church's pastor, Rosier Pile, guided him in the faith, and Alvin began passing on the Word in Sunday school lessons. He also took voice lessons so he could sing during services, and he would become known as the Singing Elder.

"So I was saved," York would later say.

3

THE PATHS OF RIGHTEOUSNESS

A nd so Alvin C. York was saved.

The world, not so much.

The year before York had come to Jesus, before he'd had his Awakening and renounced all vices, the world war that would make him famous was touched off by the assassination of the Austrian archduke Ferdinand at the hand of the Serb Gavrilo Princip on June 28, 1914, the deed providing the spark to a long-simmering and toxic miasma of jealousies, fears, hard feelings, and unilateral national priorities that would lead to the deaths of millions on battlefields from France to Russia.

A host of secretly negotiated treaties had led Russia to align with its Slav cousin Serbia should Serbia be attacked by either the Austro-Hungarian Empire or Germany; Russia had also committed to having the back of France should it be attacked; the British, French, and Russians had guaranteed Belgium's neutrality and promised to intervene should a foreign power attack it; and Germany, aching to establish its military dominance, would join with the Hapsburgs.

In response to the archduke's assassination, the Austrians demanded certain concessions from Serbia. Serbia acquiesced to most of them, and, it was thought, a general war could be avoided. But Austria, backed by Germany, wanted war. Military leaders in Germany, who had been preparing and dreaming about an invasion of France for decades, also wanted in.

Through the month of July cooler heads in countries across Europe tried in vain to avoid an all-out continental war, but like the gears of a fine-tuned machine mobilizations ensued. Finally, Austria declared war on Serbia; Russia in turn ordered a general mobilization of its armies; Germany thence mobilized, which alarmed France and caused it to order a mobilization of its forces.

Germany soon enough declared war on France and Russia. Britain, meanwhile, continued to hope to avoid being dragged in, but in early August 1914 German troops, carrying out the directives of a decades-old German blueprint for war on France known as the Schlieffen Plan, stepped into neutral Luxembourg and proceeded to cross into Belgium.

The plan's architects had deliberately made the violation of Belgian neutrality one of its key elements. They envisioned a quick march through Belgium, and thence a two-pronged attack on Paris from the north and east; the German forces would be given six weeks to defeat the French, and then pivot to the east and crush the expected ponderous Russian army plodding toward its rear.

The violation of Belgian neutrality brought Britain into the developing fray, and before long German troops found themselves fighting against French and English armies. By the end of the first year of what would come to be called the Great War, and later World War 1, long fronts had been established in the west in France, and across the frontiers to the east.

By 1915 millions of men were engaged, great battles had already been fought, and it would take another four long years of devastating and unceasing bombardments and futile frontal attacks against machine guns before the killing and misery ended in the defeat of the Central Powers.

Men dumbly went to their deaths like sheep at Loos, Ypres, Passchendale, and the Somme. In 1917, tired of being led to slaughter, some French troops rebelled and refused orders to go to the front.

Hiding in dank trenches, men endured mind- and body-numbing, weeks-long bombardments that in some instances were followed immediately by an attack by an enemy desperate to break through and end the stalemate. They endured, too, chemical warfare—clouds of phosgene, mustard, chlorine, and other gases that blinded and burned and insidiously suffocated soldiers on all sides.

And the mud—oh, the mud. And the cooties, the gangrenous wounds, the shell shock and the insane insistence on frontal attacks against an entrenched enemy wielding a Maxim, or a Vickers, or a Lewis machine gun spewing death at the rate of six hundred missiles a minute, and all for what? To gain at most a few yards of more mud, or none at all, as at the Somme in 1916, where sixty thousand Brits fell dead or wounded on just the first day without gaining a foothold in the German line. By late 1918, some 1.4 million Frenchmen were dead; so were an astounding 1.8 million German soldiers.

In the United States, meanwhile, people watched the events in Europe mostly with disinterest, considering it a Continental matter. The United States, though, maintained trade with Britain, and sent vast amounts of supplies and materiel across the Atlantic Ocean to its beleaguered cousin—a situation that before too long caught the eye of Germany's military leaders.

Hoping to starve England into submission, Germany began a submarine campaign, sending its wolf packs into the high seas to intercept and sink the merchant marine ships helping to feed and arm Britain. The U.S. warned Germany to stop such predations, and for a time it did.

But in February 1917 Germany again began trying to squeeze England, and sank more American ships. Germany also stirred up other trouble on the United States' southern border, sending a telegram to Mexico—it would come to be known as "the Zimmerman telegram"—that promised the eventual return of the American southwestern states to Mexico if it would perform enough mischief to keep American troops pinned there in the event of America entering the war. The contents were intercepted and revealed by the British, who hoped its revelation would prompt America to end its isolationist stance.

For President Woodrow Wilson, who had campaigned for a second term in 1916 on a promise to stay out of the war, it was the final straw. American ships were being sunk, American merchant marines were drowning, and now a loss of U.S. territory was threatened.

The storm clouds of war drifted in from the far eastern horizon and now were directly overhead. American men now would have to leave their homes in Pall Mall, Tennessee, or New Haven, Connecticut, or Chicago or New York or Denver, some of them to die, some to be maimed . . .

And some to become heroes.

THE TENNESSEE BACKWOODSMAN Alvin C. York would one day demand an explanation as to what the war was about and stage his own small revolt. But that would come after he found himself caught up in it, amid the killing and suffering and misery.

In the midteens of the twentieth century, little news of the great war filtered back to Pall Mall, Tennessee. A man could ignore it and get on with life, as the born-again York did, courting the teenaged local girl Gracie Williams—at fifteen a dozen years his junior—working at building a new highway for $1.65 a day, and "reading the Bible and doing church work."

What little he did know of the war did not interest him. "I had no time nohow to bother much about a lot of foreigners quarreling and killing each other over there in Europe," he would say. As for the United States, "I didn't think our country would get into it nohow . . . Even when we got into it in 1917, it seemed a long way off."

But then, on April 6, 1917, at President Woodrow Wilson's urging, Congress declared war on Germany. With a standing army of only some 125,000 men, it was obvious right away that some method of encouraging enlistments would be needed. After some debate, and with the uneasy memory of draft riots in some northern cities during the Civil War still lingering in the national memory, the federal government once more required all men between the ages of twenty-one and thirty-one to register for the draft on June 5.

About 9.5 million American men turned out for the country-wide registrations, standing peacefully in line and giving over their names, addresses, dates of birth, and other vital information to their local draft boards.

And Alvin York was one of these men. In late spring, just after Gracie agreed to become his wife, he became one of the millions of men who received a notice, "a little red card telling me to register for the draft." He was floored.

He had been saved, and the Bible's Sixth Commandment— "Thou shalt not kill"—was in his mind. Then, too, he knew his ancestors, his people, going back generations had fought for their country. He was, he would say later, "all mussed up. Everything was going from under me. Fight! Kill!" And here he was, having recently accepted the Gospel of "peace and love."

If he went to war and took a life or lives, he knew, he could not call himself "a good Christian." If he refused to serve, "according to Uncle Sam, I weren't a good American." What was a man to do?

He sought out his pastor and religious mentor, Rosier Pile, who happened to also be the local draft registrar. They talked over Alvin's situation and read the Good Book for guidance, but neither could get over the words *Thou Shalt Not Kill.*

So York in the end registered but sought an exemption from the

draft on religious grounds, writing on the draft form, which ironically was signed by his sympathizer, Rosier Pile, "Don't want to
fight." And on August 28, 1917, York went further and formally
applied for an exemption from the Fentress County draft board.

His appeal was denied. The board told him in effect that the
Church of Christ in Christian Union—whose parent group, the
Churches of Christ in Christian Union, had only forty congre-
gations, mostly in Ohio and Indiana, by 1915—was not a "well-
recognized" sect and had no specific creed other than the words
that are contained in the Bible.

Crushed, York again appealed, this time petitioning the Middle
Tennessee district draft board, and attaching affidavits from himself and Pastor Pile.

"But it weren't no use," York would say.

Still, he pressed on, appealing the denials until on October 6,
the district draft board reaffirmed its decision not to grant an exemption. Three weeks later, he was called in for a physical exam-
ination. Hard as steel at six feet tall and 160 pounds, he had no
chance of failing the exam. And on November 10, 1917, his worst
fears came true when he received a notice ordering him to be ready
for induction into the army on twenty-four hours' notice.

That notice arrived on November 14, and by the next day Alvin
C. York, one day to become the most famous and notorious doughboy in the A.E.F., found himself saying good-bye to his mother
and Pastor Pile and Gracie Williams. He traveled by buckboard
to Jamestown, where he spent two days idling while other draftees
were being assembled.

Trucks then brought the contingent from Jamestown to Oneida,
Tennessee—where at two A.M. on November 16, all boarded a train
headed south for Atlanta, Georgia, and nearby Camp Gordon, one
of sixteen training cantonments that were then springing up across
the nation as the country mobilized for war.

It was his first trip out of Fentress County, and his first train ride. Along the way, his thoughts turned to his predicament, and to the uncertain future he—and all the doughboys on that train—were facing. He decided he would simply bear whatever came his way, and he prayed "that God would show me His blessed will. And back there in the mountains Pastor Pile prayed and Mother prayed, too."

Placed in the Twenty-First Training Battalion upon arrival at the training camp, he spent his first morning policing the flat, red-dirt grounds, picking up discarded cigarette butts and other litter. The sound of hammers and saws rent the air around him as workers continued to erect what would ultimately be sixteen hundred wooden buildings—barracks, a hospital, a mess hall, and other structures.

After a month of performing squads right and squads left with other draftees, he was sent on to Company G, 328th Infantry Regiment, Eighty-Second Division. But he didn't stop agitating for an exemption from service. Still conflicted, York suffered under the weight of his beliefs, and the contrast between those beliefs and his impending employment as a killer.

After several months, he couldn't take the strain anymore and sought out his twenty-three-year-old company commander, Edward Courtney Bullock Danforth Jr., a 1915 graduate of Harvard University. York would remember telling him all about his conflicted mind, and how he belonged to a church that "was opposed to war and that I didn't wish to be placed in a position that it might be necessary for me to kill a fellow man. . . .

"I told him I wanted him to know I didn't believe in killing no-how, and that it worried me a-plenty."

Danforth seemed to believe he was being sincere. A couple of nights later he took York to see the 328th's Second Battalion commander, Maj. Gonzalo Edward "Ned" Buxton.

Though born in Kansas City, Missouri, Buxton, then thirty-seven years old, had deep roots in New England. He attended the Highland Military Academy in Worcester, Massachusetts, and then graduated from Brown University in 1902 before going on to Harvard Law School. In between he spent a year working as a reporter for the *Providence Journal*.

In 1912, Buxton was named treasurer of the *Journal*. His love of journalism, though, caused him to get a leave of absence from the paper when the world war broke out in August 1914. He went overseas as a war correspondent and remained there, reporting on the conflict in France and Belgium for six months before returning to the *Journal*.

Buxton had spent fifteen years in the National Guard by the time the United States entered the war in 1917. Because of his experience, he was able to enlist in the U.S. Army as a major and was assigned to the Eighty-Second Division at Camp Gordon. No military martinet, Buxton was sympathetic to York's philosophical dilemma.

Buxton was aware that Rosier Pile had written Woodrow Wilson asking for York's release from service "because I was a conscientious objector," York would later say. At the meeting arranged by Danforth, Buxton quickly asked York if he objected to fighting.

Put on the spot by his battalion commander, York was less forthcoming with Buxton than he had been with Danforth. "I answered, 'No, that's what I'm here for. But I wish you would tell me what this war is about.'"

The three sat for hours in Buxton's shadowy, spartan quarters, which was lit by a single bare light bulb swinging from the ceiling, and discussed York's beliefs. Buxton quizzed him, asking why York did not want to fight, about the creed of York's church, and when York replied to him by saying he believed in every word of the Bible, Buxton asked him where specifically in the book did it condemn war.

York replied: Thou Shalt Not Kill.

Buxton, though open to the idea of York claiming an exemption from service as a conscientious objector, first tried to sway York with his own knowledge of the Good Book. Jesus, he told York, had once said that a man who had no sword should "sell his cloak and buy one." He also asked York if Jesus would have stood by and allowed Belgium to be overrun.

Buxton also argued that the duty of a Christian was not just to serve his or her god, but to "render unto Caesar the things that are Caesar's." Buxton, York understood, was trying to convey to him "the duties of Christians to their government."

Touché. They went back and forth like that into the night, York becoming more and more impressed with Buxton's knowledge of biblical passages, the last of them being this from the Book of Ezekiel:

"Whoever heareth the sound of the trumpet and taketh not warning, if the sword come and take him away, his blood shall be on his own head. He heard the sound of the trumpet, and he took not warning, his blood shall be upon him. But he that taketh warning shall deliver his soul."

York was not yet convinced that might was right, but Buxton's arguments at least got him "to thinking more and more." Buxton, York would later say, "was the first New Englander I ever knowed . . . I was kinder surprised at his knowledge of the Bible. It made me happy in my soul to know that my battalion commander was familiar with the word of God."

Buxton finally told York to take some time and think some more, and to then come see him whenever he wanted. Alvin C. York thought and thought some more over the coming weeks, and finally realized he needed to clear his head in the woods and mountains back home. He applied for and received a ten-day pass, and headed back to Tennessee.

After a twelve-mile hike from Jamestown, he arrived in Pall Mall on March 21, 1918. He spent a subsequent night and a day out in the hills, praying for guidance, until, he would say, the Lord came to him and "gave me the assurance I needed . . . So at last I begun to see the light."

York decided that "no matter what a man is forced to do, so long as he is right in his own soul he remains a righteous man." If it was God's will that he be sent to war and even kill another man, God would "not hold it agin me." He decided that he was simply an instrument of God's will, and as long as he believed in the Lord he would be protected and absolved, no matter what.

As well, York came to see that the stakes involved in the war were bigger than his own "personal peace of soul." Though Buxton had offered him an out, York ultimately decided to remain a soldier.

He still wanted to understand why American men were required to leave their homes and fight on foreign soil. He once again approached Captain Danforth, who was with York's platoon commander, Lt. Kirby Stewart of Bradenton, Florida.

It was a vexing question, and one being asked in all quarters in America. But Danforth and Stewart were patient with York, and explained how Belgium's neutrality had been violated, how Germany thence marched into France and had to be stopped before they "overrun the world."

In effect, they explained, U.S. troops were needed to stop the Germans, stop the killing, and end the war. "We were to be peacemakers," a somewhat mollified York would say.

And so Alvin Cullum York went to war.

4

THE SALT OF THE EARTH

His fate settled—perhaps *sealed* is a better word—Alvin York for the first time took a look around him, opened up, and made an effort to get to know those he would be going to war with.

To a naïve backwoods hick like himself, they were an exotic bunch—Jews from New York, Irishmen, immigrant Slavs and Poles who had formerly toiled in the coal mines in western Pennsylvania, cowboys from the western plains, and young men of almost every ethnicity whose parents had left Europe behind for the promise of America, or who had left for the United States as teens of their own accord for a shot at the American Dream.

There were others, too, in this mélange, this great Melting Pot that was the American Expeditionary Force. There were small-town boys who'd been taken out of school and sent out to work to help support their families during hard times; farm boys whose families had scratched livings from the soil like the Yorks of Fentress County, Tennessee; factory and mill workers from the cities who had grease under their fingernails and street smarts on their résumés; and a small army of former clerks, porters, teamsters, and mechanics who, like all the others, had been plucked from Main Street, U.S.A., and off the country's grimy mean streets from New York to Denver.

The Eighty-Second Division's members came from forty-eight states—hence its nickname, the All-American Division—and 20 percent were immigrants, in keeping with the overall percentage of foreign-born in the A.E.F. as a whole. Though a wildly heteroge-neous conglomerate of backgrounds and languages, the division's enlisted men all had some things in common.

One, they were all conscripts. Two, few had had little formal educations.

That, at least, was something most had in common with Alvin York.

The men who would one day compose the York Patrol also had another element in common with one another: most were, perhaps coincidentally, from the northeast, and seven of the sixteen men who would achieve a measure of reflected glory—almost half—were immigrants.

Chief among them was Bernard Early, who was in fact an act-ing sergeant and in the lead of the patrol when it separated from its company and walked into the Argonne Forest to make a little history.

Early, an immigrant from Leitram, Ireland, had been a bar-tender in New Haven, Connecticut, before the war. Twenty-four years old when he was drafted, he was a five-foot-eight, 160-pound dervish with a temper, a fondness of the barroom wares he plied, and, despite his size, a predilection for brawling once properly lit.

"The amount of liquor he could put away was most amazing," the teetotaler Alvin York would recall of Bernie Early. "And when it came to fighting he jes couldn't be beat . . . In and around the camp, in the saloon or over in the front lines in France, it was all the same to Bernie. If there was a fight he was happy."

On the morning of October 8, 1918, Bernie found his fight, as did his best pal in Company G of the 328th Infantry Regiment: William B. Cutting.

No one in the patrol knew it yet, but William Cutting was actu-ally named Otis Bernard Merrithew, who had turned twenty-one years old in March 1917. The son of machinist Otis B. Merrithew

Sr., and Julia Riley Merrithew, he, like York, had lost his father. He also lost his mother, who died before Otis turned three. Otis Jr. was raised by his Irish-born stepmother, Nellie McHugh, who by 1910, when Merrithew was fourteen years old, was running a boarding-house in Fitchburg, Massachusetts; by that time, too, young Otis had been put to work as a "chore boy" on a nearby farm, his school-ing finished.

His stepmother appears to have been hard-living: in July 1912 she was arrested at the boardinghouse on Main Street after another woman, Nellie Winters, alleged that while visiting Nellie Mer-rithew, she was offered a drink and then was attacked and thrown through the kitchen door, striking her head on the open drawer of a bureau and suffering a laceration to her head.

The incident, the *Fitchburg Sentinel* reported, "has all the ap-pearances of a drunken brawl." Nellie Merrithew was charged with assault and battery, while Nellie Winters was charged with "drunkenness." The charges against Mrs. Merrithew were subse-quently dropped, while Nellie Winters was put on probation for six months.

A world war might ironically have offered young Otis Merrithew some refuge from the drama at the Merrithew home. One account says he ran away from home to enlist in the army, and upon his in-duction on October 3, 1917, gave his name as William B. Cutting, a name he had seen on a local clothing store.

Another later account says Merrithew always hated his first name, and had been teased about it as a child:

"'Otis,' the neighborhood kids had called him. 'Oh, Otis,' they would razz the skinny redhead. He would chase after them in a rage, but they'd dodge around him yelling, 'What's the matter, O-tis, can't you catch us?'

"'Otis, Otis Merrithew,' he mumbled under his breath and cringed at the sound of his real name." The young Otis Merrithew "smiled to himself as he remembered the few he had caught and whipped down to size." The adult Otis would display the same tenacity in asserting himself years later.

Interestingly enough, when he shipped out for France in May 1918, "Bill Cutting" gave Nellie B. Merrithew of Fitchburg, Massachusetts, as his emergency contact. Confusion over his real identity would cause some controversy after the war.

By design or geographical coincidence, the patrol was packed with New Englanders, including Pvt. Percy Peck Beardsley, who turned twenty-six in 1917 and came from a deep Connecticut pedigree. One writer would refer to him as "a Connecticut farmer with a zest for living," while another would paint a portrait of Beardsley as "quiet, grave-faced, almost phlegmatic"—a true Yankee.

Percy—known as "Perse"—grew up on the family farm outside of Roxbury, Connecticut. The acreage had been purchased in 1794 by his great-grandfather Nathan Beardsley, who had served in the state militia during the Revolutionary War and subsequently carried the honorarium "Captain."

Nate handed the farm to his son Thomas, and in turn Percy's father, Nate Jr., bought the farm from Thomas and took over operations. Described by one local as being "tough as a pine knot," he also began what would become a famed breeding site for Devon oxen, which were shown off at county fairs around New England and beyond, two of the oxen even winning a prize at the 1876 World's Fair in Philadelphia.

Nate also had a fondness for apple cider and kept twenty barrels of the stuff in the cellar. When he came of age, Percy learned to imbibe at the foot of his father; the two of them could drain a barrel in one month.

Percy would grow up hunting through the woods and fields on and surrounding the farm, and it was understood that he would one day himself take it over from his father. Percy was no stranger to either guns or good marksmanship, and was "not one to get excited and lose his head or do anything but shoot straight at the mark," a local newspaper would one day report.

In 1917, shortly before Percy headed off to war, the farm was invaded by a film crew out of New York. In tow was the silent-screen actress Norma Talmadge, who arrived "with a retinue of attendants and cameramen," one paper would report. For several weeks, the old Beardsley place became the African Transvaal, the setting for the film *Poppy*, about an African woman who marries an abusive husband, gets impregnated by an amnesiac, and then runs off to become a novelist. The Beardsley wagons and oxen got star treatment in the picture.

Three other New Englanders—two of them transplanted from their respective Old Countries, like Bernie Early—rounded out the core of the York Patrol.

Patrick "Paddy" Donohue, twenty-seven when drafted, had been born in County Cork, Ireland, and left home for the United States at the age of seventeen in 1906. His family left behind, he found work in a textile mill in Lawrence, Massachusetts, and was working there when the draft caught up to him. Another transplanted soldier from the Bay State was Joseph Stanley Konotski, a brawny, twenty-one-year-old native of Poland. Konotski enlisted at Holyoke, Massachusetts, when he heard that service in the U.S. Army could hasten his becoming an American citizen.

And there was twenty-five-year-old Murray L. Savage, of Richmond, New York, who would become the closest thing Alvin York had to a friend in the army. Another firm believer in the Good Book, Savage was working as a farmhand for his brother-in-law, Hollis McPherson, in East Bloomfield, New York, when he was drafted in 1917.

There were, of course, others to round out the patrol—Fred Wareing, of New Bedford, Massachusetts, who was twenty-six and working in a mill when he was drafted; George W. Wills, twenty-three, and twenty-one-year-old Ralph E. Weiler, the former a machinist and the latter a laborer who toiled for a junk dealer named Ike Blumenthal; another Pennsylvanian, William E. Wine, twenty-one, was working just outside of Philadelphia at the Frankford Arsenal when he was drafted.

There was also another New Yorker, Carl F. Swanson, twenty-one, who also had lost a father to a premature and accidental death when Swedish immigrant Amandus Swanson tumbled from a factory roof in 1905. Carl was just nine when the tragedy occurred, and as a teen he supported his mother and five siblings.

And there was twenty-three-year-old Thomas Gibbs Johnson, who shared a southern heritage with Alvin York and whose father was part of the boat crew that brought the body of the legendary Confederate general Thomas "Stonewall" Jackson up the James River for burial in 1863. Thomas Johnson was a student at the Virginia Commercial School in his hometown of Lynchburg, Virginia, when the draft called; he would not join the 328th Infantry Regiment until September 1918 when he arrived in France as a replacement.

In keeping with the exotic nature of the Eighty-Second Division and A.E.F., the patrol included four other immigrants—the Italians Michael Angelo Sacina and Mario Muzzi, both of them nearing thirty years old and transplants to New York City. And as well there was the twenty-seven-year-old Pole Maryan Dymowski—who left his job at the Crescent Belting and Packing Company when drafted—and the Russian Feodor Sok; they had found new lives respectively in Trenton, New Jersey, and Buffalo, New York. (Of Sok, York would say, "For a long time I didn't even know that was his real name. I thought it was his nickname.")

One more soldier figured in the patrol's future. That was Sgt. Harry M. Parsons, a former actor and a "natcheral-born entertainer," York would remember. Parsons, twenty-seven, would lead the men in song while on long hikes, and preferred to use a soft glove on them—most of the time. But when Parsons needed to add a little violence to his repertoire, "he made a right-smart job of it." York also said, "And when he did that somebody went down, and it was never him."

Looking back, York had nothing but admiration for his new acquaintances in his platoon, calling them "jes a bunch of hard-living, hard-fighting doughboys; always spoiling for a scrap.

"But when you got to know them, they were jes about as fine a bunch of buddies as ever got together . . . and when they got into it over there they jes kept on a-goin'." He also said, "They could out-swear, out-drink, and out-cuss any other crowd of men I have ever knowed."

In fact, though he made friends quickly with Murray Savage, once he returned from his soul-searching hajj in his beloved woods and mountains of Tennessee, York found his new mates worried about whether he would have their backs once they were thrown into a world war—and were suspicious in general of his potential as a soldier.

"They knowed I was a conscientious objector, and they hadn't much use for that," York would say of his platoon mates. "They jes didn't understand. Sometimes they got to teasing me most awful bad, but I never done any arguing with them . . . I didn't want to fight nobody and least of all American doughboys."

Without evidence, Otis Merrithew would later claim that York had been punished while in training because of his qualms about killing. And York and Early even fought over the issue until, at one point, "Bernie threatened to blow his brains out, and that had ended the argument," Merrithew remembered.

Merrithew would also recall York as a quiet man whose few utterances included moaning over his "gal friend"—Gracie—back home. Patrick Donohue remembered York as "a quiet, easy-going fellow. He never had much to say."

Through the winter and into the spring, the men of the York Patrol and the rest of the Eighty-Second Division trained at Camp Gordon. Draftees had begun arriving on September 5, 1917, and had instantly begun training under the charge of regular army men who drilled not only privates but the newly graduated junior officers fresh from officers' training schools.

Meanwhile in Europe, where men on all sides were dying by the thousands in their stinking, rat-ridden trenches or in suicide leaps into full-frontal assaults against entrenched machine guns and heavy artillery, the Allies—France and Britain—were almost despairing of victory, and urged the United States to send as many men Over There as was possible.

American military minds had at first believed that five hundred thousand men would be needed, but that figure soon swelled to one million and then beyond. Four million young Americans would be in uniform by the time the war ended, half of them in France.

In June 1917 the first contingent of Americans—the First Division, which at that time was heavy with regulars—sailed for France, and began training under the supervision of the Blue Devils, veteran French soldiers who instructed men in building trenches, throwing hand grenades, using a bayonet, and other martial arts.

The Allies, veterans of three years of almost-stationary war, leaned toward the defensive. But playing defense was not in the American playbook, and Gen. John Pershing, commander of the American Expeditionary Force, had no intention of wasting his men in the smothering bombardments of the trenches. He instead was certain his exuberant, young soldiers would take little time in gaining ground and breaking the stalemate on the Western Front.

First, though, draftees had to be whipped into shape—a difficult task at first, considering the dearth of equipment available in the camps. At Camp Gordon, men were issued the "Camp Gordon 1917 Model" rifle—a five-foot-long stick that the men carried in drill. Eventually, production of military materiel would catch up, and most doughboys would be issued Springfield rifles, bayonets, helmets, gas masks, and other items necessary to warfare on the Western Front.

By the latter part of October, those first draftees to arrive were packed off to different divisions, each company being left with its officers and noncoms, and a new wave of recent inductees began to arrive: Alvin C. York and his new "buddies" were among these.

The Eighty-Second Division's four regiments—the 325th, 326th, 327th, and 328th—set up schools to teach the use of the bayonet, the gas mask, and the hand grenade, and, once real rifles arrived in February 1918, even sniping. Where men had drilled in their street clothes, uniforms began to flood into the camp as fall progressed, "and soon the percentage of straw hats and tennis shoes at dress parade was on the decline," a regimental history says.

About the time the first rifles arrived, so did French and British veterans, sent overseas to instruct the men. The French were insistent that only hand grenades and the "Chautchaut"—a light machine gun—would be needed on the front. The Brits, meanwhile, were certain that a bayonet, a trench knife, and a gas mask were all that were needed to win the war in the trenches.

All in all, the instruction imparted the idea that the rifle was merely a holder for a bayonet. Under General Pershing, however, American doctrine relied and would continue to rely on marksmanship with the rifle, and plenty of work was put in at the rifle range.

Pershing had no intention of allowing his troops to be bogged down in trench warfare as the Allies and Germans had. He believed in a philosophy of open warfare—that once American troops had been trained in and inured to life in the trenches, they'd be able to bust out and break through the German lines.

To help effect this, he increased the size of American divisions to 28,500 men—double the size of the typical Allied or German division—believing that a larger mass of men working as one unit and under one divisional staff would be better able to smash the German line and carry through. Each division contained a brigade of two regiments each, and each regiment had three battalions made up of four 250-man infantry companies. Each regiment also carried four smaller machine-gun companies.

But, as previously noted, the rifle held sway, and it was for that reason that millions of nascent doughboys spent hours on the rifle ranges. The efforts at Camp Gordon bemused Alvin York, who had grown up with a squirrel gun in his hands and become an adept marksman. Even with a newfangled Springfield, York excelled; his platoon mates, many of them immigrants from the big cities, tended to struggle.

"They missed everything but the sky," he would say. "It weren't no trouble nohow for me to hit them great big army targets. They were so much bigger than turkeys' heads."

The men continued with trench building, the laying of barbed-wire entanglements, and other such arts that might come in handy in France. They also donned gas masks and experienced the "gas house," an enclosure filled with suffocating gas, to get an idea of how they would react when faced with the real item on the Western Front, where it had first been employed in 1915.

Such work was going on at camps across the nation, from Camp Grant in Illinois to Camp MacArthur in Texas to Fort Lewis in Washington State, all efforts aimed at getting the army up to speed and to one day flood France with able-bodied, eager American fighting men and defeat, in doughboy parlance, "the Hun," or the "Boche," and Kaiser Wilhelm, and turn back the Teutonic horde.

And across the country, in cantonments far and wide, rumors arose and persisted about going Over There; that rumor made it to Camp Gordon in early April, just as Alvin York was returning to the camp after having had his come-to-Jesus moment in his beloved Tennessee hills.

He returned in late March 1918 knowing it was likely he and his mates would soon sail for France, but he would say his meditations and soul-searching also had left him confident that the Lord would watch over him and allow him to return to Pall Mall and Gracie and a future life. "I almost felt sure of coming home, for the Lord was with me," he would say.

The 328th Infantry Regiment spent two weeks marking and packing equipment for the coming journey, and when the order to board trains for New York came on April 19, 1918, the sometimes dreaded, sometimes longed-for journey across the ocean to France began.

A "motley crew" of "tear stained wives, mothers, sisters, sweethearts and others of varying relationship" were at the station to see the men off on their great adventure, one source says. There was no such send-off for Pvt. Alvin C. York, who watched quietly and unnoticed by the civilian throng as the troop train chugged from the depot. At that moment he was just another seemingly insignificant cog in a giant war-making machine, a nobody who had riled his superiors and some of his platoon mates with his deep reservations about killing another man.

5

A TIME FOR WAR

Death was on his mind that night; his death, impending perhaps, who knew? In just a week the man who hadn't left Tennessee until he was twenty-nine years old was to board a ship and travel the wide Atlantic to France to scrap with the dreaded Hun, the Boche, the Germans, who at that moment were battle hardened and attacking, while the Allied forces facing the great gray tide were on their heels and praying that it might not be too late.

"If I get killed you can say that I Died that you might stay free," Alvin York wrote to his fiancée Gracie Williams on April 23, 1918. "I wish that me and you would of married when I was in home then I would of knowed that you would of Ben took good care of and you would have had plenty of money . . . If I never get back you would of got $10,000 . . . that would of done you as long as you live."

That night Alvin York was at Camp Upton, New York, in the midst of several thousand other young Americans wondering what they would face in France, and whether they might ever return to their lives. York had previously accepted that his Lord would watch over him and get him back in one piece; on this night he didn't sound so sure.

At that moment Americans had already died in battle, the first three at Seicheprey during a raid-in-force by German commandos on the dark night of November 2–November 3, 1917. Cpl. James Gresham and Pvts. Merle Hay and Thomas Enright, all of Company F, Sixteenth Infantry Regiment, First Division, were slain in their filthy, rat-ridden trench, and news of their deaths spread quickly among the four American divisions that were then in-country.

The First Division had indeed been the first: first to sail the sea to France, first to enter the front lines, and now, first to lose infantrymen in battle. It had been followed by the Second, Third, and Twenty-Sixth Divisions beginning in the fall of 1917, but by the first few months of 1918 only 175,000 American soldiers had been transported overseas, and the great majority of those were still learning the art of the Great War in quiet sectors of the front.

Still, the sheer specter of hundreds of thousands of Yanks arriving in France gave the German High Command pause. The Germans, who had largely given up the offensive and pulled back east during the course of 1917 to straighten and shorten their lines, were during those early months of 1918 planning a huge offensive aimed at splitting the French and British forces in the Somme region and rolling the English into the sea before America could put both feet into the fray.

Germany was helped enormously by the Russian Revolution in late 1917, and by a treaty between Russia and the Central Powers that took Russia out of the war. Eighty divisions were thus freed to turn west toward the Allies' twisting trench lines, and some of these took part in what came next.

Following an intense twelve-day bombardment of the Allied front between Ypres and St. Quentin, on March 21, 1918, the Germans launched their massive attack and within days had pushed the British back, in two days killing an untold number of Tommies while capturing twenty-one thousand more.

It was, in sum, a disaster for the Allies.

Panicked and desperate, they appealed to A.E.F. commander Gen. John Pershing to send the Americans to plug the line. Pershing had steadfastly refused through the winter to release his troops piecemeal into battle, as his sights were set on creating a homogeneous American army that would operate on its own. But with the French locked in savage conflict to the south and the Brits steadily retreating in the north, and huge German guns now raining their loads into Paris from points seventy-five miles from the front lines, the hour at last had come. Pershing, hat in hand, went to Field Marshal Ferdinand Foch, commander of the Allied effort, in late March and told him: *All that I have is yours.*

Foch could only hope that it wasn't too late to stem the tide, but soon enough Americans were leaving their quiet practice sectors and moving to meet the threat.

ALVIN YORK AND the men of Company G, 328th Infantry Regiment would join the fun soon enough, but at the end of April they were still at Camp Upton, waiting.

In the meantime, the unit was besieged by family members and friends of some of the men who hailed from New York and the New England region—among them Bernard Early, Carl Swanson, and Percy Beardsley. Their relatives implored the regiment's leaders to allow their boys passes so they could spend some precious, and perhaps last, days together. After some hesitation, passes ranging from twenty-four hours to thirty-six hours were granted.

Bernie Early made the quick trip up the Atlantic shore to 191 Franklin Street in New Haven, where he visited with his sister, Beatrice. Percy Beardsley hotfooted it to his family's Connecticut farm in Roxbury, where his father, Nate, awaited with a mug of hard cider. Carl Swanson hustled to New York City and a reunion with his mother, Carrie, and several siblings.

Some overstayed their visits and were left behind when their regiment entrained from Camp Upton for Boston on April 30, and as well when the unit sailed for France aboard the H.M.S. *Scandi-*

navian the next day. Early and Swanson were two of these dere-licts; each would ultimately find their way across on different ships in the coming days, as Swanson went over on May 11 aboard the S.S. *Themistocles*, and Early sailed on the S.S. *City of Brisbane* on May 7.

Meanwhile, the *Scandinavian* headed first to New York to join fifteen other troop transports and the cruiser S.S. *San Diego*, which were to protect the ships on their perilous ten-day journey through the sometimes submarine-infested waters of the Atlantic. Lifeboat drills added to the sense of dread for many aboard, but the trip was largely uneventful, save for the rampant rumor that a torpedo had at one point skipped between the ships without hitting anything.

On the morning of May 15 a squadron of destroyers met the ship off the coast of England, and on the next day the *Scandinavian* heaved to in the port of Liverpool. From there, Alvin York and the Second and Third Battalions of the 328th hiked to Knotty Ash Rest Camp—York would refer to it as "Knotteash"—outside Liverpool, a reception by cheering locals who lined the way putting a bounce in each man's step.

Their moods were not buoyed, though, by the sight of the numerous British soldiers that were convalescing at a camp just a few hundred yards from the battalions. Many of the Brits had lost a limb or more, and were happy to regale the fresh-faced Americans with the gory details of their experiences in battle.

At Knotty Ash, their diet changed, as British rations of jam, cheese, and tea replaced fresh beef and coffee. On May 17, both battalions of about one thousand men each entrained for Southampton on the southeastern coast of England, from which the first battalion, Headquarters Company, and Machine Gun and Supply Companies had left the previous day for Le Havre on the French coast.

After a pleasant crossing of England—which in the spring resembled "one beautiful picturesque Garden," one doughboy would write—each man received a letter of welcome signed by King George V, and were further uplifted by more cheering locals who lined the station tracks as they pulled in.

The Second and Third Battalions of the 328th Infantry arrived at Le Havre on May 20, crossing on the H.M.S. *Viper*, which was "more like a bucking mule than a boat" to a quickly seasick Alvin York. Le Havre brought another realization by the men that they were, indeed, on their way to a great war: at the docks, a long hospital train rolled up carrying more wounded on their way home to England. "One couldn't help but wonder how long it would be before he would be coming back in that manner," the regiment's history says.

After arriving in Le Havre, the men of the Eighty-Second Division learned they were to be placed under the command of the British and serve with British troops. The men were ordered to turn in their American-made rifles and were handed Lee-Enfields, the standard issue to British and Commonwealth troops during the Great War. York, who had grown accustomed to his gun, was not happy with the switch.

They were also told to throw away a goodly portion of the 250 pounds of equipment they had been allowed to carry to Europe. Each man would be allowed just fifty pounds of equipment and materiel, that number including a bed roll.

And that first evening they found themselves crammed twenty-five men to one smallish tent. The men, one source says, managed to fit inside "by putting their feet together near the center pole and their heads outside the tent, the process of turning over being done 'by the numbers.'"

On May 22, the regiment boarded trains and soon were rolling northeast through France, their destination the northern end of the Somme sector. Here, they went into reserve behind British troops who were holding the front line. On the twenty-fourth of May, Gen.

Douglas Haig, the commander of the British forces, inspected the troops. John Pershing, too, visited the division.

The 328th began rotating men into trench life in quiet sectors, where the threat of attack was low but the experience of digging, stringing wire, manning machine-gun posts, and watching the far-off flashes of the big guns was invaluable. Meanwhile, the First Division was, once again, the first to act.

In mid-April, its men entrained for Paris, and then were hustled northward to the vicinity of the tiny hilltop village of Cantigny in Picardy, where part of the great German offensive had bogged down in the face of severe resistance by French Colonial troops. The Germans held the village, while the First and Second Brigades of the First Division entered the front lines to the west and through most of the month of May began digging, laying wire, reconnoitering, and partaking in artillery duels.

On May 28, 1918, America finally went on the offensive when the Twenty-Eighth Infantry Regiment rose from its trenches at 6:45 A.M. and advanced to the east, sweeping away opposition in front of and in the village and then pushing five hundred yards beyond, where men furiously went to work digging in under heavy bombardments of shells and machine-gun bullets.

They endured this until May 31, when the regiment was relieved and the makeshift lines were taken over by the Sixteenth Infantry Regiment. The Twenty-Eighth had lost 13 officers and 185 enlisted men over its four days of battle, and another 32 officers and 837 men had been wounded or gone missing; the line, however, would be held for the duration of the war.

Farther south and east, other Americans went into action just six days after the taking of Cantigny. A new German drive launched on May 27 was moving south and west toward Paris, and by early June was just thirty-five air miles from the capital. Diverted from a planned relief of the First Division at Cantigny, the Second

Division—half marines, half army regulars—were sent to meet the threat, and elements of the Third Division took up defensive posts on the Marne River at Château-Thierry.

While the men of the Third Division beat off an attempted crossing of the Marne in early June, the Marine Fifth and Sixth Regiments slowly gathered in front of a kidney-shaped patch of woods called the Bois de Belleau, a former royal hunting ground. As Germans infiltrated the wood and began entrenching, the marines faced off against them, spreading their line from the northwest to the southeast on bare ground.

On the morning of June 6, the marines' Fifth Regiment went into action, wading through knee-high wheat and attacking the northern edge of the wood. That assault stymied, more marines from the Sixth Regiment went in on the southern end, while a single company—the Ninety-Sixth—attacked and took the strategic village of Bouresches at the far southern end of the wood.

By the end of June 6, the Marine Fifth Regiment had lost 333 marines dead, wounded, or missing—the largest one-day loss of life for the marines until the bloody 1943 assault on the atoll of Tarawa in the Pacific.

Fighting raged in front of and in the wood through most of June, until finally on the twenty-sixth an officer reported, "Belleau Woods now U.S. Marine Corps entirely." The cost of taking and holding the wood and assaulting the nearby village of Vaux was enormous: between June 1 and July 10, 1918, the Second Division's casualties consisted of 217 officers and 9,560 men either killed, wounded, or gassed.

Slowly, America was becoming involved in the maelstrom that reigned on the Western Front. But Cantigny and Belleau Wood were just the harbingers of battles to come, battles that would rage in France and cost more and more American lives through the last half of 1918.

In time, the war would come for Alvin York and his company mates, but as May turned to June, and the First, Second, and Third Divisions were being bloodied and coming out victorious from Cantigny to Château-Thierry, the Eighty-Second Division and other American units continued to train, and sample life in small towns across northern France, and hike—oh, the hikes.

Under the aegis of the British, even the simple act of bathing involved long treks. The men marched for two hours over hot and dusty roads, then at the bathhouse they were "allowed so much time to get in the bath, timed as we washed, timed as we rinsed, and timed as we dressed," one soldier would recall. After hiking all the way back, "we were not in much better shape than when we started out."

While on short leaves, the doughboys snapped up the local wines as if they were afraid they would run out. They also bird-dogged the local mademoiselles, and released other pent-up energies in café brawls, going at each other with "fists and belts," York would say.

In a local café one night, "one of the Irish boys said he didn't believe the Poles could fight nohow," York would remember. That Irishman might have been the pugnacious Bernie Early; in any event the place was torn apart as the two went at it, stopping only when the military police were called.

York, who had long since given up drinking and fighting, mostly hung by himself, reading his Bible and writing in the diary he was keeping, against regulations. He spent time, too, with twenty-five-year-old Cpl. Murray Savage, one of the few men in Company G who, as noted, shared York's deep Christian faith.

They also shared the devastation of losing a father, in Murray's case John Savage, a farmer who, learning from a doctor that he had a terminal disease, put his affairs in order and "made all the arrangements for his burial" before expiring at the age of fifty-seven on New Year's Day, 1915, a newspaper would report. Murray would suffer another blow shortly before entering the service when his twelve-year-old sister, Leona, died in 1917.

Further tragedy awaited the Savage family of Richmond, New York, before the year would be out.

AFTER THREE WEEKS of training under the British, orders suddenly came for the 328th Infantry Regiment's men to turn in their British weapons and kit, and they were once more handed American equipment. On June 16, the Eighty-Second Division boarded trains and headed first for the outskirts of Paris, then east toward Toul, above which the Twenty-Sixth Division, largely consisting of New Englanders, were holding the line on the southern face of what was known as the St. Mihiel Salient—also called the Lagny Sector—a triangular section of France that saw vicious back-and-forth fighting in 1914 and 1915 but since had largely become a rest area for various German divisions.

The men of the Eighty-Second Division arrived near Toul—which is ten miles west of Nancy—on June 16, and took to the roads, marching north for the villages of St. Étienne and Lucy; as they trained in the area rumors soon spread among the green Americans that they would see the Real Thing—real duty in real front-line trenches in an "active" sector, and no more pussy-footing around the backwaters of the war.

On the night of June 25, the Eighty-Second Division began the process of relieving the Twenty-Sixth Division, always a delicate maneuver when the slightest sound or appearance of movement brought searching German artillery to bear. And the sound of the big guns welcomed the men as they trudged forward, passing over second-line trenches and finagling their way across fields of barbed wire.

There were plenty of graves, too, somber reminders of where they were and what lay ahead, for some of them at least.

The 328th relieved the 104th Infantry Regiment on the left-center of the sector between Bouconville and Rambucourt, just to the southwest of Seicheprey, where the First Division had held the line through much of the winter, and where in April 1918 the Twenty-Sixth Division, which had relieved the First, suffered more than 600 casualties—including 81 men killed in action and another 187 men captured or missing—when a handpicked body of 2,800 Germans staged a raid-in-force on two companies from the 102nd Infantry Regiment.

As the Second Battalion approached its assigned trenches in the night, walking almost blind through the inky night, the men came under fire that was intended for the front line ahead of them but missed and passed over into its ranks.

The officers steadied the men, telling them that "they were only stray bullets; that they would not injure us, and not to mind them," York would recall. One "Italian boy" grinned at this and said it didn't matter if the bullets were stray or not: "If they hit us they would do jes as much damage as if they was aimed at us."

The whine and smack of bullets, the bitter smell of cordite, Very lights floating overhead like fireflies, bodies everywhere; they were indeed entering an active sector.

The Second Battalion of the 328th took over the five-thousand-yard front on the far left of the Eighty-Second's position, and was bounded on the left by French troops and on the right by the 327th Infantry Regiment. To their front was the looming visage of Mont-sec, a four-hundred-foot prominence from which German spotters could observe the enemy and direct artillery fire and air reconnaissance when needed.

The regiment was close to the base of the mountain, and atop it German spotters used powerful binoculars to scan the American line, searching for a hint of movement—the top of a tin hat, a careless doughboy letting his guard down—and when the spotters located a target, they brought down the wrath of the Fatherland in a cascading, probing bombardment.

"When any movement or any new camouflage or any signs of new trenches having been dug were detected by the observers from the top of this mountain they would signal the locations to their artillery and from their maps they would begin shelling," Frank Holden, a lieutenant with the Second Battalion's Company H, would recall. "This mountain was ever our day ghost."

The reliefs completed on June 29, the men in the front line began the "dreary monotony" of trench warfare, which the 328th's history would describe as sitting in a trench for days "gazing intently at the enemy lines and never see anything to shoot at, chow details, wire stringing details, trench digging details, patrols every night with monotonous regularity and at the end of several weeks to be holding the same positions with nothing apparently accomplished."

As the French said, *C'est la guerre . . .*

York and his mates did their share of said patrolling, and York was put in charge of an automatic-rifle squad. The men were handed and shown how to load and fire the French Chautchaut— York would call them "sho-sho rifles," or "portable machine guns"—heavy, clumsy automatic weapons that took three men to carry and operate and carried an eighteen-round clip.

"All you could do with them was make a lot of noise, and waste a heap of ammunition, and hope for the best," York would remember.

Being in an active sector, the men were subjected to the usual, numbing inconveniences of trench life in the Great War. German snipers were on constant lookout for targets, attacks of mustard and other gases forced the men to don stuffy, blinding masks, and artillery bombardments tore up what was left of the barren, muddy ground and shattered men's souls.

Not Alvin York's, however. Amid the shelling and the heaped dead bodies and the rank, rotting smell of death and the sting of acrid smoke and the weeklong rotations into the front lines, he was thinking, and praying.

"I believed in God and in his Promises . . . Up there in the front line I knowed as I had never knowed before what a comforting thing religion is. So I clung to my faith all the time."

But while at the front, there was a lot more than just sitting around philosophizing. Patrols were frequent and aggressive, and the doughboys explored deep into no-man's-land, leading to clashes with the Germans. As well, the patrols sometimes brought hell back from their forays, as German artillery awoke from its slumber upon discovery of American soldiers prowling in the dark and let loose on the American trenches.

On August 4, one such patrol by two companies of the 326th Infantry Regiment got into a hot firefight six hundred yards into no-man's-land; upon their return two sections of their trenches were deluged with German artillery rounds, and seventeen men were killed and fifteen were wounded.

"The trouble with our boys . . . was they would want to go out on top of the trenches and start something," York would say later. "They was wanting to get into it and get it over . . . They didn't want to lay around and do nothing . . . They was always wanting to go over the top—and keep a-going. They shore were ambitious."

Some from what would come to be known as the York Patrol participated in one particular raid led by their platoon commander, Kirby Stewart. Chafing at not having yet captured any Germans during the myriad patrolling, the 328th Infantry Regiment's commander, Edward Buxton, ordered Stewart and another lieutenant to choose fifty men from different Second Battalion platoons and follow him into no-man's-land one dark night.

Hoping to catch the Germans by surprise, the patrol crept ever closer to the German wire that had been laid to repel just such an incursion. Suddenly, a German trench-mortar shell exploded overhead, followed by a cracking, bright flare. German machine guns swept the ground in front of the Americans as they ate dirt and tried to make themselves small. Rifle fire coming from the trench soon cackled, joining the nightmarish cacophony. All the doughboys could do was remain in place and wait for orders from Buxton. He and his two subordinates quickly agreed that any chance of surprise at that point was gone, and so the patrol was ordered to about-face and crawl for their lives in the dark intervals when the brilliant, burning flares had flamed out.

Kirby Stewart, meanwhile, bravely crawled about fifty yards away from the group and emptied his pistol into the air in the hope of drawing German fire from the patrol. "When Lieutenant Stewart joined his platoon again he had two bullet holes in his overseas cap, one where the bullet entered and the other where it went out," Frank Holden recalled. Stewart et al. made it safely back to their lines.

In case there were any lingering doubts that they were now at war, there were also some casualties incurred in the trenches, some from friendly fire. Nervous sentries on duty in the black, dark French nights would shout *Halt* and shoot in the same motion, usually missing but on occasion finding a friendly target out in the night.

Other Company G men suffered accidental wounds, including Pvt. John D. Holt, who was evacuated to a hospital for an undetermined injury, and Pvt. Earl W. Keating, who broke one of his legs while on patrol outside of Bouconville in July. All told, the Eighty-Second Division incurred 352 casualties, including one officer and 43 men who were killed in action or died of wounds, while in the sector.

For them, the war was over; for Alvin York and the rest of Company G, it was only beginning.

6

FROM PARADISE TO BATTLE

As the 328th Infantry Regiment manned the trenches at Seicheprey, the war turned.

In the early-morning hours of July 15, 1918, the Germans opened a new offensive eighty miles to the west of where the Eighty-Second Division held its line, punching a hole between Reims and Soissons and quickly hurtling across the Aisne River and south toward Château-Thierry on the Marne River. Once again, the Germans had the initiative, and once more it appeared that Paris might fall.

But where others saw looming catastrophe, Field Marshal Ferdinand Foch and Gen. John Pershing saw opportunity. The lightning advance of the Germans had created a bulge that hung like a sagging balloon between Soissons and Reims, and both men aimed to move fast and pierce through it with a counterattack of their own. At best, a surprise assault across the neck of the bag below Soissons could entrap the enemy forces; at the least, the Allies would regain the initiative with a successful offensive and cause the Germans to withdraw.

To that end, two American divisions—the First and the Second, whose men were battle-hardened veterans now—were turned over to Foch and with the colonial First Moroccan Division were made part of the French Tenth Army. On July 16, all were put on the move toward a carefully selected jump-off point in the Retz Forest below Soissons, and on the night of July 17–July 18 they assembled in a driving rainstorm to await the 4:35 A.M. start on July 18.

Strung out from north to south with the First Division to the north, the Moroccan division in the center, and the Second Division on the south, the assaulting forces jumped off heading east and followed a light rolling barrage. By midmorning great gains of up to four miles through the German lines were made, the Germans not having had much time to dig in during their brief stay within the pocket.

The great battle—it would come to be known as the Battle of Soissons—raged through July 18 and over the next three days, until finally elements of the First Division managed at great cost to capture the village of Berzy-le-Sec, high above the Crise River, on the morning of July 21, 1918. With that, the great surprise offensive came to an end.

With that stroke, the railway and highways supplying the pocket were cut, and a general German withdrawal began. In ensuing days, other American divisions—the Fourth, the Thirty-Second, the Twenty-Sixth, the Twenty-Eighth, and the Forty-Second—pushed north from Château-Thierry to Fismes, west of Reims. Hard fighting lasted through the month of July and into August until the hanging pocketful of Germans was squeezed off.

The battle would be remembered as the "Turning of the Tide" on the Western Front of the Great War, and the Germans would only lose more and more ground to the Allies as summer faded into early fall.

ALVIN YORK, PERCY Beardsley, Bernard Early, and others in Company G of the 328th Infantry Regiment continued to hold the line on the southern face of the St. Mihiel Salient until the Eighty-Second Division was relieved by the Eighty-Ninth Division between August 5 and August 7.

Reliefs were often fraught with danger, and this one was no exception. Any noise—a cough, the clank of a canteen, the collective trudging and stumbling of thousands of men coming and going in the night—brought the ire of German machine gunners and artillery. As well, there was always the chance of a sudden German attack being launched out of the blackness, just as men were leaving the protection of the lines.

Indeed, the Germans launched just such an attack on the night of August 7. As troops of the Eighty-Ninth Division were entering the positions formerly occupied by the Eighty-Second's men, the Germans bombarded the front line with gas shells. Seventeen Eighty-Second Division machine gunners awaiting their own relief were made casualties, and the Eighty-Ninth suffered "very heavy casualties," according to the Eighty-Second's history.

Still, the six-week stay in the trenches had introduced all to the monotonies and horrors of the war, to gas and snipers and bombardments of artillery and mud and "cooties"—lice. Upon being relieved, each man was more assured of his ability to endure and survive, and, as one veteran would write, "that feeling of confidence which differentiates the experienced soldier from the rookie."

Part of the Eighty-Second Division now entrained south toward Château-Thierry on the Marne River, but soon was recalled and rejoined the division, which was ordered to relieve the Second Division around Pont-à-Mousson, at the eastern apex of the St. Mihiel Salient.

Bounded on the east by the rushing waters of the Moselle River, the area was also known as the Marbache sector. It was considered a "bon" sector, in the parlance of the doughboy; outside of a few shells being lobbed back and forth across the lines, and the constant threat of a raid by the so-called Hindenburg's Traveling Circus—a unit of German infiltrators who had carried out the attack on the 102nd Infantry Regiment in April—the area offered some peace for men just in from the front lines.

Though mountains of barbed wire were strung in the no-man's-land between the American and French lines and those of the Germans, and each side occupied tunnel-fed outposts in a few bombed-out buildings, the village had been largely unscathed by the war. Then the Second Division showed up in early August, and suddenly the natives fled.

Fleeing citizens had left behind their fruit and vegetable gardens, so fresh food was bountiful. There were fat fish in the Moselle, which the men went after with hand grenades, plopping them into the slow-moving water and collecting the stunned victims that floated to the top.

Pvt. Alvin C. York would remember the area as a sort of "earthly paradise," where it was difficult to remember that one was "still in the war . . . We bathed and rested there. And got us some good fruit and laid out in the sunshine until we felt sort of re-made all over again."

The usual rotation-by-battalions into the forward line was employed again, each unit manning the trenches for about a week before heading for the back line. Alvin York and the Second Battalion of the 328th manned the front line from August 16 to August 24, when the frontline regiments were relieved. Five days later, "an event" occurred in which a four-man patrol of the 325th Infantry Regiment's Third Battalion was ambushed "and never returned," the Eighty-Second's history says.

Only one man, a corporal who was taken prisoner, would be seen again, returning to Company L after the Armistice. The others were all killed. Eleven days after the ambush, the 328th's Second Battalion returned to the front line. Its men could not know it, but they were about to go into real action.

The American command had had its eye on the triangular St. Mihiel Salient almost since its troops began arriving in the summer of 1917. Pershing had long dreamed of an all-American army operating independently as a homogeneous force, and the salient, which jutted its western point almost twenty-five miles into the zigzagging trench system that marked the Western Front, seemed a natural theater for Americans to act on their own and show the world what they could do.

The crises of the spring and summer had precluded such an operation, but now attention once more turned to the area. In late summer, Pershing created the American First Army and urged the Supreme War Council to allow him to attack and reduce the salient. Once rid of its German occupants, the salient could serve as a springboard for an assault on the vital German rail center of Metz, to the east.

The Allies initially approved of the move, but Sir Douglas Haig, commander of the British Expeditionary Force, envisioned a larger, all-out operation across the Western Front. In his view, the Germans had created one large salient that split northern France in two, and he argued that a coordinated push by the Allies from the North Sea almost to Switzerland would be more effective in winning the war.

The British would push eastward on the northern flank, the French in the center, while the Americans would attack northward on the right flank between the Argonne Forest and the Meuse River. As imagined, a reduction of the St. Mihiel Salient that culminated in a move on Metz would actually take the Americans away from where the all-encompassing battle should be fought.

Foch ultimately agreed with Haig and began laying plans for the American push north to begin on September 15. Pershing, his eyes still on the prize, assured Foch that if the general offensive could be pushed back ten days to September 25, he could attack and level the salient, then have his troops withdraw and head sixty miles to the northwest and be on the jump-off line in the Meuse-Argonne with time to spare.

It was a gamble: several divisions that were slated for action in the salient would also be needed for the Meuse-Argonne offensive. Pershing tapped his chief of operations, George C. Marshall—later to become famous for the post–World War 2 Marshall Plan that kept Western Europe supplied with food and materiel—to work out all of the transportation and other issues involved.

With the question of the advance through the Meuse-Argonne settled, Pershing and his staff selected September 12, 1918, for the jump-off into the salient. Seven American divisions—from left to right the First, Forty-Second, Eighty-Ninth, Second, Fifth, Ninetieth, and Eighty-Second—were to take part in the advance north from the salient's southern face. The Twenty-Sixth Division, meanwhile, was to advance east from the western edge of the salient, and hook up with the First Division.

While some divisions spent several days traveling at night and then assembling on the southern face of the salient, the Eighty-Second on the far right remained in place. As of September 9 the Second Battalion of the 328th Infantry Regiment held the front line, while the Third Battalion took up places in the supporting trenches two miles back and the First Battalion sat five miles to the rear.

All knew something was up; a constant rumble of transports and artillery caissons and tanks could be heard all along the line, and rumors were rife that a big offensive was in the offing. On the afternoon of September 11, the rumors were confirmed when orders were received saying that a drive would begin early on the next morning.

The Second Battalion was ordered to stand fast in its trenches but send out patrols after H-hour, while the First Battalion was ordered to shift left and just behind the junction of the 328th Infantry Regiment and the 360th Infantry Regiment, Ninetieth Division to the left.

At 1:15 A.M. on the twelfth, three thousand pieces of artillery began laying the first of more than one million shells—"the greatest barrage of the war, up until that time," according to the 328th's history—and then the rolling barrage began at 5:30 A.M., and the men of the American First Army stepped into no-man's-land across the fifteen-mile front.

"It was a great sight, that broad expanse of country dotted everywhere with men and tanks, bursting shells, rockets rising and bursting into white, red, green stars, Mont Sec looming up dark and forbidding and showing here and there on its sides white puffs of smoke which told where our big 8 inch guns were dropping their shells—all in the gray light of early morning under the broken storm clouds against which the fast, low-flying airplanes were sharply silhouetted," one American major would recall.

Alvin York, too, was awed by the sights and sounds that morning. "The air was full of airplanes, and most of them American planes . . . ," he recalled. "They were diving and circling around all over the place like a swarm of birds. We seed several right-smart fights away up there above us."

The timing of the offensive was impeccable: Even before the seven American divisions jumped off, the Germans had been busily pulling back, intending to evacuate the salient. On the night of September 11–September 12, German frontline units pulled back to secondary positions that had been fortified with wire, leaving isolated, mostly token outposts at the front.

As the Americans surged forward, many encountered little resistance; on the 328th's front, the men encountered "uniform severe resistance" while scattering German outposts in no-man's-land. On the afternoon of the twelfth, a patrol of Company F was sent forward on the west bank of the Moselle River to see whether the Germans on that line had pulled back.

They hadn't, but they were soon pushed out of a stronghold known as the Maison Gauthier; at about the same time, a patrol from Company F moving farther to the west encountered bitter resistance at the outskirts of the village of Norroy. After finally deciding his force was too small to roust the defenders, Lt. Charles Harrison was killed while extricating his men. All told, the Second Battalion took about twenty-five casualties on September 12.

All along the American line that day, general movement through the salient was swift. On the left, the First Division swept aside some feeble resistance and took the village of Nonsard in the early afternoon of September 12. At 7:15 A.M. on the thirteenth, scouts from the Twenty-Sixth and First Divisions met at Hattonchatel, and the salient was split. In the center, the Second Division also quickly covered the five miles to the village of Thiaucourt, its first-day objective.

Alvin York and Company G encountered little resistance on its patrols, and York would complain that the Germans simply melted away on their front. "But fast as we went forward the Germans kept on moving backwards, faster," York, who was promoted to the rank of acting corporal before the offensive, would recall with some frustration. But the Americans of the Eighty-Second Division didn't shirk in their first real fight: "They wanted to push right on and not stop until they got to Berlin."

On September 13, the 328th's Second Battalion was ordered to assemble and protect the right flank of the Ninetieth Division as it attacked through the Bois de Prêtre; its further orders were to seize the village of Norroy two kilometers to the north. Leaving its position after it was dark, the battalion had to pick its way through mountains of barbed wire, but Companies G and E soon arrived at Norroy, from which a battalion of the Sixty-Eighth Landwehr, 225th German Division had just fled.

Edward Buxton and the Headquarters Company soon followed, and encountered Alvin York and his platoon mates. "Just before we reached the outskirts of Norroy, we heard voices a little to our right.

We found it was Lieutenant Kirby Stewart talking to his platoon, getting them through some bad places," Lt. Frank Holden recalled.

"We entered Norroy through a hole in a stone wall that a shell had made, and walked up a side street into the main street of this town. The only noise that we heard was the running of water in the little fountain in the middle of the main street and a few barks from a lonely dog."

The Americans found warm, cooked food lying on tables, and military maps and other documents that had been left carelessly lying about. There were also some older residents who had lived under German occupation for the duration of the war.

When the Germans took Norroy in 1914, they captured some of its citizens who had not had time to flee. Some of these were sent to work in munitions factories, while others remained to perform menial duties for the occupiers. The Germans on September 13 took with them as many inhabitants as they could find as they withdrew—but some were able to hide, many in cellars throughout the town.

That night, the young Americans enjoyed their share of German cigars, cigarettes—and beer. Some of the men also liberated several barrels of wine, opened them, and drank their fill. As a result, "they were fuller of fight than ever," York recalled.

Alvin York and his platoon dug in that night on a hillside just north of the village. They encountered no resistance but confirmed on arrival that the Germans were pulling away from their immediate front. Hungry after a long day's advance, they also scrounged grapes from a nearby vineyard—until they were spotted by a German observation balloon.

Shells soon rained down, and orders went around to stay away from the grapes. But York couldn't resist; he slipped away to the vineyard, which brought another shell down almost on top of his head.

"I jumped and ran and I done run right into my own Captain," he recalled of E. C. B. Danforth. "He liked grapes, too . . . and we both fled."

Heavy and harassing German artillery rained high-explosives and gas shells on Norroy and vicinity throughout September 14, the Germans hoping to cause at least some damage before they continued to retreat north. The 328th's men were forced to put on their stuffy, almost-suffocating gas masks, and keep them on for hours.

The Germans, who had weather experts tasked with assessing the winds and the terrain, sent three hundred gas shells into the town's northwestern corner. The vapors, meant to make its victims sneeze so violently they could not keep their gas masks on, drifted throughout the village. Then came a bombardment of high explosives and mustard gas, an oily, deadly, and dreaded form of chemical attack that caused burns and blindness.

"They were trying to scatter it so that the liquid would spatter on us, burning our flesh before it evaporated into fumes when it would burn our lungs," Holden, the second battalion's gas officer, would write. On top of the gas, shrapnel-filled shells flew in as well.

Few in Company G were affected, and none were killed. However, Sgt. Joseph Fowler and Pvts. Ettore Palombi and William Voiles were wounded and evacuated, while Cpl. Lewis Hamilton of Branford, Connecticut, became a casualty of gas. York, Early, Swanson, and the rest of the seventeen who were to gain some measure of fame later on in the war were all unscathed.

Still, the strain of advancing and fighting with little rest and no hot food for two days was beginning to exhaust the men of the Second Battalion. As a further advance was being rumored, the regiment decided to have the 328th's Third Battalion take over from the second battalion and move on the village of Vandières, north of Norroy, on September 15.

The Third Battalion descended the north face of the Norroy heights at one P.M. and walked into a maelstrom in the valley below, as German artillery to the east quickly spotted it on the level, open ground and poured it on.

"The attack was made with practically no artillery preparation and our forces were at all times in plain sight of the enemy to the front and right flank; consequently we were heavily shelled throughout the advance by enemy artillery firing at point blank range," the regiment's history says.

Men advanced, and fell right and left. Plumes of rock and dirt filled the air, as the survivors struggled on across the killing field. By the time the leading elements reached the southern outskirts of Vandières at about 3:30 P.M., 275 men had been wounded or killed, including two captains and two lieutenants. It was the Eighty-Second Division's most severe, and deadly, test to date.

There were heroes among the Third Battalion. While trying to consolidate and reinforce the battalion's lines at Vandières, the Eighty-Second's divisional machine-gun officer, Lt. Col. Emory Pike, would earn the first of two Medals of Honor that would be awarded to the Eighty-Second Division.

Pike moved hither and yon, grabbing soldiers who had become disoriented from the heavy barrages of German artillery and organizing the defense. When a young soldier was wounded by a shell, Pike personally attended to him, "encouraging all by his cheeriness." Before long another shell plunked down near Pike, and he, too, suffered a severe wound, one that would ultimately kill him.

If not for their luck in having been relieved the previous evening, the man who would one day become the most famous doughboy in history and his platoon mates might also have had their war end on that day.

THAT NIGHT, THE 328th's First Battalion, which had remained in Norroy in support for the day's attack, moved forward and relieved the bloodied Third Battalion. German artillery probed and roamed the dark during the relief, until finally the First Battalion retreated from Vandières and took over some formerly German trenches that had faced to the south.

Engineers quickly went to work and reoriented them to face the enemy to the north. The men of the 328th Infantry Regiment held their position just south of Vandières until three A.M. on September 18, when the 360th Infantry Regiment, Ninetieth Division slid to its right and took over.

Acting Cpl. Alvin York and his mates had seen real action, been through a terrible battle, and lived to see another day. John Pershing had seen his all-American army leave the protection of its trenches and perform open warfare, which had long been his ambition. As at Soissons, American soldiers attacked and pushed the enemy back, and scored a brilliant, if limited, victory.

Reflecting after the push at St. Mihiel, one as-yet-unknown hick acting corporal from Nowhere, Tennessee, would shower his appreciation on the man who led him and his unit. "The St. Mihiel offensive must have been as complete a drive and as well arranged as ever could have been by any general of any army," York would gush.

"The feeling of the majority of the boys was one hundred per cent, for General Pershing. As a whole the Army was back of him, believed in him, and would follow him anywhere."

No longer deeply conflicted about the war and his part in it, Alvin York instead reveled in the victory, and his small role in it. He would soon have the opportunity to follow John Pershing into a larger and much-deadlier "anywhere."

7

TOWARD THE UNKNOWN

Having proved its mettle in the relative cakewalk that was the St. Mihiel offensive, elements of the American First Army now pivoted and raced to meet the appointment John Pershing had set for it in the Meuse-Argonne, formerly virgin territory in this big, great war but soon to be an area ringing with the sounds of battle, the sounds of rifles and machine guns and artillery echoing through deep woods and over hill and dale across a twenty-mile front, a place where badly wounded men on both sides crawled away into the deep woods and brush to die, alone, their bodies never to be found; a battlefield where gas was plentiful and found its victims in gullies and ditches, collecting and pooling and suffocating and blinding; a site where green American boys not yet bloodied found their war, and where twenty-six thousand American youth would find Death waiting for them.

It was also a place where some men would find fame awaiting them, including a hick from Tennessee who had come through his first real taste of battle untouched and the soldiers in his platoon who'd shared the discomfits of battle and deprivation and who now wondered what fresh ordeals awaited them—and wondered as well on what new battleground they might face them.

Alvin York and the York Patrol wouldn't have to wait long to find out.

By September 21, the entire Eighty-Second Division had been relieved from its lines by the Sixty-Ninth French Division and camped around the Marbache sector. Units were reorganized, re-placements for the 950 men who had been killed or wounded in the previous nine days were folded into the four regiments, and the survivors of the assaults on Norroy and Vandières rested and licked their wounds.

Meanwhile, the great offensive that had been postponed so Pershing could have his cherished attack on the St. Mihiel Salient was being put into motion.

The Meuse-Argonne area had been handed to John Pershing for the employment of his American First Army, and his chief of staff, George Marshall, had had just a few weeks to figure out how to attack the St. Mihiel Salient, then withdraw some of those troops and put them on the road fifty miles to the northwest.

More than 200,000 men needed to be transported from the St. Mihiel area to the staging area in the Meuse-Argonne, while some 400,000 other men also had to be delivered to the site of the new offensive. Meanwhile, the 220,000 Frenchman then holding the southern face of the offensive zone had to be moved out.

To get the men from St. Mihiel, Marshall employed two main roads, with heavy trucks and artillery traveling northward on one road and transports delivering foot soldiers on the other. Move-ment could be made only at night to maintain some semblance of secrecy, and the men slept in woods during the day; before long, the huge assembly of men, horses, and machines converged into frustrating traffic jams that had to be sorted out by military police.

Nine American divisions plus six more meant for reserve—the First, Third, Twenty-Ninth, Thirty-Second, Eighty-Second, and Ninety-Second—were to congregate on the southern edge of the Argonne Forest in the west and the heights of the Meuse River in the east. Facing them above and across the front was an enemy strongly entrenched within some of France's most difficult terrain, a place of high hills and patches of woods and farms and slashing, deep ravines—territory in which the Germans had had four years to string wire, build concrete machine-gun emplacements, and throw up other obstacles to anyone even thinking of invading.

The area was vital to the German war effort, protecting the supply lines that ran from Metz in the southeast to Belgium in the north. Were it to be taken, the lines of communication from Flanders to Switzerland would be compromised, and the flow of German men and materiel across the Western Front would be interrupted; if it fell, the German armies across the front would be choked and starved; if it fell, Germany would lose the war.

It was also considered to be the toughest nut to crack, and for that reason no Allied force had even made a stab at piercing its defenses. As the famed war correspondent Frederick Palmer wrote, "No sector in the old German lines was considered more redoubtable than the Meuse-Argonne sector."

A fortified line running from Grandpré in the west through the Romagne Hills to Damvillers on the Meuse River was particularly problematic for the assaulting Americans. Called the Kriemhilde Stellung, this main line of defense—the strongest of a series of defensive lines that made up the Hindenburg Line—would pose a formidable obstacle to the aim of pushing the Germans back to and over the Meuse River in the north.

All in all, as Hugh Drum, chief of staff of the American First Army, would say, "This was the most ideal defensive terrain I have ever seen or read about. Nature had provided for flank and crossfire to the utmost in addition to concealment."

Still, ambitions within the American army were high—perhaps ridiculously so. The entire area was thought to be held by just five German divisions, and plans called for the assaulting divisions to be on the Kriemhilde Stellung within thirty-six hours, and thence to carry through that obstacle and continue north before German reinforcements could arrive.

Once through the Kriemhilde Stellung, the terrain of the Meuse-Argonne would be much more favorable; it featured rolling hills and fields and patches of woods much of the way to the Meuse River. Only one major obstacle, the Freya Stellung strung across Barricourt Ridge five miles north of the Kriemhilde Stellung, would stand in the way of a rout of the German forces.

The American plan of assault called for the Thirty-Third and Eightieth U.S. Divisions to advance along the Meuse River, and with the Fourth Division compose the III Corps in the eastern sector under Gen. Robert Lee Bullard. Meanwhile, from left to right, the Ninety-First, Thirty-Seventh, and Seventy-Ninth Divisions— which composed the V Corps in the center under Gen. Hunter Liggett—in conjunction with the Fourth Division on their right, were to envelop either side of the 1,122-foot-tall eminence of Montfaucon, which perched in the middle of the sector just north of the American jump-off line and whose heights offered German artillery a vast field of fire to work over.

On the left of the advance, the Seventy-Seventh, Twenty-Eighth, and Thirty-Fifth Divisions, from left to right, made up the army's I Corps, and were to bite deep into the heart of the Argonne Forest. The Seventy-Seventh was to jump off at the western edge of the offensive, while the Twenty-Eighth Division on its right was to force its way forward along the west bank of the Aire River. On the eastern bank of the Aire, the Thirty-Fifth Division was to aim for the Romagne Hills above the village of Exermont, just south of the Kriemhilde Stellung.

All of the assaulting divisions plus nearly two hundred French-produced Renault tanks were in place by the night of September 25, when American officers, who dressed in French overcoats and helmets to deceive the enemy, reconnoitered their lines.

At 11:30 P.M., heavy guns far south began pounding the areas to the rear of the German front lines; at 2:30 A.M. on September

26 the deep night erupted as 2,700 artillery pieces—all that had been devoted to the front—began a three-hour barrage. And at 5:30 A.M., officers shrieked their whistles, and the leading waves of the American First Army—some two hundred thousand men—began slipping from their trenches and other defensive fortifications and moved cautiously behind rolling barrages, inching forward over fog-enshrouded ground toward the unseen German defenses.

On the far right, the Thirty-Third Division made good time, and attained its first-day objective in just more than three hours, aided by the extraordinary actions of three soldiers.

Sgt. Sydney Gumpertz, who had enlisted at the age of thirty-eight in the summer of 1917, jumped off with Company E, 132nd Infantry Regiment into a thick fog on the west bank of the Meuse River. Headed for the Bois de Forges, he and several of his men became separated from their unit and quickly found themselves facing a half-concealed German trench. He tossed a smoke grenade in; fifty hacking, coughing German soldiers soon came out as prisoners.

Hearing the chatter of a German Maxim machine gun, Gumpertz led two privates, one armed with a Chautchaut, in a rush on the emplacement. The ground suddenly opened up, and after falling into a trench he soon had another fourteen prisoners. German artillery fire soon killed Gumpertz's mates, and, his blood up, Gumpertz attacked a final German machine-gun nest by himself. There, he killed two Germans and captured sixteen more—plus two guns, to boot.

Gumpertz's company commander, George H. Mallon, was also busy that morning. With nine strays he would call his "little army," Mallon attacked and reduced nine German machine-gun nests and captured a battery of four .155 howitzers before pausing to take a breath.

Moving on, the *petite armée* encountered even more machine

guns, and the forty-one-year-old Mallon employed the hammer-and-anvil tactic of sending his men on the flanks while he—the hammer—made direct assaults on them. Mallon and company captured some one hundred prisoners and eleven machine guns and howitzers without the loss of a single American soldier.

Another member of the 132nd Infantry Regiment, twenty-seven-year-old Sgt. Willie Sandlin of Company A, rushed a whopping three German machine-gun nests that morning and killed at least twenty-four men. He, Gumpertz, and Mallin would eventually be awarded Medals of Honor.

Farther west that morning, the green Seventy-Ninth Division, whose men had not even been on a front line until they assembled for the Meuse-Argonne push, faltered while moving directly on the massif of Montfaucon.

While the divisions to right and left had been able to advance past a German-held piece of open ground called the Golfe de Malancourt, the 313th and 314th Infantry Regiments of the Seventy-Ninth lost their rolling barrage, and as a result were pinned down by severe machine-gun fire and had to go to ground at midmorning.

To the west, the Seventy-Seventh and Twenty-Eighth Divisions advanced steadily on the left bank of the Aire, as did the Thirty-Fifth Division on the east bank. The Thirty-Fifth, made up mostly of Missourians and Kansans, covered six miles of ground in the first few days, and captured the villages of Cheppy and Varennes.

At Cheppy, as in the Bois de Forges, there was plenty of valor to go around. Held up by German machine guns before the village, Pvt. Nels Wold of Company I of the 138th Infantry Regiment asked permission to work his way around one of the nests. Permission was granted, and soon gunshots rang from a thicket; Wold then emerged with three prisoners.

Wold performed this act three more times, each time killing the gunners or taking them prisoner, then waving to his companions to signal them to move. But his luck ran out during a fifth attempt; the twenty-two-year-old was killed.

Wold's company commander, Alexander Rives Skinker, also showed his mettle that day; but like Wold, his Medal of Honor would be posthumous. Skinker, thirty-four, carried a Chautchaut as he led several men forward toward a German gun emplacement, firing as he went, but fell dead before he could reduce it.

For several days, the advance across the front was swift; by September 27, the Seventy-Ninth Division finally managed to take Montfaucon, and the village of Nantillois fell to the same division the very next day. But as September turned, German resistance was stiffening, and none of the nine divisions had been able yet to reach their first-day objectives on the Kriemhilde Stellung.

After four days of rapid advance, the Thirty-Fifth Division was by the end of the month smarting, having lost six thousand men who'd been killed, wounded, or gassed. Its men on September 29 had briefly taken the village of Exermont, at the base of the Romagne Hills, but were soon put to their heels by a strong German counterattack, and had to leave their dead and wounded behind as they took to a running flight for a refuge several kilometers south.

Besides the hardening German resistance, the choppy, difficult terrain over which the soldiers had had to pick their way was proving to be a problem. As well, communication and supply became more and more difficult, units became separated and lost, and commanders lost contact with their men. After hearing disheartening reports from across the front, on September 29 Gen. John Pershing ordered a pause in the movements east of the Aire, and also ordered fresh, or at least more experienced, blood into the fray.

On the left, the veteran First Division was attached to I Corps and took over the former Thirty-Fifth Division area south of Exermont and east of the Aire. In the center, the Seventy-Ninth Division was relieved, and the veteran Third and Thirty-Second Divisions moved in to compose a new V Corps, which was to advance on the First Division's right and take the central Romagne heights. The Fourth, Eightieth, and Thirty-Third Divisions remained intact as the III Corps on the right of the advance, and were charged with taking the Cunel heights west of the Meuse.

Estimates vary, but one says that during the first phase of the Meuse-Argonne drive the American First Army incurred nearly seventy-five thousand casualties—mostly from artillery shrapnel—without even reaching any of its first-day objectives.

And as had been feared, the Germans reinforced their defenses, and now numbered 125,000 men manning the lines from the Meuse in the east to the depths of the Argonne Forest in the west.

After a four-day pause to reorganize and refresh, on Pershing's orders the second phase of the operation commenced on October 4. His directive was simple: the American First Army, he said, needed to "drive forward with all possible force."

That, it would attempt to do. But it would need the particular talents of a born-again, almost conscientious objector named Alvin York before the week was out.

8

LOST BOYS

The wonders of a world war could be large and small. Large when considering the carnage, the booming of artillery, the waves of men advancing to almost-certain death, the mustard gas that blinded the eyes and clung to flesh and caused agonizing burns, the newfangled tanks that clattered and roared up roads choked with mud and doughboys lining either side, the aerial duels that streaked across the sky and left behind twisting and turning contrails, the smell of death that pervaded the woods and roads and byways and formerly bucolic pastures now churned to thick muck, the fear and musing over mortality in each participant's head, and the killing—oh, the killing that went on and on and on.

But there were small wonders as well, one being the way a man's mind turned and changed while among others facing the same peril and ordeals as oneself. Every foot soldier suffered, every man hoped to God he would somehow live, and in the end most men came to the realization that he wasn't fighting so much against an enemy but *for* the man next to him, the man beside him in a trench or gas-ridden funkhole, the man keeping his head down and silently praying while artillery rounds sought their victims, the man sharing a smoke or a joke or a can of monkey meat or even his deepest feelings about the damnable predicament he found himself in.

Acting Cpl. Alvin York, who had hardly traveled out of Fentress County, Tennessee, before being drafted, had, early on, sought some way out of the predicament of having to kill a fellow man while serving with others who had fewer qualms about it. But York was beginning to develop new feelings about his lot.

War, he knew, brought out the worst in men, and turned them into "a mad, fightin' animal." But there was also the small wonder of camaraderie he felt toward the men of Company G and even the men in his own platoon who had jeered and laughed at his attempts to be designated a C.O.

The shared experiences, the shared privations and ordeals, created a religious sensation that for the first time in his fairly sheltered life made him appreciate the Poles and Greeks and Jews and Italians and Irish—Bernie Early and Paddy Donohue and Michael Angelo Sacina and Mario Muzzi, to name a few—and all of the men in Company G, 328th Infantry Regiment, and his platoon.

War, he would later admit with some wonder, "also brings out something else, something I jes don't know how to describe, a sort of tenderness and love for the fellows fightin' with you . . . I knowed men could be strong and rough, but I never understood before that they could be so tender and loving, and I jes couldn't [bear] to think of anything happenin' to them. It was too awful to think of them-there boys being wounded or killed."

York would do "a lot of thinking and praying about these things as we moved out into the Argonne."

The Eighty-Second Division, though destined for a reserve role while nine other divisions jumped off on September 26, had begun pulling out of the Marbache area on September 24, headed for Clermont-en-Argonne, some forty miles to the northwest of Pont-à-Mousson.

The artillery led the way, followed by one hundred camions carrying the infantry. On that ride, Alvin York was introduced to another of the world war's small wonders—the colorful transport drivers, colonial Annamese from southeast Asia whom York would refer to as "Chinamen." In July these had counted among their number one Nguyen That Thanh, who had helped deliver the Second Division to its jump-off lines at Soissons and who one day would be known to the world as the Communist Vietnamese leader Ho Chi Minh.

On September 25, the long train of wagons, artillery, and transports arrived at the headquarters of the American First Army. After the offensive launched the next morning, the Eighty-Second moved up a little at a time, and on October 1, its men watched as elements of the Thirty-Fifth Division, beaten up and put to rout just a few miles north, sullenly marched through them, headed south to lick their wounds.

All understood then that ferocious battle awaited them, and soon.

"Men must be tiring," the authors of the Eighty-Second Division's history noted. "Fresh Americans must be needed to replace the appalling wastage."

Fresh Americans had indeed been called upon, as the First Division took over the Thirty-Fifth's former zone on the east bank of the Aire River. While the men of the Eighty-Second Division waited to learn their fate, Phase Two of the fight for the Meuse-Argonne began on October 4 all along the line.

The First Division attacked north toward Fléville and Exermont, which the Thirty-Fifth had briefly taken before being kicked out by a strong German counterattack. Its task was daunting, as German artillery on high ground across the Aire River easily probed and pounded the area around the two villages.

To the division's front, rows of hills blocked their way, each manned with entrenched and desperate German soldiers and smothered with pockets of brush and deep woods. In the center, directly above Exermont, loomed the steep slopes of Hill 240, also known locally as the Montrefagne; behind it stood Hills 263, 269, and 272, each named for their height in meters above sea level, which formed a bowl around a stead called Arietal Farm.

At first light, the strongly held Montrebeau Wood below Exermont was assaulted by the Twenty-Sixth and Twenty-Eighth Infantry Regiments, while the Eighteenth Infantry Regiment moved on deep Exermont Ravine just to the west and the Sixteenth Infantry Regiment attempted to take Fléville, just east of the Aire. Everywhere, men approached over a carpet of dead Thirty-Fifth Division men.

At the Twenty-Eighth Infantry Regiment's jump-off line, Lt. Herman Dacus of Company L encountered Lt. Maury Maverick of Company I. They shook hands, wished each other luck—and then led their men forward toward the Montrebeau Wood.

Maverick would later write that there were "no bugles, no flags, no drums, and as far as we knew no heroes." But there was plenty of steel, as German artillery found the men and created a "great noise like great stillness . . . We hardly knew where the Germans were. We were simply in a big black spot with streaks of screaming red and yellow, with roaring giants in the sky tearing and whirling and roaring."

It wasn't long before one of the German guns found its mark, and Maverick and his four runners were enveloped in a shell burst. Maverick lost a piece of his shoulder and collarbone, but he was relatively lucky; all four runners perished.

Maverick couldn't know it, but there was indeed at least one hero on the field that day.

At Montrebeau Wood, the Twenty-Eighth Infantry Regiment was held up by strong machine-gun fire coming from within. Pvt. Sterling Morelock, of Company M, quickly went into action, grabbing a couple of runners from the Headquarters Company. They were soon racing across the open ground before the wood, and then plunged into its depths.

One by one, Morelock and company sought out and erased five machine-gun nests, each one of which held one to five guns. His company companions wounded, Morelock instructed the ten prisoners he had taken to carry them back for aid. When his company commander arrived on the scene, he was quickly wounded by a shell, and Morelock tended to him.

But while doing so, he himself was severely wounded when a shell exploded nearby. He would endure a decades-long odyssey of hospital stays but would at least have some solace: a Medal of Honor.

The Sixteenth Infantry Regiment on the far left, meanwhile, advanced more than two miles and forced its way into Fléville, but at a terrible price: one battalion lost all but two officers and 560 enlisted men killed or wounded. After gaining a toehold in the village, the survivors were forced out by heavy German shelling from the heights across the Aire River and took up a defensive line south of town.

The Eighteenth Infantry Regiment, meanwhile, attained Exermont Ravine and took the abandoned village of Exermont. The regiment moved up the slopes of Hill 240, which loomed just above the village, and into withering sheets of machine-gun fire.

They finally achieved the heavily wooded crest, but soon also became targets for the German artillery across the Aire, and were forced to retreat to the massif's southern base. The Twenty-Eighth and Twenty-Sixth Infantry Regiments, meanwhile, managed to force their way through Montrebeau Wood and several German-fortified farms and went into line on the right of the Eighteenth Infantry Regiment.

The First Division's attack resumed at 6:30 A.M. on October 5, the day's mission to once more take Hill 240 and Hill 272 beyond and to the north. While the Twenty-Sixth Infantry Regiment advanced across the valley below Hills 272 and 269, the Eighteenth and Twenty-Eighth Infantry Regiments stormed Hill 240 and pushed the Germans off.

Sgt. Michael B. Ellis, a twenty-three-year-old Missourian, advanced into the thick morning with Company C of the Twenty-Eighth Infantry Regiment, and soon outpaced it. He moved into the thick brush and woods at the base of Hill 240 and in quick measure encountered, flanked, and reduced three German machine-gun nests, killing two defenders and capturing forty-one more to boot. By midday, he had located four more guns and bagged twenty more Germans. Altogether, during an action that would earn him a Medal of Honor, Ellis—who would come to be known in the press as "Mad Dog"—captured sixty Germans and ten machine guns.

Others, of course, were doing their own essential, if perhaps less dramatic, work that morning, plunging into the dripping woods and chasing the German defenders north. By afternoon, the Eighteenth and Twenty-Eighth Infantry Regiments were on the crest of Hill 240, and paused before attempting to take the broad, grassy-sloped Hill 272; heavy fire from German artillery and machine guns beat them off. "Enfilade and frontal fire wiped out entire platoons," one American officer wrote.

The Twenty-Sixth Regiment, meanwhile, assaulted Arietal Farm in the center of the bowl that was ringed by Hills 240, 269, and 272. Despite heavy fire from artillery and fifty machine guns on the looming Hill 272, the farm was ultimately taken.

"Veritable sheets of steel from the machine guns on the hill across the valley and from the Farm d'Arietal swept knee-high over the ground, mowing down the advancing ranks and killing them after they fell," Capt. Lyman Frasier recalled.

"Hand-to-hand fighting raged for a short time in le Petit Bois and at the Farm d'Arietal. Artillerymen were bayoneted at their guns. Machine gunners fell on the piles of their empty shells." The attack was incredibly costly: in Frasier's battalion alone, sixteen officers were killed or wounded, as were 590 enlisted men—more than half the battalion.

Across the First Division's line, men now held their lines under severe shelling from the German batteries across the Aire River. For the next three days, the division's men dug in and tended to the wounded, and sent out patrols to keep apprised of their enemy's whereabouts, while the First Army's brass sought a solution to the vexing problem of how to eliminate the overpowering German artillery that had stymied the division's forward progress.

THE BEST MINDS in the A.E.F. were at the same time also trying to figure out how to save a mixed contingent of the Seventy-Seventh Division that had become cut off and virtually surrounded in deep, wooded terrain in the midst of the Argonne Forest on the far left flank of I Corps.

While the offensive had paused east of the Aire River for several days, the Seventy-Seventh and Twenty-Eighth Divisions stopped for just a day to regroup and take in replacements. On October 1, 1918, Maj. Charles Whittlesey led his First Battalion of the 308th Infantry Regiment plus elements of the 307th Regiment and the 306th Machine Gun Battalion north through dense woods about five miles southwest of Fléville.

By ten A.M., the Americans found themselves at a crossroad east of the village of Binarville. Whittlesey's men attacked a strongly fortified hill to their front, but were unable to push the German defenders out. On the morning of October 2, Whittlesey's men made another attempt, advancing behind a rolling barrage, but once again could make no headway. However, his scouts explored a north–south ravine to the east that led all the way to the battalion's objective at Charlevaux Mill.

At one P.M., the mixed battalion moved out, its men advancing single file up the thickly wooded ravine. Reaching the area of the mill, the men moved past a swampy lowland and on to higher ground on the other side. There, Whittlesey established a perimeter, and though French soldiers attacking north from Binarville and the 307th Infantry Regiment to his right had not kept pace with his men's own advance, he was ordered to hold his exposed position for the night.

The next morning, Company K of the 307th—then containing about ninety-five men—under Capt. Nelson Holderman arrived to reinforce Whittlesey. However, they would be the last that were able to get through; Whittlesey found that the Germans had strung wire across his way north out of the ravine, and enemy soldiers blocked him to the south and on his flanks.

By nine A.M. on October 3, the roughly five hundred men, sitting ducks, found themselves enduring heavy barrages of artillery. German soldiers then attacked the pocket in midafternoon, approaching behind a salvo of hand grenades. Beaten off, they again attacked from the front and sides at five P.M.

On October 4, Whittlesey sent patrols out to try to find a way forward. They returned to report that a heavy German presence was still blocking the way. That afternoon, American artillery, in reply to a message Whittlesey had sent out by carrier pigeon, began shelling the German positions southeast of the men—but then all watched and waited in horror, burrowing as far as they could into foxholes scratched into the earth, as the shells began creeping northwest and into their position. Once the shelling ebbed, the Germans once more attacked from the ridge above them and were beaten off by rifles and Chautchauts.

More shelling and attacks followed on October 5, but by then the American command was aware of the plight of the unit that would become known as "the Lost Battalion." Out of food and water, cold, wet, and miserable, its men were slowly being decimated by shot and shell, and there were real concerns that the entire unit would be lost; there were worries, as well, about what its loss would do to morale among Americans both fighting in France and worrying at home.

As the suffering of the men continued amid more barrages and German attacks, the staff of I Corps and the American First Army brainstormed a solution. Simultaneously but independently, the head of I Corps, Gen. Hunter Liggett, and Col. Ralph Ward of the First Army's operations division arrived at a bold plan—one that, if it worked, could save the Lost Battalion *and* eliminate the heavy German guns that had stopped the First Division's progress east of the Aire River.

They proposed to have a large American force—an entire division—attack west across the Aire and into the Argonne Forest, and force the Germans to withdraw. The move would be a huge gamble, as the right flank of the Americans would be, to use a common military expression, "in the air" and exposed to fire from the German forces manning the hills west of Fléville.

In a war that saw only limited innovations in strategy and was marked mainly by dumb-headed, full-frontal assaults and the mantra *forward,* it would be a bold and, if successful, brilliant move. But the proposed action could easily result in disaster, given that this attacking force would have to cross the fronts of two American divisions—always a dangerous action given the itchy trigger fingers of the average sentries—and assault over unknown ground that contained unknown obstacles and dangers. But there was a lot riding on a successful outcome, chiefly the rescue of the Lost Battalion and the resumption of the First Division's advance northward.

At noon on October 6, even as the Lost Battalion's men were fighting off more German attacks, Liggett and his staff met with First Army Chief of Staff Hugh Drum and Maj. Gen. James McAndrew, headquarters chief of staff, to discuss the proposition. Most of Liggett's staff disapproved of the idea, but Drum and McAndrew reacted positively. John Pershing, too, gave the proposal the green light.

The First Division had in the fighting of October 4 and 5 pushed the German line above Exermont and into the surrounding hills, creating a salient south of the Fléville-Exermont line and leaving room for a large force to move west and above the still-advancing Twenty-Eighth Division on the west bank of the Aire River. It was through this area that the rescuing new force of Americans would attack. The Eighty-Second Division, then in corps reserve, was selected to do the job.

The first step was notifying Brig. Gen. Charles Rhodes, in command of the 157th Field Artillery Brigade, to begin moving his guns north from the vicinity of Clermont-en-Argonne toward Varrenes. Rhodes and the Eighty-Second Division's commander, Gen. George Duncan, were then ordered to report to Liggett at I Corps headquarters southeast of Varrenes.

There, Duncan—who only two days before had taken command of the division after Gen. William Burnham was relieved and named military attaché to Greece—learned of the pending move, and of his division's part in it. Brig. Gen. Malin Craig told Duncan that the assault was a "military necessity."

Racing to his own headquarters, Duncan called together his brigade, regimental, and battalion commanders and told them of the planned attack—and further told them that the division's 164th Brigade, consisting of the 327th and 328th Infantry Regiments and the 321st Machine Gun Battalion under Brig. Gen. Julian Lindsey, would carry it out.

As the brigade immediately began assembling for a night march over congested roads and though a cold rain, Lindsey and his staff reconnoitered the planned staging area south of Exermont. Lindsey then was ordered to visit the headquarters of the First Division at Cheppy, just a few kilometers from Clermont-en-Argonne, to coordinate between that division and the 164th Brigade.

Lindsey and Col. Gordon Johnson of the I Corps staff met with Gen. Charles Summerall, commander of the First Division, and Brig. Gen. Frank Parker, commander of the First Division's First Brigade. They consulted maps of the Eighty-Second's line of march and planned attack area, and afterward both of the veteran First Division leaders just shook their heads.

"The First Brigade couldn't do that in one night and that means no other brigade in the army could do it," Parker told Lindsey and Johnson.

Added Summerall: "The First [Division] couldn't do that and I wouldn't ask them to."

Nevertheless, orders were orders: Alvin York and the rest of the 164th Brigade's men, mostly still green and, if truth be told, untried and untested, would be called upon to execute a night march over clogged roads and then attack into heavily defended territory none had ever laid eyes on. It was probably better that none of them knew that even veterans thought it would be suicidal.

Their numbers called, all the men of the 164th could do was answer.

9

TO KINGDOM COME

Drizzling rain, the flash of the big guns to the northwest, the smell of death, the clanking rumbling of the artillery caissons, and the sodden tromping of muddy boots and the dull clomp of horseshoes; shells surprising and plopping left and right and even on the road ahead and in the eerie, shadowy light of flares the shattered, gnarled trees guarding the approach like hideous gargoyles and eight miles to go on an October Sunday night, a day of rest—hah!—the Lord's day, October 6, 1918, soon turning into Monday morning and marching and tromping and they've gone too far . . .

Sunday evening, October 6, 1918. The 327th Infantry Regiment moved east from its position just west of Varennes at ten past six, led by its First Battalion and followed by the regimental machine-gun company, Stokes mortar platoons, the Second Battalion, and, bringing up the rear, the Third Battalion.

At the junction of what was called the Main Army Road that fed men into the Argonne fight, the column turned north and headed for La Forge, a tiny village on the east side of the Aire River, where it was to be met by guides from the Twenty-Eighth Division and led across the river to a position just north of Chatel-Chéhéry.

It was from there that the 327th's First Battalion was to jump off to the west at dawn. The 327th's Second Battalion, meanwhile, was to continue marching up the the Main Army Road to a support position farther north, while its Third Battalion went into division reserve around a munitions dump.

The 328th Infantry Regiment, too, was supposed to jump off south of the 327th Infantry Regiment's zone at dawn, while elements of the Twenty-Eighth Division to the south would also pivot from their northward slog and begin pushing west. The 328th began leaving its camp near Clermont-en-Argonne at eight P.M., the First Battalion in the lead, followed by the Second and Third Battalions with the machine-gun company in the rear.

But in the dark, amid all the noise and the confusion and the mingling of artillery and foot soldiers, the 328th Infantry Regiment missed its guides and the turn-off at La Forge and continued to plod north almost all the way to Fléville before it discovered its mistake. The regiment was turned around.

The Main Army Road ran from south of Varennes to Fléville, and on this night was clogged with materiel and men meant for the Twenty-Eighth Division to the left and the First Division ahead. The mass of trucks and horses and men created a nightmare in the pitch-black night; at times, the entire northward-bound column would stop for half an hour at a time while military police vainly tried to sort out the tangle.

At one point, the 328th Infantry Regiment's commander, Lt. Col. Richard Wetherill, and Capt. Adone Tomasello, the regiment's operations officer, "pulled a dead man and his dead horse off the road" to help the motor traffic to continue, the Eighty-Second's history says.

Meanwhile, the first battalion of the 327th reached La Forge at about three A.M. on October 7, and began fording the three-foot-deep Aire River an hour later. Companies C and D jumped off at five A.M., headed west toward a bare rise known as Hill 180. It took the hill "in a rush," the 327th's commander, Col. Frank Ely, would later write, and captured forty-six Germans.

The battalion then turned its attention to the village of Cornay just beyond. The soldiers made good progress initially, but the attack bogged down under machine-gun fire coming from the south on sparsely wooded Hill 223—which the 328th Regiment was to have attacked in line with the 327th but had failed to do so. Taking heavy casualties, the First Battalion of the 327th swapped their rifles for shovels and scratched holes into the muddy French soil.

Frank Ely notified brigade headquarters of the 328th's failure to appear on the battlefield to support his left flank; the brigade "reported the 328" Inf. as being lost," a clearly still-irked Ely would write in 1927.

The failure of the 328th Infantry Regiment to attack, or even appear, was "fatal to the fullest success," Ely complained. But the 328th had had a tougher time reaching the battleground than Ely knew—it had left its position near Clermont-en-Argonne two hours later than the 327th, and had farther—fourteen kilometers—to go to reach its jump-off line opposite Hill 223. It was also held up by the jam created by the artillery train.

The unceasing traffic, the mud, the shelling—all combined to reduce its movement to a crawl, and its assigned assault battalion, the First, didn't reach the Army Road–La Forge turn-off until after five A.M., just as the men from the 327th were storming Hill 180.

"At times the congestion was so great our officers would have to find a hole and call to his men as it was too dark to see any thing except vague shadows," Charles M. Day, senior lieutenant with Company B, would recall.

When the 328th did arrive, Companies A and C of the First Battalion prepared for the coming assault on Hill 223, to the eastern face of which the village of Chatel-Chéhéry clung. The Corps objective was a railway—called the Decauville railway—two kilometers to the west that supplied the German effort in the Argonne. With that line cut, the Germans would have to begin withdrawing from the Argonne. Or, as brigade commander Julian Lindsey put it in a field message: "Who wins the railway . . . wins the war."

The First Battalion of the 328th took cover in Des Granges Wood. Looking west, heavy fog obstructed the view, but the Germans, "finding something was afoot," began shelling the wood. Confusion continued to reign, Day would write.

As the fog lifted, the German pounding increased, so Companies A and B "were ordered to take cover till it could be found out just what was to be attacked."

"We were to attack west, but we didn't know where from," Day would write, adding that the fact that the battalion's men were "green" didn't help matters.

Wetherill was as confused as anyone that morning. He returned to La Forge and attempted to get a view of his objective. For a short time it was thought that another hill—Hill 244, just southwest of Chatel-Chéhéry—was Hill 223.

But infantrymen from the Twenty-Eighth Division were spotted "clinging" to that hill opposite the village, and it finally was determined that the target was the high rise just to the west of Chatel-Chéhéry and about a kilometer to the south of Hill 180.

As the hours rolled by, the German artillery shelling the wood began to take a toll. Ten to 15 percent of the men in Company B alone were killed or wounded. Because Companies A and C were closest to the edge of the wood, they would have to form ranks under direct observation of the Germans; the decision was made to instead send Companies B and D toward Hill 233.

The men moved out at 11:15 A.M., splashing through the Aire and then climbing its steep western bank, heading for Chatel-Chéhéry. At about noon, Company B and two platoons from Company D raced for a spur that flowed out from the northern side of Hill 223, while Company D's other two platoons made for a gap on the hill's southern end.

By the time they attacked, the fog had completely lifted and the attackers were in plain view of German observation posts on high ground around the village of Cornay to the northwest. "Consequently we were shelled heavily the entire distance. We also came under [machine] gun fire from the ridge overlooking Chatel Chehery," Day would write.

Company H of the 328th, meanwhile, was ordered to push west along the southern edge of Hill 223. Racing across open ground in full view of the enemy on Hill 244 to the south and German artillery positioned around Cornay, men fell to the right, left, and front as they advanced under intense German artillery fire.

Watching from Hill 244 south of the action, a corporal with the Twenty-Eighth Division—itself no stranger to battle—described the company's halting advance.

"The [company] starts in perfect alignment and reaches the middle of the first field," Harold Pierce would write. "Over in the German horizon there is a 'crunmph,' the telltale whistles as a salvo speeds to them. Most of them take it standing up, another sign of green troops.

"The next salvo of seventy-sevens comes and before the shells burst the entire line disappears in the tall grass. They rise a little disorganized and press on . . . Soon they are all running forward all formation gone as the shells search the ground and find many victims." While the still-living bravely pressed on, behind them "men [were] moving slowly back, limping, carrying others while many more must be sprawled out dead."

Luckily facing no opposition from the German infantry, Companies B and D were able to take the east side of Hill 223. There, Company B's commander, Capt. Richard Douglas, was shot in the foot. Suddenly, Day found himself in command of the unit.

At about two P.M., Companies B and D made a move into a valley that lay at the hill's western edge. They soon came under intense fire from the front and from both flanks, with the heaviest fire coming from a heavily wooded hill to the southwest. Day sent a message to battalion headquarters, saying that artillery would be needed to effect any further advance.

While he was reconnoitering the position and reorganizing the defense, the Germans launched a counterattack from the west and north, using the cover of a machine-gun barrage as they advanced.

Falling back to the crest of Hill 223, the men dug in behind some old German wire. The Germans came again later that evening, advancing "so close we were both using grenades as well as pistols and rifles," Day wrote.

Both companies took "severe" casualties, the Eighty-Second's history says, and at one point a runner stumbled back to regimental headquarters to report that Companies B and D had been annihilated.

In fact, the First Battalion held on and beat off the German attacks, but soon came under heavy fire from German artillery. During the night, Companies A and C were hustled across the Aire to Chatel-Chéhéry as a precaution, as were three platoons of the regimental machine-gun company and a few platoons of trench mortars.

Day One of the bold stroke closed with the First Battalion barely hanging on to its hard-won ground. The rain, traffic snarls, misinformation, and stiff German resistance had put the entire operation in peril; Day Two, it seemed, would need some kind of miracle if the plan was to succeed.

WHILE THE 164TH Brigade spent much of October 7 attempting to break through the German defenses west of Chatel-Chéhéry, the day brought the bone-weary, starving survivors of the Lost Battalion a demand for their surrender from the Germans.

Carried by an American soldier who had tried to collect foodstuffs that had been air-dropped outside of the battalion's perimeter but had been captured, the note instilled not despair but hope among Charles Whittlesey's men and officers, who took it as evidence that it was German, and not American, resolve that was weakening.

The day also brought a renewed attack on their forlorn position, this time by *Strosstruppen*—storm troopers—and once again featured the usual cover of hand grenades and rifle fire; it also featured a chilling new facet: the use of flamethrowers to try to fry the men out of their lines.

With the Seventy-Seventh, Twenty-Eighth, and the Eighty-Second Divisions pressing their defenses, the attack that afternoon would be the Germans' last, though Whittlesey's men couldn't yet know it. All they knew was that they wanted to live, and as the commandos rushed their position, emaciated and wounded and now-riled Americans crawled from their filthy funk holes and fought back furiously, dropping Germans to left, front, and center, and turning the tables on those carrying liquid fire by shooting the tanks of fuel on their backs and watching in delight as their would-be tormentors' flesh turned black and blistered as they slowly burned to death.

The Lost Battalion's ordeal was almost over by the evening of October 7, but the fight in the Argonne Forest was far from finished. The attack would be pressed again the next day; this time it would include a man from Tennessee who had once balked at the idea of killing another man, who was still trying to figure out why the world was at war and why he had been sucked into it, and who on the evening of October 7 was laying low, just trying not to get killed, until orders came to the Second Battalion, 328th Infantry Regiment, at eleven P.M.

"We layed in some little holes on the roadside all Day that night we went and stayed a little while and come Back to our little holes and the Shells Bursting all around us," Acting Cpl. Alvin York wrote in his diary that night, employing his usual half-literate mix of upper and lower cases. "I seen men just Blowed up By the Big German Shells Which Were Bursting all a round us. So the order came for us to take hill 223 and 240 the 8th."

The Second Battalion had remained east of the Aire River during the day of October 7, when it was designated as the support battalion for the attack on Hill 223. It was out of the fire but still close enough to get burned. As York would note, men were killed and wounded by artillery fire all through the day as they hunkered in holes scratched out of the earth to either side of the Main Army Road.

At dark the flashes of German guns firing their salvoes toward the Americans lit up the sky, and their booming sounded like an approaching thunderstorm. Wounded, pallid and limp, passed on stretchers, dead men lay about, their glassy eyes staring at nothing and their open mouths giving mute testimony to the horrors of modern warfare.

"And it was wet and cold and damp," York would remember. "And it all made me think of the Bible and the story of the Anti-Christ and Armageddon."

At about two A.M. on October 8, Company G's commander, E. C. B. Danforth, appeared out of the inky dark night with new orders for his men: they were to advance to Hill 223 and at 6:10 A.M. pick up the 328th's attack west toward the Dacauville railway.

And so it was that Alvin York, Bernard Early, Otis Merrithew, and the rest of the Second Battalion of the 328th Infantry Regiment assembled in the dark and headed for the Aire River crossing, where the only available bridge had shortly before been blown to bits by a German artillery barrage.

The going was tough as they approached the steep hill that led up to Chatel-Chéhéry.

"It was so dark and everything was so mussed up and the going was so rough that it was most awful hard to keep contact and to find the hill," York would say. "But we done kept on a-going jes the same. We were marching, I might say floundering around, in column of squads."

The advance to the jump-off was challenging all along the line. Col. Frank Ely of the 327th Regiment had sought to have his Third Battalion released from brigade reserve and support the continued advance of his First Battalion. When the Third Battalion couldn't be found in the chaotic night, brigade commander Julian Lindsey instead released the Third Battalion of the 328th Regiment for Ely's use.

That battalion "advanced noisily to a crossing of the Aire River opposite Hill 180," Ely would remember. Fire from German machine guns found its men in the half-light of dawn, and two companies—L and M—were dispersed; as a result, less than half of the battalion crossed the river and arrived in time to support the pending advance of the 327th's First Battalion.

The movement of the 328th's Second Battalion, even through the dark, also was detected by the Germans, who soon responded with a heavy barrage. The Second Battalion passed through battered, limb-shorn trees and over and past the dead and the wounded of the First Battalion, many of whom had been ripped to shreds in the Des Granges Wood the previous morning.

The carnage, the incoming shells, and the desolate forest filled with the dead and the dying made home in the Valley of the Three Forks of the Wolf River seem "a long, long way off," York would say.

It had been hoped that the balance of the 328th's Third Battalion could make it to Hill 180 before daylight arrived, but in the end the majority of its men didn't find Hill 180 until much later—too late, in fact, to support the coming attack, and some would not report until the afternoon of October 8.

By then, many of the men in the 328th Infantry Regiment were themselves lying splayed on the ground with their dead eyes open, their skin pallid and white, while others were streaming back in disorganized flight. By then as well more than two hundred German prisoners were being marched back to the regimental headquarters at Chatel-Chéhéry, a tall, thin, fundamentalist yokel from the backwoods of Tennessee leading the way.

10

DAY OF DAYS, PART ONE

Cain slew Abel, and David, Goliath. On October 8, 1918, Germans with the 120th, 122nd, and 125th Landwehr Infantry Regiments slew Sgt. John G. Hink, of Tempe, Arizona; Pvt. Harry Baker, of Orange, Massachusetts; Pvt. Joseph Graham, of Cleveland, Ohio; Pvt. John Liedtke, of New Haven, Connecticut; and Pvt. Comer J. Hughes, of Dublin, Georgia.

And they slew more, many more, including Lt. Kirby P. Stewart of Bradenton, Florida, who led Alvin York and Murray Savage and Carl Swanson and Otis Merrithew and fifty other soldiers with Company G, 328th Infantry Regiment down the west slope of Hill 223 and into the teeth of a firestorm of shot and shell coming from the left, from the right, and from the center; from thick, dark green and wooded hills flecked with red and orange that hid their guns and provided a field for deadly fire at the doomed, halting American line pushing through a misty, bloody hell, advancing and dropping, dropping then advancing, step by step, through knee-high grass and past the bodies of the dead and the soon-to-be-dead, bending forward as through a hailstorm as German bullets thudded young flesh to the right and front and left as the thick, moist, October air hummed as if alive with bees, stinging, deadly bees.

As dawn emerged on October 8, the Second Battalion relieved the battered and bloodied survivors of the first. The gray light of morning brought German sniper fire upon them as they did so, and whiplash bullets from machine guns hidden in the grass and small depressions to their front did their own damage. Men limped away and fresh meat for the slaughter arrived and went to ground and waited and watched and tried not to die too early in the day.

To their right was the First Battalion of the 327th, already bruised somewhat in the previous day's taking of Hill 180 and the attempt on Cornay. To their left was the 110th Infantry Regiment of the Twenty-Eighth Division, which was to advance in step with the 328th Infantry Regiment and protect its left flank. The jump-off was set for ten past six in the morning, the direction ten points north of west and farther into the Argonne Forest.

All were to advance behind a heavy barrage; as happened too often in the course of the war, the barrage never came. There would be, however, the solace of an overhead barrage of bullets from the regiment's machine-gun battalion.

No matter; it was theirs to do or die. And so across the plateau and into the valley, ten points north of west except not for the 327th Regiment, whose orders were changed *after* its jump-off to attack north between Fléville, at which big German guns continued to pour their shells, and Cornay to the west; the 328th's Second Battalion, too, was supposed to push north toward the hills ringing Cornay; its orders to do so, though, lay concealed in the coat pocket of a Second Battalion runner who lay dead near the regimental command post south of Hill 233.

And so the 328th would move with its right flank in the air, as they say, opening a one-kilometer gap between it and the 327th and making that flank vulnerable to German fire once the regiment slipped past the tail end of the 327th's advance. On the left, the 110th Infantry Regiment would also fail to move, "so that our attack was launched with both flanks exposed" and under "most adverse conditions," the 328th's history casually notes.

Within the 328th, Company G was placed on the left and Company E on the right. Alvin York and his mates were on the farthest left, two hundred yards behind and in support of the leading wave. At ten past six, with the air on fire and an abominable, cacophonous din ascending, "we done went over the top, as ordered," York would say.

And so into the valley of death walked one-half of the brave men of the Second Battalion, 328th Infantry Regiment. Hills ranged to the left, front, and right, from which the Germans had no trouble finding the soft flesh of the advancing Americans. "I'm a-telling you that-there valley was a death trap," York would remember.

There were also machine guns to their rear on Hill 223. After the two waves of doughboys passed, German soldiers came out from hiding and let rip. In response, Sgt. Harry Parsons motioned to the automatic-rifle squad on the right of the advance to pivot and head back up the slope to find the source of the fire. The squad quickly spotted the offending gunners and captured eight Germans and two weapons.

Soon enough, though, the fire from the three sides of the valley became too much; the first wave took numerous casualties before finally going to ground. The second wave cautiously approached through the rain of bullets sent its way by machine gunners and riflemen. But many Germans found their marks.

Down soon enough and never to rise again went Walter L. Fox, Adelard Dupuis, Everett Howard, and Stephen Miricki. And down went 2nd Lt. Kirby Pelot Stewart of Bradenton, Florida, who was twenty-seven years old and was actually a *first* lieutenant, though he didn't know it; his promotion had been approved on August 17, 1918, but had not yet reached him.

Stewart had enlisted in the Florida National Guard, and in 1916 he was sent with his unit to the Mexican border, where he was promoted from private to sergeant. In 1917, he attended the first officers' training camp at Camp McPherson, Georgia, and upon graduation was assigned to the 328th Infantry Regiment.

By the morning of October 8, 1918, he was just west of Chatel-Chéhéry, leading the third platoon of Company G, when "he was shot through the leg but this did not stop him, and he bravely continued to lead his men forward," Pvt. Michael Tornsello would report. Alas, another bullet would find him, "this time through the head, which shot caused instant death."

The German fire that morning seemed to be coming "from everywhere," York would remember. "I'm a-telling you they were shooting straight, and our boys jes done went down like the long grass before the mowing machine at home. Our attacks jes faded out. We had to lie down flat on our faces and dig in . . . We jes couldn't go on."

Like Union general George Meade at Gettysburg in 1863, the Germans had the high ground—in fact, three Round Tops from which to pour lead into the advancing Americans. But here, the woods concealed the origins of the German fire, except for brief, bright flashes from the muzzles of their guns hidden deep in the shadows. The worst fire seemed to be coming from the left, on the unprotected flank where the 110th Infantry Regiment was supposed to be advancing.

"We knowed then that them-there machine guns would have to be put out of action before the advance could go on," York would say. "We also knowed that there was so many of them and they were in such commanding positions that a whole battalion couldn't put them out of action nohow by a frontal attack . . . But they had to be takened somehow."

The battalion's progress slowed, and then stopped as both assaulting waves went to ground in the face of increasing German machine-gun fire. In the midst of the maelstrom, Sgt. Harry Parsons bravely "exposed himself again and again, trying to locate exactly where the machine guns over there on the left front were firing from," York recalled.

With the company's commander, E. C. B. Danforth, out of sight somewhere to the right with the leading assault platoons, and Kirby Stewart lying dead with a bullet through his brain, it was up to Parsons to find some way forward—or some way out.

Parsons did act, and split the men under him into "combat groups," he would remember. He also decided to use one of those groups to try to reduce the German guns raining death on them from the left flank.

Crouching under a hail of German lead, he called Acting Sgt. Bernard Early over and through and over the din managed to order him to lead three squads back to the east, then enter the woods to the south to locate the offending machine guns that were causing such havoc.

Parsons was certain it was a suicide mission, but someone had to go. Something had to be done to stop the slaughter on Hill 223.

Early called his corporals—Murray Savage, Otis Merrithew, and Alvin York—to him and explained the plan. All told, the reconnoitering party consisted of four noncoms and thirteen privates; they soon were working their way back and then to the south, where they entered the woods at the base of the hill in single file.

And so was born the legend of the York Patrol, which in fact originated as the Early Patrol.

Early was on point, leading Murray Savage's squad, which consisted of Savage and Pvts. Maryan Dymowski and Ralph Weiler. Otis Merrithew led his squad, consisting of Pvts. Fred Wareing, Feodor Sok, Michael Sacina, Patrick Donohue, George Wills, and William Wine.

Alvin York led the automatic-rifle squad: Pvts. Carl Swanson, Mario Muzzi, Percy Beardsley carrying the Chautchaut, Joe Konotski, and Thomas Johnson.

The seventeen men were soon swallowed up by the brush and saplings at the base of the hill. Parsons followed them for a time, looking above him for any sign of German snipers. "Suddenly I looked down, and directly ahead of me two snipers were picking our boys off in the valley," Parsons would recall.

"I immediately dropped down on the ground and shot one of the snipers dead. I also wounded his partner, who missed me with his first shot. But with the shelter of a tree trunk he continued firing at me."

The morning mist had mostly burned away by the time Early's party began ascending the wooded hill, and the Americans were spotted by machine gunners on the slopes before Cornay, six hundred yards across the valley to the north. But the heavy underbrush, the screen of trees, and the distance prevented all from being hit—though bullets fell all about them as they exerted themselves up the hill and toward the southwest.

As they ascended what the Germans called Hill 2, the promised American artillery barrage finally opened on the German front line, causing disarray to the Boche but giving cover to the patrol.

Toward the top, the men encountered what they believed was an old German trench, but in fact was more likely a ditch that was dug to mark a property boundary. They jumped in and followed it to the crest of the hill, and then descended, the furious sounds of battle ebbing some as they did.

Moving cautiously and picking their way with care, the patrol's members encountered no one as they continued on, now behind the German line. A footpath leading farther to the left appeared, and so they followed that, veering to the southwest once more. A new, fresher path leading to the right appeared, and the patrol stopped to consider its options.

Now three hundred yards behind the German line, some of the men vouched for a flank attack to the right, at about the point where German machine guns could be heard firing ceaselessly from the top of the commanding ridge above them. But Bernie

Early, York, and others of the men argued to keep prowling further to the southwest, to get deeper into the German rear. This they ultimately did, spreading out among the brush and trees in skirmish formation and continuing to move slowly and cautiously, on the lookout for the enemy.

THEY SOON ENCOUNTERED a small stream, which was clear of brush and trees on both sides. They continued on until suddenly, Cpl. Murray Savage, in the lead with Early, called out. "There are the Boche!"

Ahead of them and racing away down the path were two German medical men wearing Red Cross insignia. They were ordered to surrender but took off running instead, "like two scared rabbits," as York would recall. Shots now leapt from several American rifles as the doughboys took off after them.

Murray Savage and his squad, in the lead with York and his men behind him, followed the Germans into a clearing, where dozens of German soldiers were espied "just sitting around a campfire gabbing," Otis Merrithew would recall. Savage reported back to Early to say that he had "found something much more interesting" than the medical men.

Early now led the entire patrol down the slope. At the bottom, the patrol spread itself on either side of the stream, and before long were confronted with the sight of from twenty to seventy Germans—accounts differ—gathered on a hillside around a small, rough shack, where a heavy-set officer was speaking to them. They had just finished eating, and some were lounging and smoking and resting, evidently prepping themselves for a day of battle. Carelessly, none of them were near their weapons.

The patrol edged closer, Early in the lead followed by Savage and his men and then York and his, with Merrithew's squad bringing up the rear. Early instructed all to crouch in the brush for several moments, and then he gave the order to fire.

"We surprised them, I guess," Early said. "While we were deciding what to do someone fired a shot and everyone joined him."

Sharp reports leapt from the muzzles of the Americans' rifles, and the lazing Germans sprang for their own weapons that had carelessly been laid aside. The fusillade caused confusion in the ranks of the Germans, who had no idea how many of the enemy were firing on them. "Many of them threw up their hands and surrendered, while others set out on the run," Early would remember.

Others still fell to their knees, put their hands behind their heads, and yelled "Kamerad! Kamerad!" Early told his men to stop firing. "This is murder," he said.

Germans now warily eyed the Americans, who were spread out and leveling their rifles at their prey. Early walked over to Lt. Paul Vollmer, the German battalion commander who spoke some English, and told him to begin getting his men lined up in preparation for removal from the ravine.

Those Germans who had been lounging about rose to their feet, and York would remember the ground about them being covered by a "mess of beefsteaks, jellies, jams, and loaf bread." The Americans, he added, "were [almost] as surprised as they were, coming on them so sudden.

"But we kept our heads and jumped them right smart, and covered them and told them to put their hands up and to keep them up . . . And we fired a few shots just to sorter impress them. I guess they thought the whole American Army was in their rear. And we didn't stop to tell them any different."

THOUGH PINNED DOWN by heavy German machine-gun and rifle fire coming from the left, center, and right, the advancing

Americans could not know how desperate the plight of their enemy was on that morning.

Its outposts guarding the western slopes of Hill 223 had been put to flight by the 328th, the men scurrying to the dubious safety of the tree line to the German center and left flank, where the 125th Landwehr Infantry Regiment (LIR) was busily attempting to repel the Americans.

On the German right was a thin line of soldiers with the First Battalion, 120th LIR, which had endured a devastating American artillery bombardment on the morning of October 7 and suffered "tremendous losses," the operations officer of the Second Landwehr Division would report.

The American salvoes and resulting casualties forced the German defenders to be spread thin. Lacking the necessary manpower because of the bombardment, the Germans "put up strong points and machine gun posts at vantage points in the terrain," the officer would add.

The 120th LIR's survivors would now be facing off against the 250 men of Company G, 328th Infantry Regiment who were advancing toward them. One of those surviving Germans, Lt. Karl Kübler, commanded a platoon of the Fourth Company, 120th LIR. On the evening of October 7, he posted his men in positions directly west of Hill 223, then set out to make a final inspection of his sector.

He became immediately concerned at his platoon's isolated position. "I saw that we had no contact on our right flank," he would later write. "Immediately I sent out patrols to establish this liaison."

Those patrols came back and reported that the Second Machine Gun Company was, in fact, posted to his right. But the gap between his men and the machine gunners worried him.

"I regarded our situation as very dangerous," he wrote, "for the Americans could easily pass through the gaps in the sector of the 2nd Machine Gun Company and gain our rear."

Kübler reported his concerns to his company commander, Lt. Fritz Endriss. Endriss in turn sent a message to the First Battalion's commander, Lt. Paul Vollmer, warning of the "critical situation" and asking for permission to relocate the platoon in a ravine farther south.

"Unfortunately, my proposal was not approved," Kübler would note, with Vollmer coldly replying: "You will hold the position to which you have been assigned."

In fact, though, Vollmer—who had spent some time in Chicago before the war—himself was worried about the Fourth Company's isolated position. Just that morning (October 7) Vollmer's battalion had been pulled out of the line it had held since September 30 and marched west to assume a position in support of the forces facing the American assault on Hill 223.

But as the day's attacks intensified, and the 328th First Battalion gained a foothold on Hill 223, Vollmer on his own volition decided to turn his battalion back east; he encountered his regimental commander on the way to the front and received an enthusiastic endorsement of the move.

In the afternoon of October 7, Vollmer and his men came to a halt some distance south of Humserberg Hill, which was defended by the 125th LIR. Noticing that the sector at which he arrived was "occupied by very weak forces," Vollmer ordered Endriss and his Fourth Company to take up positions at the edge of the woods "and establish contact with the adjoining sectors."

Vollmer himself spent the night of October 7–October 8 with his reserve companies in the rear, but the situation at the front gnawed at him. Early in the morning of October 8, he went to the headquarters of Capt. Karl von Sick, commander of the Third Battalion.

Sick had also absorbed the regiment's Second Battalion into his command, and had his headquarters on Hill 244—known as Hohenbornhoehe Hill to the Germans—which was on the southern end of the battlefield and in the Twenty-Eighth Division's assigned sector.

Sick asked Vollmer to take command of the defensive area south of the 125th LIR, and told him he would have under his command not only his First Battalion of the 120th LIR, but the Seventh Bavarian Sapper Company and the Prussian 210th Reserve Infantry Regiment, elements of which had been sent forward to reinforce the front during the night.

Vollmer returned to the point where he had placed his Fourth Company at the edge of the woods facing Hill 223. Unaware that the American advance of October 7 had already forced the 125th LIR to retreat to the west and north, Vollmer was surprised to see that "the enemy apparently had moved up closer under the cover of darkness."

To the northeast, he could also see German prisoners being herded east from Hill 167—Humserberg Hill to the Germans. Vollmer correctly surmised that these prisoners belonged to the 125th LIR. The sight of them only exacerbated Vollmer's concern for his own defense.

Either by chance or design, the Fourth Company's position was at the exit of a wooded ravine just to the southwest of the firing line. While some men prepared to fight in the open against the advancing Americans, others, smartly, had found defensive positions that were better concealed behind natural depressions and woods. The terrain was virginal, a new battleground, and there had been no time to entrench.

There were other concerns. Lt. Karl Glass, Vollmer's adjutant, and a few other staff members had approached the position from the west that morning, and as they entered the ravine to the Fourth Company's rear they encountered "several groups of men who belonged to another regiment"—the 210th Reserve Infantry, part of the Forty-Fifth Reserve Infantry Division.

These men were lounging about, bushed after having spent much of the night marching to the front. "Their arms and bolts laid aside, these men were eating breakfast," Glass recalled. "When we expressed our surprise over their carelessness, the men declared that they had 'hiked' all night and, first of all, needed 'something to eat.' We knew that these were the first arrivals of the support division which was promised us."

Moving from the ravine, Glass reported to Vollmer at the edge of the wood and told him of the lackadaisical behavior of their reinforcements. Vollmer returned to the ravine with Glass. By now, they could see American troops—probably those of Company G, 328th Infantry Regiment—advancing toward them, then disappearing into the undergrowth.

Vollmer instructed Glass to move forward and find out where these Americans had gone, while he began trying to urge the men of the 210th Reserve Infantry to move out. But Glass found it difficult to make time through the dense underbrush. About 150 yards from the German line, Glass saw Americans coming on in two waves, some crossing the grassy western slope of Hill 223 and some "pushing on deeper and deeper into the woods" at the northern base of Hill 244.

After four years of war, the very sight of American soldiers boldly advancing was dispiriting to the average German soldier. The opportunity to win the war before the United States could enter it in force had been squandered, and the doughboys, fresh-faced and new to the conflict, moved with an élan that had long been beaten out of the Germans and their French and British counterparts.

Still, German soldiers throughout the Meuse-Argonne continued to put up a stiff fight against their American counterparts, many of whom entered the fight green and untested. And among these relative newbies to the war were Alvin York and Bernard Early and Carl Swanson and fourteen other young Americans, now coming on with the intent of saving their comrades out on that open, grassy slope who were being cut to pieces by German soldiers who were proving on October 8, 1918, that they still had plenty of will to resist.

11

DAY OF DAYS, PART TWO

For a few peaceful, breathless seconds, Americans faced Germans, and Germans Americans, in a dark, shaded ravine in France while steps away, steps above them, the cacophony of war—rifle shots, the *put-put-put* of hot, firing machine guns, the screams of those hit and those dying—echoed on the gently sloping plain that spread west from Chatel-Chéhéry and lapped up on the very eastern edge of the Argonne Forest.

In that ravine and among those young Americans from Company G, 328th Infantry Regiment there was a nervous euphoria; they had surprised their enemy, they had captured dozens of them without hardly firing a shot, they had done their duty and relieved the pressure on the other young Americans advancing toward them on the morning of October 8, 1918.

And for the next few seconds there were smiles among the Americans and frowns of deep worry and consternation on the faces of the Germans, none of whom had any idea of just how many Americans had surprised and taken them.

There was Alvin York, tall, redheaded, and thin, now beaming; Cpl. Otis Merrithew, slapping backs and laughing with his squad; fresh-faced Pvt. Carl Swanson, leveling his rifle and wondering what would come next; Pvt. Percy Beardsley, who'd traded in a cattle yoke for a heavy and cumbersome Chautchaut, suspiciously eyeing his German prizes; and there was the diminutive, square-jawed Acting Sgt. Bernie Early, barking orders to his patrol, whose other members—among them the tough Pole Joe Konotski and the Italians Mario Muzzi and Michael Angelo Sacina and the somewhat bewildered Pvts. William Wine and Fred Wareing—began roughly surrounding the Germans and forming them into a column of twos in preparation for turning about-face and getting the hell out of that ravine.

As they readied to head out with their prizes, Early told Konotski to stay close to the Germans on the march back to the American lines, lest the doughboys become easy prey for snipers. Almost as he said it, a cry rang out in German from the leafy hill above—"*Heruntersteigen!*"—Get down!—and the Germans ducked while whipcords of machine-gun fire thudded into Early and Merrithew and Mario Muzzi was grazed in a shoulder.

Others weren't as lucky. When the German command rang out and their charges quickly plopped to the loamy forest floor, they, for a moment uncomprehending of what was happening, froze in their places. The fire from above streamed into six of them; each toppled to the ground mortally wounded.

In the center of the mass of prisoners, Cpl. Murray Savage of upstate New York had been left as forlorn as a scarecrow in November when the Germans he was guarding flopped; Alvin York's best pal in the platoon was torn apart as nine bullets entered his body and nearly tore all his clothes off.

Four Americans standing guard on the Germans in the center of the prisoners behind Savage were also quickly felled like sheaves of wheat; all fell in a heap like thrown-away rag dolls, their lifeblood draining into the rich, leafy detritus on the floor of the ravine.

Down in an instant and never to rise went Pvt. Fred Wareing of New Bedford, Massachusetts; Pvt. Maryan Dmowski of Trenton, New Jersey, who in a letter sent upon his departure had promised his family, "I'll be home after I kill fifty Germans"; Pvt. Carl Swanson of Jamestown, New York; and Pvt. Ralph Weiler of Hanover, Pennsylvania.

One more, Pvt. William Wine of Philadelphia, had been standing apart and to the left of the center group. He, too, felt the sudden, deadly sting of a German machine-gun bullet and keeled over, dead.

Bernie Early was down near the four dead men in the center but still alive, with one bullet in his left arm and three in his left side. For him, the fight was over. Otis Merrithew, too, was hit in his left arm, and went to ground and lay still as Early plaintively called to him to help him if he could.

After the initial bursts of machine-gun fire from above, there was a lull as the German gunners tried to locate more victims hidden below. Alvin York, farther up the hill in the center of the mass of prisoners, used them and some brush to hide from the guns. Pvt. Percy Beardsley managed to hide behind a tree with his Chautchaut, though his two loaders were dead and would be of no use.

The rest of the survivors—Pvts. Michael Sacina, Feodor Sok, George Wills, Joe Konotski, Thomas Johnson, Mario Muzzi, and Paddy Donohue—managed to get low and hide themselves, all while keeping their weapons trained on their prone German captives.

The Americans, both the quick and the dead, had made a huge mistake after encountering the German force in the ravine. Unseen above them, thirty yards up the slope of the ravine, German machine gunners had been firing toward the east at the oncoming doughboys of the 328th Infantry Regiment.

When the Americans let loose with several volleys at those Germans trying to escape from their grasp, and while these same were lining their captives up, several of the gunners swung their weapons around, saw events unfolding below, and after shouting to their comrades to hit the dirt let loose.

The Americans, still greener than meadow grass, had in effect blundered into a trap and been undone by their sheer excitement and hubris. Six of them now lay dead among the weeds along the small stream that drained through the forest floor; their blood, trickling through that same vegetation, now joined that trickle of water as their comrades ate dirt and wondered what in the hell would happen next.

THE CAPTURED GERMAN officers would in 1929 offer their own account of the action that day in the Argonne Forest.

Lt. Karl Kübler, in command of a platoon of the Fourth Company, 120th LIR, was with his men at the edge of the forest, facing Hill 223 and the oncoming men of Companies E and G, 328th Infantry Regiment. "We greeted the enemy with a lively fire," he would recall.

As the Americans came on, Lt. Paul Vollmer, commander of the 120th LIR, and his new adjutant, Lt. Karl Glass, arrived at the Fourth Company's location for an inspection. "Just at that moment a tremendous bedlam broke loose in the rear," Kübler would say later.

The American artillery barrage, coming too late to help those dead on the western slope of Hill 223, enveloped the German back line, killing and wounding an unknown number of soldiers.

Vollmer ordered Kübler to lead his platoon to the edge of the woods and confront the doughboys coming from the east. Besides the twenty-five men from the Fourth Company, Kübler also had with him about forty men from the 210th Reserve Infantry and twenty Bavarian sappers.

The barrage that had enveloped the Fourth Company was the same that had fallen as the York Patrol ascended Hill 2 unseen on the Germans' right. Because of the casualties incurred among the

Fourth Company, Vollmer knew he needed the help of the 210th Reserve Infantry more than ever, and he headed to the ravine to get more of those men up and moving.

As he did, he glanced toward Hill 2 and saw a line of American troops coming on from the south. Though the range was long, he ordered several soldiers with him to open fire. When they did, shouts came from the ravine: "Don't shoot, there are Germans here!"

Reaching the German soldiers in the ravine, Vollmer found that the men of the 210th Reserve Infantry were once again about to remove their belts and sidearms, apparently convinced that they were soon to be captured. Vollmer "at the point of [his] pistol" ordered them to resume fighting.

But it was too late. As Vollmer exhorted his troops, the York Patrol continued to advance through the ravine toward them.

"Suddenly several American soldiers came toward me constantly firing their rifles," he would report. "I returned the fire as well as I could under the circumstances, until I was surrounded— and alone. I had no choice but to surrender."

One anonymous German soldier from the Fourth Company would concisely confirm Vollmer's recollections, reporting that he and about a dozen of his mates had returned to the back lines to pick up some food rations. Despite regulations, they were not armed.

"We were about to hurry back to our company, when about eight Americans came running down the hill in our rear . . . The enemy kept firing on us and killed several men of our party." All were made prisoners by Bernard Early and company.

Lt. Karl Glass, meanwhile, had been ordered by Vollmer to seek out the whereabouts of the Americans who had been spotted advancing on the Germans' right flank.

"I could see the Americans a short distance away from me

crossing a small meadow at the edge of the woods," Glass would remember. "Advancing in single and double waves, the enemy was pushing on deeper and deeper into the woods."

He retraced his steps, unaware of events in the ravine. "In passing, I warned the various groups and especially the machine gun crews that they were being attacked in flank and rear," Glass said. "I then looked for the Battalion Commander and learned that he had gone to the rear, some 70 meters behind the line."

Eventually, he saw Vollmer standing—apparently by himself—a few meters away. Glass remained oblivious to the scene that was unfolding in the ravine.

"I rushed up to him and had hardly started to make my report, when I was suddenly surrounded by a number of Americans . . . Not until then did I see that Lieutenant Vollmer had been captured.

"I am not definite whether there were still more prisoners, nor how many Americans there were present. On the other hand, I still have in my mind a fairly clear picture of the American soldier in charge; it was he who kept his pistol aimed at me.

"He was a large and strong man with a red mustache, broad features and, I believe, freckle-faced."

In other words, Acting Cpl. Alvin C. York, Company G, 328th Infantry Regiment.

Interestingly, some of the German and American accounts barely mention what occurred between the initial capture of the Germans and their delivery to the American rear. The omissions, we shall see, were made for various reasons. All are at the crux of the making of the legend that is Sergeant York, America's greatest hero of World War 1.

12

AN EPOCHAL EXPLOIT

And so the man who just wanted to know what all the fighting was about, the man who did not want to kill another man, the man who'd had his come-to-Jesus moment and sworn off violence and smoking and drinking and his wild past, found himself in a bit of a predicament on the morning of October 8, 1918.

He would remember the sensation of being utterly alone, of squeezing the trigger of first his rifle, and then his .45, popping off rounds at the Germans above him just as he used to knock off the heads of turkeys back in Fentress County, Tennessee. He would remember a dull awareness that while the Germans above him were trying vainly to knock him off with their machine guns and rifles, someone to the rear of him was also firing vainly with a pistol, *pop-pop-pop-pop-pop-pop* to no avail, and out of the corner of one eye he could see the damp leaves flying and the twigs snapping and he could hear the dull thuds when the errant shots crashed into the forest floor.

And he would remember the steely gray sky and his assailants silhouetted against the browning October leaves and above all his surprise at his own grim determination, a determination born of a wanton need and desire for survival against all odds; he fought for his own survival and for the survival of the others, how many at that point he could not know, could not even know if there were *any* others still alive out of the seventeen young men who just moments before had been captors, but who now were just barely and grimly hanging on in the face of the fire of what seemed to be one hundred machine guns probing the thickets and brush for their soft bodies, bursts of fire tearing up earth and soil and grass and loamy moist dark soil all around them.

Many people today hope for their fifteen minutes of fame. For Alvin York, fifteen minutes of sharp, hot action on the morning of October 8, 1918, would endow him with an entire lifetime of fame and notoriety.

He was still a nobody corporal, a hick from Whosits, Tennessee, when Acting Sgt. Bernie Early gave his three corporals and thirteen enlisted men the order to begin lining up their prizes, the seventy or so German soldiers that they had surprised at the bottom of a steep, western-facing slope in the Argonne Forest. But the call in German to "Get down!" from up on the skyline had quickly disrupted that act, and in just seconds six men of the York Patrol had been ripped apart by bullets as their prisoners hit the earth and tried, too, to get lower than the spray of lead coming from above.

In that instant Cpl. Murray Savage's squad had been wiped out, and now Savage lay bloodied and quiet among the detritus of the autumn forest, as did his charges, Pvts. Maryan Dymowski and Ralph Weiler. Cpl. Otis Merrithew had been wounded and the two others from his small unit, Pvts. Fred Wareing and William Wine, lay limply in the repose of death. In York's squad, Pvt. Carl Swanson had been killed almost instantly, while Pvt. Mario Muzzi was wounded in a shoulder.

And now they were coming for him, these Germans, while he squatted low behind a gaggle of their brethren and waited with his rifle at the ready for the enemy above to show themselves.

Which they did, soon enough.

"By this time, those of my men who were left had gotten behind trees, and two men sniped at the Boche," York would say in the official report of the action. "They fired about half a clip each. But there wasn't any tree for me, so I just sat in the mud and used my rifle, shooting at the Boche machine gunners."

Later, he would recall, "I had no time nohow to do nothing but watch them-there German machine gunners and give them the best I had. Every time I seed a German I jes teched him off."

The enemy above consisted of some Bavarian sappers who, while racing toward the front, noticed the to-do in the ravine and had stopped, unnoticed by the Americans below, to aid their captured mates.

There were men, too, from the Fourth Company of the 120th LIR. One or some one of these had ordered the captives to go to ground, and the first bursts of fire from the ravine lip had killed not only six Americans but some prisoners as well.

As the firing continued and the commotion went on, more Germans came in from the forest edge to have a whack at taking out the tall American who lay prone at first and seemed to be the only one of the enemy who was still alive. But there were more Americans, hiding behind the prisoners or behind trees or in the brush, though York couldn't know where they were or what they were doing.

And meanwhile, York kept busy. Hidden by a clump of brush at first, he sidled forward early in the fight, still keeping the German prisoners between him and the men on the ravine edge. "There was such a noise and racket all around," he would remember.

Patiently, York waited for the enemy to show himself thirty yards above. Because of the steepness of the slope, the gunners above had to raise up to get a good look at what they were trying to kill. Every time one did, York "teched" him off.

Except for the cover of the prisoners, York was in an exposed position. But the Germans just couldn't hit him—not even Lt. Paul Vollmer, who, York was dimly aware, had not been relieved of his pistol in all the commotion and emptied it at York while he himself was aiming and firing.

Now unafraid of being hit, York raised up and began shooting "off-hand, which is my favorite position . . . ," he would say. "I used up several clips. The barrel was getting hot and my rifle ammunition was running low, or was where it was hard for me to get at it quickly. But I had to keep on shooting jes the same."

He would also recall, "The Germans were what saved me. I kept up close to them, and so the fellows on the hill had to fire a little high for fear of hitting their own men. The bullets were cracking just over my head and a lot of twigs fell down."

And he didn't know it, but he did have some help.

Pvt. Percy Beardsley, the Connecticut Yankee, had dodged behind an oak tree at the bottom of the ravine when the shooting first started. His position placed him between the lifeless bodies of Dymowski and Wareing.

"We were up against a whole battalion of Germans and it looked pretty hopeless for us," Beardsley would attest. "We were scattered out in the brush, some were guarding a bunch of Germans who had begun to surrender, and three or four of us fired two or three shots at the line of Germans on the hillside."

Beardsley managed to fire and reload his clumsy Chautchaut, a difficult task for a single soldier to perform. He sprayed the hillside above as best as he could, popping out from behind the tree and then dodging back behind it to avoid the hot German fire. He also later resorted to his pistol, he would attest.

"The German machine gunners kept up a heavy fire, as did the German riflemen on the hillside with the machine gunners," Beardsley recalled. He would later say he was certain that he killed at least "a few" of the enemy.

But he would credit York with the lion's share of the dead, which eventually would run to somewhere around twenty-five Germans.

Others of the survivors would also credit York for his actions that morning—at least in the immediate aftermath of the fight. Pvt.

Joseph Konotski, the Pole from Holyoke, Massachusetts, said York "rallied the men and closed in on the enemy, using his rifle as long as he could conveniently reach his ammunition. He then resorted to his pistol with which he killed and wounded no less than fifteen of the enemy."

Beardsley and Konotski were the only men, besides York, who witnessed his action that day (York would later tell his former battalion commander, Edward Buxton, that he vaguely remembered Konotski shooting at the Germans). Several of the others—Pvts. Michael Sacina, Patrick Donohue, George Wills, and Feodor Sok— would say that while York was firing, they were guarding prisoners and he was out of their sight.

Otis Merrithew and Mario Muzzi, both wounded, "froze in the brush with their wounds, while the enemy gunners on the hill paused to see if something might move to make a fresh target," one account of the action based on an interview with Merrithew would say.

"Now three enemy gunners stuck their heads up while [Merrithew] wondered what had happened to Cpl. Alvin York. A rifle spoke from the brush three times and three bodies tumbled down the hill."

Percy Beardsley and, possibly, Joseph Konotski were the only witnesses besides York to the firefight's denouement—a doomed charge down the hill by a handful of men under the command of Fritz Endriss, commander of the Fourth Company, 120th LIR.

York would variously say that Endriss had with him either five or six men. From the corner of his left eye York could see the squad of Germans creeping toward him; when just twenty yards away from him they leapt from a natural depression in the hillside and came toward him single file, Endriss in the lead.

His remaining stash of rifle ammunition out of reach, and there being no time to lose, York unholstered his .45 automatic.

York would give credit to an old turkey-hunting trick for what occurred next. Knowing that if he shot Endriss first the others would flee for cover, he aimed for the last man in line and shot him, and then shot the man to his left and so on, until finally he put a bullet in Endriss's stomach.

"Got the lieutenant right through the stomach and he dropped and screamed a lot," York would say, adding: "At that distance I couldn't miss."

Beardsley, for one, would report that he witnessed York's action in taking out Endriss and his charging men. "The officer whom Corporal York shot was leading a charge of some riflemen with bayonets fixed down the hillside toward us . . . He fired rapidly with rifle and pistol until he had shot down a German officer and many of his men," Beardsley would attest.

As the German lieutenant, Endriss, writhed in agony, his wound mortal, the Germans manning the guns above went silent. York now yelled for them to surrender, though it's likely their English was none too good. But after a moment, York saw that headed his way was Lieutenant Vollmer, who "could speak English as well as I could."

As Vollmer approached York during the lull, he asked of York, "English?"

York replied, "No, not English. American."

"Good Lord!" Vollmer replied.

"I reckon he had done some shooting at us himself, because I heard firing from the prisoners and afterward I found out that his pistol was empty," York recalled. "He put his hand on my shoulder . . . and said to me in English: 'Don't shoot anymore, and I'll make them surrender.' So I said 'All right'; and he did so, and they did so."

Just as Pvt. Michael Sacina was about to shoot at Vollmer from his concealed position, Vollmer blew his whistle, the signal for surrender. The Germans on the hillside and those already in the ravine "held up their hands and begun to gather around," York would say.

But as the Germans began descending the hill to join their previously captured brethren, one of them reached to his belt and pulled out a small hand grenade he had concealed. Red-faced and angry, the German quickly reached back and with his right arm tossed the grenade in York's general direction; the small bomb missed York and instead exploded among the German prisoners, wounding one.

It had not been a bright move on the part of the German. York would later say casually, "I had to tech him off. The rest surrendered without any more trouble."

Beardsley affirmed that Vollmer surrendered himself and his men to York, and added that as soon as the Germans began milling down the hill York called over the seven remaining privates and told them to situate themselves in the middle of the growing column of prisoners, and remain close to them in an effort to blend in and dissuade any trigger-happy German snipers from taking a whack at one of the doughboys.

The Americans had quite a haul. Otis Merrithew would remember bagging more than one hundred German enlisted men, plus four officers (among them the severely wounded Fritz Endriss). Another twenty-five or so Germans lay on the ground dead. Finally, a makeshift stretcher was constructed for Bernard Early, while Merrithew and Mario Muzzi bound their own wounds.

"Then began our unique parade of 110 Germans, guarded by ten doughboys heading for the front line," Merrithew would say.

It had all taken fifteen minutes to half an hour. Eleven Americans had captured well more than one hundred Germans—and were still well behind enemy lines.

Now the question was how to get back to their own lines alive—and with the prisoners.

LT. MAX THOMA of the Seventh Bavarian Sapper Company had been ordered by Vollmer to man a wide gap in the line at the edge of the woods. Leaving one platoon at the edge of the ravine, he brought another platoon forward to face the Americans coming on from Hill 223.

"The firing line was located on a slope covered with beech trees and undergrowth," he would recall. "On the left flank, I met a machine gun; its crew, I believe, consisted of only one man. This particular point afforded excellent observation."

Thoma spread his men to right and left, and decided to remain with the machine gun. Spotting some doughboys to the left, he ordered the machine gunner to fire until he discerned that the Americans were herding German prisoners to the east. He and his men, however, continued to fire at the advancing American line.

He could hear "the sound of lively rifle fire" from his men who had been ordered to take places on his right, but wanted to confirm they were in the correct place.

"I had advanced but a few steps when I heard shouting in the woods and the command, given in German, 'take off your belts,'" he recalled. He quickly grabbed several of his men and made a beeline for the place from which the order had originated, "all the while calling out loud, 'Don't remove your belts.'"

Advancing with fixed bayonets, Thoma and his men ran into a herd of captured Germans—among them Lt. Paul Vollmer. Vollmer told Thoma the right rear of the German position had been enveloped. "In order to prevent further useless bloodshed," he ordered Thoma to surrender.

Thoma refused. "I won't let them capture me," Thoma said. Vollmer replied, "It is useless. We are surrounded."

Lt. Karl Glass remembered the encounter between Thoma and Vollmer slightly differently. As the prisoners were being herded east, "Suddenly a German officer and several men with fixed bayonets jumped up on our left, that is, from the direction of our lines," Glass recalled.

"Of all the shouting and yelling that ensued, I recall only the words exchanged between the officer and Lieutenant Vollmer: 'I will not surrender!'—'It is useless!'—'I will do so on your responsibility!'" With several Americans now approaching him, Thoma finally acceded, and joined the mass of prisoners.

Some in the York Patrol had worried that they would encounter German opposition on the way to the rear. York also had to deal with some pessimists among the patrol who considered their plight to be hopeless.

"One of my men said it was impossible to get so many prisoners back to the American lines," York would recall. "And I told him to shut up."

The English-speaking Lieutenant Vollmer understood all, and soon became suspicious. He had been convinced that he and his men had surrendered to a large force of infiltrating doughboys, and asked York how many men he had. "I told him I had a-plenty," York told him.

York told Vollmer to get his men lined up on the hillside. He then had Vollmer order several of his men to pick up Bernard Early and carry him on a makeshift stretcher. Merrithew and Mario Muzzi, meanwhile, "patched up our wounds as best we could with pieces of cloth," Merrithew recalled.

York then put Vollmer at the head of the column and took a place right behind him, his pistol at Vollmer's back. "I poked the Colt in his back and told him to hike," York would say. "I guess I had him bluffed."

Otis Merrithew would remember Vollmer continually asking York, "How many men do you have?"

"I remember York replying, 'Shet up and keep marchin' and if one of your men makes a move to escape, we'll tetch off the whole lot of you.'"

But which way to go? German troops were still in place and fighting along the line to the north, and it was in that direction that Vollmer suggested the prisoners be taken. York, realizing that the prisoners taken were in the German second line, had no intention of trying to get through the German first line. He decided to march back the way the patrol had come just an hour or so before.

There was no time to lose as the battle continued to rage around them, and the six dead Americans from the York Patrol, among them Cpl. Murray Savage, had to be left where they lay. As York would recall, "Him and I were cronies—he was my bunkie—but I had to leave him there. I didn't dare to take my eye off the mob of prisoners."

The entourage ascended out of the ravine and onto the field above. As they approached Hill 2, they encountered Max Thoma.

Here, York's version of events clashes with that of the Germans. He would say that the Americans and their prisoners chanced upon a first-line German machine-gun nest that the patrol had not been aware of earlier, and that he told Vollmer to order the gunners to surrender or he would shoot him.

Vollmer "blowed his whistle and they all done surrendered," York said. "All except one."

Vollmer, he added, told the recalcitrant German twice to surrender, and was twice refused. York shot the man. "I hated to do it," York said.

Lt. Karl Kübler disputed this account, saying that American soldiers were already mingling at the exit to the ravine at the tree line, and one squad of doughboys was standing in a trench that had been occupied by some of his machine gunners.

Kübler would also dismiss some of the drama of the march back. "I saw Lieutenant Vollmer and the other officers surrounded by eight Americans who, flourishing their pistols, were describing a regular Indian dance round their prisoners."

Lt. Glass, too, disputed York's account. "I did not see . . . that this American shot the companions of Lieutenant Thoma."

Glass did, however, remember seeing Lt. Fritz Endriss, who had been carried from the ravine and laid on the field. "The man was on his back; it looked as if he had been shot from the rear," Glass testified. "Two Americans were taking care of him.

"While I failed to recognize the wounded man, Lieutenant Vollmer informed me later that he was Lieutenant Endriss, the Commanding Officer of the 4th Company."

Glass and the several men who were with him joined the parade, as did another fifteen or so machine gunners York and company subsequently ran into. Ordered by Vollmer to surrender, they gave up without a struggle.

The headquarters of the 328th Infantry Regiment had followed the halting advance that morning, and was now on the southern end of Hill 223. York worried now that the approaching column of Germans would be mistaken as a German counterattack. He was relieved when he saw soldiers from the 328th approaching to help guard the prisoners and they recognized the patrol's members as Americans.

At the regimental HQ, the column stopped and milled about, as the Americans wondered what to do with their prizes.

"The Americans stood us against a tree and carried on a lively conversation among themselves," Glass recalled. "Suddenly some other Americans appeared and addressed our guards in a highly excited tone of voice."

Among those other Americans was Capt. Adone Tomasello, the 328th Infantry Regiment's intelligence officer. As the patrol members and the captured Germans milled about, York walked over to Tomasello and calmly asked: "What shall I do with these prisoners?" Tomasello told York to get the Germans together and take them toward the rear.

"Even then I couldn't quite believe they were prisoners," Tomasello said. "York returned to where the Germans waited, herded them up, made them collect their machine guns and weapons, then marched them back as coolly as if he were taking his own squad to dig a trench."

But first, Tomasello and his officers needed information. They ordered Vollmer to sit and began interrogating him. Other Americans, Glass would claim, went to work on Vollmer's overcoat, cutting off the shoulder straps and then opening it to reveal the lieutenant's Iron Cross.

"To his protests and attempts to defend himself, Lieutenant Vollmer received as [the] only reply the words, 'hold still,'" Glass said. Vollmer relented, but asked if the mortally wounded Lt. Fritz Endriss could be carried to the back lines. His request was granted.

The intelligence officers, meanwhile, found in one of Vollmer's pockets orders he had received to counterattack the Americans at ten A.M. that morning. Another German prisoner carried a message from Vollmer to his superiors saying that his preparations for the attack had been disrupted by the American attack, leaving him helpless.

Lt. Joseph Woods, the Second Battalion's adjutant, appeared and ordered York and his men to escort the gaggle of Germans to regimental headquarters in Chatel-Chéhéry.

Glass had estimated that he was one of about eighty German prisoners; Woods told York he counted the prisoners as they passed him, and later attested that there were 132. Other Germans captured by Company G's Captain E. C. B. Danforth farther north in the sector of the 125th LIR—some forty-four soldiers—arrived, adding to the haul.

It had been, indeed, a day of days. It had begun in a haze of euphoria and with the supposed capture of a large number of enemy soldiers by a small patrol; it had turned tragic when six among that patrol had subsequently been cut down; but it turned triumphant because of the actions of a quiet and humble man who had wanted nothing to do with war, and who had been adamant about not wanting to kill another human being but had been required to kill two dozen lest he, and the men with him, be wiped out.

It was a day that had witnessed the greatest individual performance of the Great War, though, ironically, it would take some time for the importance to sink in. Even as York and the others in his patrol herded their charges toward the rear, no one had any clue as to how York's actions that morning would color not only his life, but the lives of all of the men in the patrol and in the 328th Infantry Regiment—and as well the lives of an adoring, hero-hungry public back home.

"None in the regiment, above all myself, realized then that we were actually eyewitnesses to an epoch-making exploit," Tomasello would say.

Bernard Early and Otis Merrithew could have no idea, either. Early and Merrithew, whose helmet sported bullet holes in the shape of a cross and whose left arm hung limply, were sent on to a field hospital, accompanied by Pvt. Paddy Donohue. There, surgeons removed some of the bullets from Early's body, after which he was sent on to a larger hospital.

(Donohue, ironically, would be wounded at the aid station when a piece of high-explosive shell sliced into one shoulder just outside the door. He joined Early and Merrithew as a patient and would not rejoin Company G until November.)

On the way to Chatel-Chéhéry, the Americans and their cap-
tives came under heavy artillery fire coming from a knoll above
Cornay to the north. York ordered the line to double-time, and the
Americans had some trouble keeping the Germans from scattering.

The column held together, and finally all broke into a run to get
out of range of the German guns. After arriving at the regimental
HQ, York was told there was no place to put so many prisoners
and was ordered to hike them farther south to the 164th Brigade's
headquarters at Varennes.

There, brigade commander Gen. Julian Lindsey came out to
witness their arrival. "Well, York," Lindsey said. "I hear you have
captured the whole damn German army."

No, said York.

"I only have 132."

13

WHAT WOULD YORK DO

Capt. E. C. B. Danforth knew nothing of what had occurred on the far left of his line on the morning of October 8, 1918, and as the York Patrol ascended the hill on the company's far left he had been trying, with his men, to continue to advance west through the valley of Death and to the Decauville rail line beyond the screen of low hills and woods to his immediate front.

But, he would remember, "At some time during the morning the fire from the left flank slackened and we were enabled to gain the hill to our immediate front, capturing a great many machine guns and driving the enemy to the west."

Two platoons from Company F had been sent forward when the attack had stalled in midmorning, and at midday some more help arrived, as the First Battalion's Company D came up in support, as did two platoons of Company H. At 3:30 P.M., the attack was renewed with greater vigor, and with greater numbers.

"One by one we crossed this valley," Company G's Sgt. Harry Parsons recalled. "We did not lose a man. After reaching the top of the hill directly to their front, suddenly all hell seemed to open up. We had reached the machine gun nests. We all dropped on the ground and the machine guns stopped but the artillery started."

One shell exploded directly above Parsons and his remaining men, and the remains of one man who was hit were "blown in our faces but he was the only casualty from that shell."

The advance resumed, and finally they reached the Decauville railway at five P.M. Companies D and G were placed on the eastern bank of the railbed and faced west, while the flanks of Company E and part of Company F were refused so that they faced north. Company D was later that night ordered to rejoin the First Battalion.

The Second Battalion remained in position on the railway through the night, and twice repelled counterattacks aimed at reopening the crucial line so troops and materiel could be evacuated from the pocket that the 164th Brigade attack over the past two days had created.

On the morning of October 9, Companies E and F once more attacked, this time toward Champrocher Ridge to the north. Moving across a valley reeking with phosgene gas, the men assaulted the steep ridge but, seriously depleted by the previous day's fighting, they were unable to consolidate any ground gained. When the two companies returned to the railway line, a count was made of the "effectives" left in the Second Battalion; there were only eighty-eight men out of the original thousand that were still able to fight.

One of them was Alvin York, whose disappearance on October 8 had been noted by Danforth.

"The Captain asked me where I had been," York would say. "I told him of the fight with the machine guns around on the left flank; of how the other non-commissioned officers had been killed or wounded; and how I had takened command and marched them prisoners away back behind the lines."

Danforth, still oblivious to the York Patrol's feat, asked York why he hadn't just dumped his prisoners at the battalion's headquarters and then returned to join the rest of the company as it slogged west. York explained that no one would take the prisoners off his hands, and he'd had to go all the way back to brigade headquarters at Varennes.

Danforth asked York how many prisoners he'd taken. When York replied, "he looked at me with a funny-like expression in his face." It would only slowly dawn on Danforth that it was because of the actions of York and the rest that "the fire from the left flank slackened," as Danforth would report, enabling Company G and the Second Battalion to advance.

York's deed in the ravine had been born of an impulse to save his own skin, and that of as many others in the patrol as he could. The actual result was much larger—larger than even he could know on the morning of October 9, 1918.

By bagging so many Germans and unknowingly disrupting a planned counterattack, York had enabled the leading waves of Companies G and E to advance west to the Decauville railway and seize and hold it. The railway was vital to supplying men and materiel to the German defenders in the Argonne; with its capture, the Germans would have no choice but to begin withdrawing from their positions.

As well, the York Patrol's coup had had an immediate effect on the Germans.

Capt. Karl von Sick, commander of the Third Battalion of the 120th Landwehr Infantry Regiment (LIR), had his headquarters about one kilometer to the south of the ravine in which Alvin York and company encountered the First Battalion, 120th LIR and the other assorted German troops.

In the late morning on October 8, he received a message from the Second Battalion of the 120th LIR on his left saying that "the enemy has penetrated our lines north of my position and is advancing in dense waves." Alarmed, he decided at 11:30 A.M. to withdraw his battalion to the west.

And with the Decauville railway cut, the German High Command on the morning of October 9 did indeed order an evacuation of troops out of the Argonne and above the Aire River, which flows northeastward through the eastern edge of the forest before turning sharply west just below the village of St. Juvin.

The October 7 assault on Hill 223 and Cornay had also caused the Germans to nervously relax their death hold around the pocket where the Lost Battalion had suffered for almost a week. Elements of the Seventy-Seventh Division were able to reach Charles Whittlesey and his men on the evening of October 7, and he and his men—those who could still walk, anyway—began the march out on the morning of October 8.

The Germans were on the run for certain, but the fight was far from over. The failed attack of Companies E and F, 328th Infantry Regiment, on the German positions on Champrocher ridge on October 9 demonstrated the German will to continue fighting.

So did the ensuing action on October 9.

On October 8, even as Alvin York and the 328th's Second Battalion was attacking west across a killing field, the 327th Infantry Regiment—the brigade mate of the 328th—was ordered to attack Cornay ridge, north of Hill 180. The Third Battalion of the 328th Infantry Regiment was also ordered in as support for the 327th.

Col. Frank Ely, commander of the 327th Infantry Regiment, once again selected his First Battalion—which had been bloodied while seizing Hill 180 the previous day—to carry out the attack. However, after it jumped off at six A.M., orders came changing the direction of the assault from northwest to due north, aiming straight for the village of Cornay.

After reorganizing almost in the face of the enemy, the First Battalion resumed the advance in the face of murderous machine-gun fire from Fleville—still not taken by the First Division—to the east and the ridges west of Cornay.

The fighting coursed through the morning and afternoon, but finally at dark what remained of Companies A and D, 327th Infantry Regiment, plus one platoon from the Third Battalion of the 328th, obtained a toehold in Cornay. Patrols subsequently were sent out and the village was cleared of Germans, while another small detachment of the 328th's Third Battalion also reached the town.

Unfortunately, friendly fire from American artillerymen forced the doughboys to retreat to the town's southern end, where they huddled precariously through the night amid a rain of shells. Meanwhile, fresh troops from the Forty-First German Division arrived; its commander would remain ignorant of the order to withdraw from the Argonne until after his men put a beating on the 164th Brigade.

"Prisoners captured later stated that the whole Division had been sent down to retake Cornay, and to beat off the flank attack on the Argonne," the 327th's history says.

The Americans launched an assault on October 9 aiming to retake the village, but were soon counterattacked by Germans who had infiltrated through the woods to the west of Cornay and an orchard to the east. The doughboys retreated to the southern edge of Cornay, but now found themselves surrounded on three sides. Taking up positions in ruined houses, they waited for the Germans to reprise their attacks.

"Our men fought with rifles and machine guns and Chautchauts from doors and windows killing great number[s] and suffering heavy losses," Ely would write in a field message to the 164th Brigade.

Late in the morning, some Germans wearing Red Cross insignia and flying Red Cross flags approached the American positions carrying a stretcher. As the doughboys watched, the stretcher was put down in a shell hole—and soon the muzzle of a machine gun popped up and began firing.

That signaled a renewed effort by the Germans, who also brought up trench mortars, which "soon knocked holes in the walls of the occupied houses," the 327th's history says. Many doughboys were killed or wounded.

Capt. Charles Brown of Company A of the 327th was severely wounded in a leg during the bombardment, so Capt. Howard Mc-Call of Company D took command. The Germans, meanwhile, made a final push and completely enveloped the forlorn group.

McCall decided to end the carnage and save some lives. "We have done all we can men, we shall all be killed if we stay," he told his men. Many of the survivors stopped firing and laid down their weapons, but a few men from the 328th Infantry Regiment made a run for it, despite the odds.

"Captain McCall permitted a number of men to attempt to escape by jumping from a window and running down the road to the south," the Eighty-Second Division's history says. "These men were shot down almost immediately."

Still, two officers and an enlisted man from the 328th Infantry Regiment told McCall they wanted out. "A German prisoner was sent out of the house to wave a towel and all enemy fire was stopped," the Eighty-Second Division's history says.

During the lull, the trio of Americans bolted from the house and raced down the road. They took refuge in a shell hole outside of town until darkness, when they made their way back to friendly forces on Hill 180.

Ninety men of the 327th were captured. More than one hundred others had been killed or died of wounds. Some 675 were wounded or gassed, and another one hundred men came down sick.

Cornay remained in German hands—but not for long. Finally getting word of the general retreat to above the Aire River, the Forty-First Division withdrew during the night of October 9–October 10, taking its American prisoners with it.

The next morning, the 325th Infantry Regiment, having relieved the 327th and 328th Infantry Regiments, assaulted Cornay at seven A.M.

"No severe resistance was met," the 325th's commander, Col.

Walter Whitman, would write. "The objective was occupied before noon."

Patrols from the 325th were sent out, and went all the way to the Aire River without being contested. "The flank attack of the 82nd Div. resulted in driving the last vestige of the enemy from the Argonne forest and made possible the advance of troops east of the Aire," Whitman would write.

That was certain; on October 9, with the Germans withdrawing their artillery from the heights above Cornay, the First U.S. Division carried on its attack after a three-day respite and finally took Fléville and the Romagne Hills above Exermont on the eastern edge of the Aire. Its men perched on Hill 263 could look north toward a plain and a series of small hills marking the Kriemhilde Stellung—the last bastion of defense for the German army, and the last serious obstacle to the A.E.F.

They could thank Alvin York and his patrol members for their finally being able to break out.

ACTING CPL. ALVIN York of Company G, 328th Infantry Regiment, had not inspired much faith in his war-making abilities until the morning of October 8, 1918. Because of his conflicts about killing other men while at Camp Gordon, some in the York Patrol had continued to mistrust him as a soldier right up to that fifteen-minute blast of cool and contained fury.

Cpl. Otis Merrithew would claim that York, even after arriving in France, continued to be beset with doubts about the war and his place in it. And even as Company G advanced west down Hill 223, Merrithew had his own doubts and suspicions about the hick from Possum Crotch, Tennessee.

"What would York do now, I wondered," Merrithew would say years after the fact. "Would he run and leave us exposed? Would he fight? I didn't know, and not knowing bothered me, for he was protecting the platoon's left flank in the midst of heavy enemy fire."

York himself did not know until that morning just how he would react in battle. By noon on October 8, 1918, he had found out.

But the newly gained knowledge of his capabilities, of his own bloodthirsty will to survive, gnawed at him in the days after. He also suffered from survivor's guilt, and wondered why and how he had made it through that morning unscathed when six others had been killed and three more wounded—one, Bernie Early, severely.

"It seemed sorter hard to believe that I had done come through alive," he would say. "Two men on both sides of me and two others right behind me were killed, and I hadn't been touched."

On the morning of October 9, 1918, York continued to ponder it all, and he also began to wonder whether all of the six men who were cut down were in fact dead. The action, and the subsequent rounding up of prisoners, had happened so quickly that on reflection he worried some might have actually survived the battle and would now be lying in the ravine, bleeding and waiting and hoping for help.

So Alvin York asked his captain, E. C. B. Danforth, if he could leave Company G for a time to go back to the scene of the firefight and make sure no one had in fact been left behind.

"I felt I jes had to go and look for them," he would say.

Danforth agreed to let him go, and allowed a small detail of orderlies and stretcher-bearers to go with him. When he arrived, he found that the regiment's salvagers had already been through to pick up discarded weapons and other materiel. Otherwise, the place was a shambles. The trees, the bushes, even the ground— everything was torn up by bullets.*

---

* York would claim in his autobiography—written ten years after the fact— that the bodies of Dymowski, Wareing, Savage, Wine, Weiler, and Swanson were already buried, but that isn't so. The dead lay where they fell until Oc-

"The ground in front and on both sides of where we done stood was all soft and torned up with bullets," York would say. "The brush on either side was also torned up and there was a sort of tunnel cut in the brush behind" where he had fired at the Germans above.

York mourned all of his dead comrades, but none as much as Cpl. Murray Savage. "My best pal, dead . . . ," York would ruefully say. "I would never share the same blanket with Corporal Savage. We'd never read the Bible together again. We would never talk about our faith and pray to our God . . .

"I prayed for the Greeks and Italians and the Poles and the Jews and the others. I done prayed for the Germans, too. They were all brother men of mine. Maybe their religion was different, but I reckon we all believed in the same God and I wanted to pray for all of them."

tober 24, 1918, when they were interred by a burial party led by Chaplain John O'Farrelly of the 303rd Engineer Regiment, Seventy-Eighth Division. The bodies were subsequently disinterred and moved to the American cemetery at Romagne. York might have been experiencing a false memory in recollecting the scene in the ravine on October 9, 1918.

14

A TIME FOR PEACE

For Alvin York, still an unheralded acting corporal in Company G of the 328th Infantry Regiment, the war continued on through October as the Eighty-Second Division now pressed north, the Seventy-Seventh Division on its left and the Forty-Second "Rainbow" Division to its right.

In the western portion, the first week of the second phase of the Meuse-Argonne offensive had been a huge success; with no small thanks to the York Patrol, the Decauville railway had been cut, forcing the Germans to begin a slow retreat north; the First Division also had taken the Romagne Hills on the eastern side of the Aire River and on October 11 was relieved by the Forty-Second Division.

In the center and to the right, American divisions comprising the III and V Corps were also advancing, pushing the German defenders back begrudgingly and lapping up at the Kriemhilde Stellung, at which the final great battles of the American offensive would be fought in mid-October.

In conjunction with the Meuse-Argonne offensive, British, French, and other American divisions had attacked the main Hindenburg Line in the north; on September 27, British forces attacked near Cambrai and took some thirty-three thousand Germans prisoner in one day. On September 29, the Twenty-Seventh and Thirtieth U.S. Divisions, which had been attached to the British, attacked the fortified German line at the St. Quentin Canal. The

Twenty-Seventh made little progress, but the Thirtieth breached the canal and the Hindenburg Line, and its success was followed up by advancing Australians.

On October 8, Alvin York's day of days, three British armies renewed the attack on a twenty-mile front between Cambrai and St. Quentin, and took ten thousand prisoners; just days later, the French kicked the German defenders out of Laon; a separate British-French offensive into Belgium resulted in a gain of eighteen miles of formerly German-held ground and the capture of twelve thousand German prisoners.

All along the Allied line, there were hopes for a final victory in 1919; it would not take nearly that long for hostilities to end.

And Alvin York and the other survivors within the York Patrol would once more be part of the still-unfolding offensive in the west. On October 11, even as the three battalions of the 328th were converging on a ridge running west from Cornay, the Eighty-Second's fight was being carried above the Aire and toward the fortified villages of St. Juvin and Grandpré, on the river's north bank. Beyond lay a "switch" of the Kriemhilde Stellung, half a mile above the river.

The Third Battalion, 325th Infantry Regiment early on October 11 hit the road running north from Fléville and toward St. Juvin, marching beneath an ominous, dull gray sky and across rain-soaked, brown countryside under the blessing of a heavy fog.

The fog, though, lifted at about six A.M., and the line of Americans encountered German troops to their front that had moved south during the night and were well into the regiment's designated jump-off point.

"They opened a withering fire on this helpless column," Col. Walter Whitman, the 325th's commander, would recall. He called up two companies in the back of the column and ordered them to advance while the lead companies hugged the road bank.

Once the immediate German threat had faded, the battalion as a whole moved on a ridge beyond the Sommerance–St. Juvin road, where it "plunged through the German wire" and fought its way to the top. "It captured the enemy machine guns though at an appalling price," Whitman would write.

The Eighty-Second's three other regiments had also gone over the top. But the 327th on Whitman's right had soon bogged down in the face of heavy enemy fire, while the 326th, with Alvin York and the 328th in support, also failed to advance in line with Whitman's men.

"The 325th was alone on the ridge with both flanks in the air," Whitman remembered. He ordered his First and Second Battalions to hustle to the front, and the reinforcements helped establish a foothold on the ridge—though the Germans tried to dislodge the Americans in four separate and doomed counterattacks.

Any thoughts that the Germans were giving up the fight easily were dashed on that lonely hill. "On the contrary; he had evidenced a grim purpose to hold a terrain so admirably adapted for defense," the division's history says. "In the four counter-attacks launched on us . . . the enemy had shown the utmost prodigality in expending his infantry and selected machine gunners." Still, the Germans were beaten back, leaving "substantial numbers" of prisoners in American hands.

The 325th would remain in place on the ridge until October 14; the 326th and 327th Infantry Regiments also stood fast to the left and right, respectively, while the 328th Infantry Regiment was pulled out of its support position and marched east to the vicinity of Fléville.

It was not there for long. Late on October 13, the Eighty-Second's advance was resumed, and the 328th Infantry Regiment came under heavy artillery fire as it moved north toward Sommerance, which the 328th's First Battalion reached just after midnight;

it relieved a battalion of the 327th Regiment that had taken and was holding the village.

The First and Second Battalions of the 328th Infantry Regiment were placed along the Sommerance–St. Juvin road west of Sommerance. Morning's light brought a new vista to the Eighty-Second's men strung out between the two villages. Where they had spent the previous week in the battered and leafy area west and north of Chatel-Chéhéry, here they could look north across broad, naked, rolling uplands marked here and there with copses of dark trees.

It was near Sommerance that Acting Cpl. Alvin York, the man who had endured the attack of more than one hundred German soldiers and streams of hot machine-gun fire in that ravine west of Chatel-Chéhéry, had what he would call, with no irony, his closest brush with death during the war.

Positioned in an apple orchard west of Sommerance, he and his mates were digging in when suddenly a heavy German artillery bombardment found them. As the big shells crept nearer and nearer, York and his company mates dug with more and more fury—"I'm a-telling you, the dirt was flying," he would say.

"And then bang!—one of the big shells struck the ground right in front of us and we all went up in the air. But we all come down again. Nobody was hurt. But it sure was close."

At 8:30 A.M. on October 14, the 328th's First Battalion went over the top and right into a concentration of German machine-gun, rifle, and artillery fire. Companies A and C led the assault, with Companies B and D in support.

On its left, the 163rd Brigade of the Eighty-Second Division also attacked, while on its right a brigade of the Forty-Second Division, which had relieved the bloodied First Division on October 11, also went over the top—and right into the attack zone of the 328th. The attack stalled as Col. Richard Wetherill of the

328th spent two hours trying to convince the Rainbow warriors to move to the east.

The advance continued, the firing increasing in intensity as the doughboys pushed through the Germans' defensive wire. Lt. Charles Day, in charge of Company B, led his men up a rise and toward the Ravine aux Pierres, which held numerous Germans, when all hell broke loose.

German machine gunners fired unending volleys of bullets from a few hundred yards on the left, while riflemen poured it on from the bottom of the ravine. Companies A and C worked forward slowly, methodically reducing machine-gun outposts in patches of woods and undulations in the otherwise flat ground. Finally, the two units pierced the wire of the Kriemhilde Stellung, while Companies B and D followed in close support.

By midafternoon, Lt. Charles Day's Company B had moved beyond the 325th Infantry Regiment to the left, and lost its protection on the right flank when Company D fell back after briefly gaining the wire of the Kriemhilde Stellung, which in the Eighty-Second's sector consisted of shallow trenches, cross-firing machine-gun posts, and heavy wire situated on and within ridges and patches of woods.

"We were unable to go forward and I think would have been practically wiped out had we tried to retire so we did about the only thing we could do which was [to stay] where we were," Day later wrote.

The Germans sent shrapnel shells Company B's way through the afternoon, but luckily for Day and company the shells overshot their forlorn position. Day tried to send a message to First Battalion headquarters "to please send some help" to try to flank and reduce a particularly troublesome German redoubt in some woods to his right front.

A lieutenant with Company D intercepted the message, and

promptly and bravely gathered about forty of his men. They crept toward the wood and fired a deluge of rifle grenades into it but were unable to dislodge the defenders. There was now little more Day and his men could do but "hug the ground. About all who didn't were immediately killed or wounded."

The 328th's Second Battalion, in support, was finally called into action, and came under severe shelling as it attempted to reach the First Battalion's forward line. Company G, along with two platoons of Company H, passed through the First Battalion's lines and continued the attack.

Alvin York and the rest of the Second Battalion would also just barely pierce the wire of the Kriemhilde Stellung, where after dark the men went to ground and began digging for their lives as the First Battalion withdrew. In Day's Company B, just twenty-five enlisted men and one officer—himself—remained fit for duty.

Company B's numbers were later increased when stragglers and sick soldiers reported, but the unit still only had about forty men to its name; the Third Battalion of the 328th, meanwhile, remained back at the Sommerance–St. Juvin road, its numbers reduced to a paltry ninety men.

It was at least fortunate that the Second Battalion had the protection of the German wire immediately to its front to help stave off any German counterattacks that might be launched. The night, though, was long, as men on the front line hugged the earth in their shallow holes and hoped for deliverance.

"The Germans was shelling us awfull with big shells also gas and the boys laying there that they couldn't burry," York recalled. "Oh my I cant tell you how I felt and when those big shells would come over and burst then I heard my comrades crying and mourning."

The morning of October 15, drizzly and foggy as usual, brought new orders to advance behind a rolling barrage. The attack was scheduled for 7:30 A.M., but at seven A.M. the Germans laid a heavy barrage on the American front line, followed by an infantry assault fifteen minutes later.

"The German fire held our men on the exposed ridge, flattened in fox holes, and a swarm of the gray-uniformed enemy was on top of our outposts before the combat groups a little in the rear could grasp the full significance of the peril," the Eighty-Second's history says. "A desperate fight of an individual character followed at hand-to-hand range."

The left of the 328th Infantry Regiment and the right of the 325th took the brunt of the attack, and some of the American defenders were forced back almost to the Sommerance–St. Juvin road. There soldiers with the 328th left their prone positions, stood up, and fired into the ranks of the Germans.

"The spirit of resistance which our men everywhere evinced shattered the enemy assault and inflicted very heavy losses. In about fifteen minutes the German survivors were running back, pursued by American fire," the division's history says.

Despite the Germans' attack, the Eighty-Second's assault went forward on time. However, the 166th Brigade of the Forty-Second Division was held up on the right by German defenders. The 328th sent a "strong patrol" under Lt. Charles Day to help, and its men returned with prisoners and word that most of the defenders had fled.

The Germans, though, continued to fight back throughout the day, attacking the dangerous salient held by the Second Battalion. Machine guns raked and artillery pounded the battalion, and rain and swooping, strafing enemy planes added to the misery.

It was impossible to move.

"Holding our first line against heavy artillery and machine-gun fire," a 7:30 P.M. message from the front to the Eighty-Second Division's headquarters said. "Repulsed counter-attack on left flank this morning. Our troops exhausted. Can not continue advance."

The Second Battalion was relieved by the tattered 327th Infantry Regiment—which numbered just more than five hundred officers and men, or just a fifth of its normal strength—and fell back. At six A.M. on October 16, the 327th once more went over the top and forced its way three hundred yards across the battleground.

But because the Forty-Second Division to the right could not make any headway, the regiment soon had its right flank in the air. The men refused the line, and elements of the 328th were brought up in support. The 327th's commander pleaded for relief in a message sent at 10:50 A.M.:

"I again call to your attention the physical condition of the men of my command. I strongly recommend their relief to-night. To men in their condition, the weather conditions of last night were very trying. They will be in no condition to-morrow morning for any strenuous operation."

Alvin York and the equally battered Second Battalion meanwhile headed back toward Sommerance, its four companies reduced from the standard 250 soldiers to twenty to forty men and one or two officers. Upon reaching Sommerance, they plopped, exhausted, into rain-filled foxholes for several nights, before returning to the front once more to relieve what remained of the Third Battalion.

York's superior, Sgt. Harry Parsons, would praise York for his work above Sommerance.

"York stuck like glue," Parsons told his hometown newspaper. "He is a man, every inch of him. He would carry out his orders to the word. I can say he is a stanch, true and reliable friend."

The Eighty-Second's commander, Gen. George Duncan, visited the front at about noon and was appalled at what he found. He, too, pleaded for the relief of his division in a message to I Corps, saying "because of physical fatigue, I don't believe these men can go forward anymore. I think we have got to hold what we have got."

He would add: "The men of this Division have behaved splendidly and have lost heavily. There are not fifty men to a Company and these are practically at the end of their strength. Their spirit is fine but to-day they are at the end of their physical endurance."

In response, I Corps commander Gen. Charles Summerall directed Duncan to employ just one battalion per day in the front line, and to rotate the battalions from the front, to support, and then to reserve on a daily basis.

Gen. Julian Lindsey, commander of the 164th Brigade, sympathized with the state of his men but in an order sent on October 17 told them flat-out:

"Howsoever great the necessity, the indications are that there will be no immediate relief. All officers must, therefore, exert themselves to the utmost toward reorganizing their commands. Conditions are never so bad but what they can be hopefully improved by rejuvenated effort."

Though not exactly the hoped-for relief, the method of rotating by battalions "bore immediate results," according to the authors of the Eighty-Second's history.

On October 18, Company G of the 328th was ordered to march west along the line and extend the regiment's sector on the left by one kilometer to protect the right flank of the Seventy-Eighth Division, which had relieved the Seventy-Seventh Division two days before.

Capt. E. C. B. Danforth had his few men connect with the right of the Seventy-Eighth Division and the left of the 163rd Brigade, and over the next twelve days patrols were sent out at night; during the day men huddled low to escape being strafed by German planes.

All expectations were that another push was in store, but meanwhile the "men and officers patiently and with good spirits stuck to their posts while the wearing-out process continued to take its toll," the 328th's history says.

The second phase of the Meuse-Argonne offensive was winding down, and plans were being laid for the third and—it was hoped—final phase.

Artillery, ammunition, and "partially rested" divisions were en route to their jump-off places as the frontline units of the Seventy-Eighth, Eighty-Second, and Forty-Second Divisions "continued to exist in cold mud and water-soaked fox holes, always subjected to harassing artillery and machine-gun fire," the Eighty-Second's history notes.

New fodder was also being forwarded to the Eighty-Second's front—five thousand to six thousand barely trained recruits from replacement divisions. But these would be spared any action; on the night of October 30–October 31, 1918, the Eighty-Second Division was finally relieved after spending twenty-five consecutive days in the line.

During those miserable days in the Argonne, the Eighty-Second Division had seen thirty-seven officers and 865 enlisted men killed, among the latter the six men of the York Patrol—Swanson, Wareing, Savage, Wine, Dymowski, and Weiler—who now rested where they fell in freshly dug graves in that ravine one kilometer west of Chatel-Chéhéry.

Almost five thousand of the Eighty-Second's soldiers had also been wounded or gassed, while 185 men had been taken prisoner. Twenty-five men had gone missing in the deep woods of the Argonne and on the rolling, ravine-pocked ground above the Aire.

THE ALL-AMERICANS OF the 82nd Division had done their job. They had attacked west into the Argonne Forest and attained the Decauville railway, cleaving the German defense in two and forcing the enemy's retreat. They had effected the relief as well of the Lost Battalion, and then pushed the German line north of the Aire.

And it would be difficult to argue that any individual soldier among the All-Americans had done more than Acting Cpl. Alvin York and the men with him—Bernard Early, Percy Beardsley, Thomas Johnson, Michael Sacina, Feodor Sok, Mario Muzzi, George Wills, Otis Merrithew, plus the six men who lay in temporary graves in that forest—to break the German line, and ultimately the German will.

On the morning of November 1, 1918, the last phase of the Meuse-Argonne offensive began. Seven American divisions—from left to right the Seventy-Eighth, Seventy-Seventh, Eightieth, Second, Eighty-Ninth, Ninetieth, and Fifth—went over the top, aiming for the Meuse River.

More heights remained to be overrun, and men once more slogged through fog and driving, cold November rains, many chilled and feverish, and most utterly miserable and war-weary.

By then, however, the German will to resist was crumbling. The German military mastermind Erich Ludendorff, himself tired of the war, had resigned on October 26. Turkey left the war on October 31, Austria-Hungary on November 4. Kaiser Wilhelm fled Berlin on October 30, and the Channel ports were in Allied hands.

The end of the war was nigh, and an Armistice was discussed on all sides. Gen. John Pershing, commander of the American Expeditionary Force, instead argued for carrying the war out to its bitter end and forcing Germany to surrender unconditionally. If that couldn't be obtained, he was agreeable, he wrote, to an Armistice with such harsh terms that Germany would never be able to make war again.

By November 1, the war was also over for Alvin York, Joseph Konotski, Percy Beardsley, and the eight other survivors of the York Patrol, who had certainly done their bit to hasten the demise of the German defenses in the Argonne.

On November 1, they and the rest of the men of the Eighty-Second Division were relieved from their muddy, water-logged funk holes by the Seventy-Seventh and Eightieth Divisions, which would carry the fight north to the Meuse River, fighting alongside the Seventy-Eighth Division and the Second Division, whose marines had gained everlasting glory at Belleau Wood almost five months before.

York, writing in his diary, only nonchalantly marked the end of his part in the war. "Argonne Forest," Alvin York would write in his diary upon being relieved. "So we came out of the lines to a germans rest camp and there we got something to eat."

He also got some new stripes—those of a sergeant. A ten-day leave followed, and York and some pals took the train to Aix-les-Bains, far to the south of the Argonne Forest in the foothills of the French Alps. York went to church, and visited baths built by Romans; he also popped over the border into Italy for a look.

"And then it all come to an end," York would note in his diary. "All of this killing and destroying."

At the eleventh hour of the eleventh day of the eleventh month—November 11, 1918—the guns went silent across the Western Front, and an almost-eerie stillness replaced the booming of the artillery and the *pup-pup-pup* of the machine guns.

Men continued to die right up to the penultimate hour, 127 of them American soldiers who had been ordered to cross the Meuse River in the early hours of the day only to be cut down on the makeshift bridges their engineers threw across.

But at eleven A.M. the madness stopped, and rain-soaked, grimy men from the North Sea to the Swiss border gathered around campfires to quietly toast their luck, and to mourn comrades fallen and left behind during the last six months of 1918—more than 1,400 killed and 6,600 wounded in the Eighty-Second Division alone. All told, some 26,000 American soldiers lost their lives in the fight

The site of the York Patrol's firefight seen in early winter, 1919.
(*U.S. Army Signal Corps*)

Alvin York in full uniform.
(Sergeant York Patriotic Foundation)

A mustachioed Pvt. Alvin York, seated
in the second row, far left, during
training at Camp Gordon, ca. 1918.
(Courtesy of Carol Schulthies)

Alvin York aiming his favorite shotgun. As a boy, he honed his shot hunting turkeys in the backwoods of Tennessee.
(Sergeant York Patriotic Foundation)

Carl Swanson.
(Sergeant York Patriotic Foundation)

Maryan Dymowski, seated.
(Courtesy of Carol Schulthies)

Murray Savage.
(Sergeant York Patriotic Foundation)

Otis Merrithew, aka William B. Cutting.
(Sergeant York Patriotic Foundation)

Though York received the lion's share of the glory, there were sixteen others with him in the Argonne Forest that day.

Fred Wareing.
(Sergeant York Patriotic Foundation)

G. Edward Buxton Jr.
(Rhode Island Heritage Hall of Fame)

George Wills.
(Sergeant York Patriotic Foundation)

Percy Beardsley.
(Sergeant York Patriotic Foundation)

Ralph Weiler.
(FindAGrave.com)

Alvin York can be seen standing, second from the right, while Maryan Dymowski is seated fourth from the right in a photo taken during training at Camp Gordon, ca. 1918. The two men would encounter very different fates on October 9, 1918.

(Courtesy of Carol Schulthies)

Alvin York and Pvt. Carl Swanson at Camp Gordon, ca. 1918.

(Sergeant York Patriotic Foundation)

A confident group of men in the 325th Infantry Regiment, Eighty-Second Division on their way to the front lines on June 25, 1918. *(U.S. Army Signal Corps)*

Men with the 328th Infantry Regiment—the York Patrol's outfit—being trained by a French officer in the fine art of grenade throwing. *(U.S. Army Signal Corps)*

The ruins of the village of Cornay, as seen in November 1918.
(U.S. Army Signal Corps)

The view north from Hill 244 toward Chatel-Chéhéry and the central slope of Hill 223 as seen in November 1918.
(U.S. Army Signal Corps)

The battlefield grave of Cpl. Murray Savage, buried where he fell after being killed by German machine-gun fire on October 8, 1918. His Enfield rifle is at his left side, and his helmet is covered by the blanket thrown over him. Savage's body was disinterred in 1921 and reburied in the Meuse-Argonne American Cemetery at Romagne, France.

(U.S. Army Signal Corps)

The battlefield graves of four members of the York Patrol: left to right are Pvts. Fred Wareing, Maryan Dymowski, Carl Swanson, and Ralph Weiler. The bodies of Wareing, Dymowski, Weiler, and William Wine were exhumed in 1921 and reburied in the Meuse-Argonne American Cemetery at Romagne, France. The body of Swanson was sent home for reburial in a cemetery in Jamestown, New York.

(U.S. Army Signal Corps)

Alvin York in early 1919 at the site of the York Patrol's firefight. George Pattullo, whose 1919 story "The Second Elder Gives Battle" would transform York's life, lurks in the background at the left edge of the frame.

(U.S. Army Signal Corps)

York during his whirlwind tour of New York after his return from France in May 1919.

(Sergeant York Patriotic Foundation)

Gary Cooper won an Academy Award for his portrayal of York in this 1941 biopic, which was the highest-grossing film of the year.
(Heritage Auctions)

Alvin York pictured with his wife, Gracie, and his mother, Mary York, at the York family farmstead in Pall Mall, Tennessee.
(Sergeant York Patriotic Foundation)

York and his new bride, Gracie, following their wedding on June 7, 1919.
(Sergeant York Patriotic Foundation)

Alvin York, center, at the ceremony at which Bernard Early received the Distinguished Service Cross on October 5, 1929. To York's right is Gen. Charles P. Summerall; to his left is Secretary of War James William Good. *(U.S. Army Signal Corps)*

Bernard Early shakes hands with Assistant Secretary of War Patrick J. Hurley on October 5, 1929, after receiving his Distinguished Service Cross for his actions with the York Patrol on October 8, 1918. *(U.S. Army Signal Corps)*

York in his later years.
(Sergeant York Patriotic Foundation)

A pensive Alvin York.
(Sergeant York Patriotic Foundation)

The graves of Alvin York and his wife, Gracie, at Wolf River Cemetery in Pall Mall, Tennessee. *(Brian Stansberry)*

The French village of Chatel-Chéhéry, seen looking north in 2019.
(Courtesy of the author)

Hill 244 seen from Hill 223. The York Patrol ascended the hill's western spur on the morning of October 8, 1918, and soon found themselves behind the Germans' lines.
(Courtesy of the author)

The top of Hill 180 as seen from Cornay, to the north. The hill was taken by the First Battalion, 328th Infantry Regiment on October 7, 1918—the day before the York Patrol's battle in a ravine to the south.
(Courtesy of the author)

A portrait of Alvin York showing his Medal of Honor (on the left) and French Croix de Guerre (on the right).

(Sergeant York Patriotic Foundation)

for the Meuse-Argonne; a total of 116,000 were killed in action, or died of wounds, disease, and accidents.

Still in Aix-les-Bains when the Armistice took effect, now-Sgt. Alvin York stayed in his room while his buddies partied through the night to celebrate the end of the war. It was noisy, he would remember, as French and Americans got drunk together, and whooped and hollered until dawn.

His feelings about the war's end, he would recall, "were like most all of the American boys. It was all over. And we were ready to go home."

15

WAITING FOR THE HERO

George Robson Pattullo was under strict orders. Anticipating an impending return to France, he wrote to a friend from New York's Seville Hotel on East Twenty-Eighth Street on November 1, 1918, to explain that George Horace Lorimer, the editor-in-chief of the *Saturday Evening Post*, had no more interest in blood-and-guts war stories, but was looking for Pattullo to write more of his colorful in-the-trenches-with-the-boys tales. These types of stories had served Pattullo and Lorimar well over the past year and a half. They carried headlines such as "Dirty Work at the Cross Roads," "A.W.O.L.," "Hellwood"—an account of the U.S. Marines at Belleau Wood in the early summer of 1918—and "The First Raid," about a German raid-in-force on the First Division's lines in November 1917 that left three Americans dead.

"My instructions are to lay off the battle stuff, unless something tremendous breaks," Pattullo wrote, "just plain, homely stories that will bring the man with the pack and rifle close to the people on this side. Of course that is what I have done, mostly, anyway."

A Canadian, Pattullo had been born in Woodstock, Ontario, in 1879. He attended the local Woodstock Collegiate Institute and afterward began writing for various papers and publications in Boston, London, and Montreal.

In 1908, he was assigned to write a story on Erwin E. "Tex" Smith, a photographer from Bonham, Texas, who was known as "the cowboy sculptor" and who was then studying art at the Museum of Fine Arts in Boston. They hit it off, and Smith suggested to Pattullo that he should leave Boston and head back to Texas with him "and try his hand at writing Texas ranch stories which he, Smith, would illustrate with photographs," the Bonham, Texas, *Daily Favorite* reported in 1924.

Then in poor health, Pattullo decided to accept the offer, hoping that the dry air of the southwest would be good for him. So he left his job as the Sunday editor of the *Boston Herald* to head southwest to the J.A. Ranch outside of tiny Clarendon, Texas, about forty miles southeast of Amarillo. While there, he produced his first western tale, "Blackie: A Texas Night Horse." Tex Smith indeed provided photos for the story, which Pattullo sold to the *Saturday Evening Post* for $150.

Encouraged, Pattullo kept churning out dime-store cowboy tales, and he and Smith left Texas to travel about the American west and even Mexico. They rode herd for ranch bosses in New Mexico and Arizona, and Pattullo's health returned. Pattullo would spend each summer on the ranch, and then return to Boston in the winter months to write up his stories.

Among the tales he created were "A Cow-Puncher Widow," and "Frenchy"—a drama of ranch life that in 1914 was turned into a film by the Majestic Motion Picture Company. He also wrote novels, among them *The Untamed* and *Natalie Graves*, which he offered to the *Saturday Evening Post* with no luck but which was published by *Women's Stories* and earned Pattullo the princely sum of $2,600.

"It was rotten and I will admit it," Pattullo said later of the story.

Distracted from his craft while in Boston, he ultimately moved back to Bonham, and while visiting Boston friends in Dallas he met and fell for Lucille Wilson, the daughter of a Dallas businessman.

Pattullo and she were married in 1913 and they had a home built in Dallas.

The next year, the world war broke out, and "the fiction market went 'blooie,'" Pattullo would recall. "My income, as a result, was greatly reduced; and there was many a night that I did not sleep well wondering how I was going to meet my payments on my house."

Then, "by the grace of God" the revolutionary Pancho Villa and four hundred of his marauders raided a U.S. Army garrison in Columbus, New Mexico, on March 9, 1916. Pattullo saw an opportunity.

"I went down to the border, first for *Collier's* and later for the *Post*," Pattullo recalled. "Inside of six months I had practically cleared off my debts from the sale of border articles."

He was well known enough by then to have his arrival at the border noted in the newspapers.

"George Pattullo of Dallas, famous for his realistic western stories, particularly the border fiction which is unique in its understanding of Mexican and frontier types, is in El Paso," the *El Paso Morning Times* reported on March 20, 1916—just a few weeks after Villa's raid.

By then, an expedition, led by future A.E.F. commander John J. Pershing, had entered Mexico in search of Villa.

One of Pattullo's first border stories was titled "Women the Pack Trains and Cooks of the Mexican Army," an account of how Mexican women were accompanying their soldier husbands in the field. Pattullo would turn his attention to the American soldiers, and that reporting would stand him in good stead the following year when the United States declared war on Germany on April 6, 1917. George Pattullo, western writer, would become George Pattullo, war correspondent.

He traveled to an officers' training camp at Leon Springs, Texas, and from there provided stories for the *Saturday Evening Post*. Soon enough, the *Post* offered him steady work as an overseas correspondent in France.

With two brothers Over There with the Canadian Army—J.H., with the Seventy-Second Seaforth Highlanders, and Andrew, with the Winnipeg Artillery—Pattullo's early efforts focused on the Canadians while the Americans were getting up to speed through the summer of 1917.

His first effort was titled "Fightin' Sons-of-Guns." "It was rather a hard job covering the subject of the Canadians in one article—but that was all the space they could allow in these wondrous times," he wrote his father, George Pattullo Sr., on September 18, 1917.

"Have been working hard—four articles and a short story already accepted since I came over and another one about done," Pattullo added. "Lorimer cabled, 'Fine work,' so I feel encouraged."

His movements were noted back in south Texas, where on October 16, 1917, it was revealed that he had been "wounded in action."

"I jumped into a six-foot deep trench and got a stonebruise on my heel," he said in a letter to an El Paso friend. Half-facetiously, he would add: "A lot of heroes in this war have done less, at that."

But he soon glommed on to the First Division, entering the trenches at Lunéville with it in the fall of 1917 and writing "The First Raid" and other stories before being struck down by a case of the mumps.

From the Thirteenth Field Hospital, he wrote to his father in February 1918:

"Here sits a busted hero! Your gallant son, after marching up with the troops when they went in; after wearing blisters on his feet until they bled; after five night and four days in the front trenches, dodging shrapnel and three-inch shells in the daytime and a Boche machine-gunner of nights; after going out stealthily to our wire just to show what a daredevil he was; after wearing a gas mask in the pitch-black of midnight-hours every time a doughboy smelled his comrade's pedal extremities and turned in a gas alarm; after all this, I say, I had to come out of there with mumps. Oui; yes; ja; si."

While in the hospital, Pattullo and the other patients endured an air raid. A whiny German plane approached the hospital in the evening and came under fire from antiaircraft guns. Lying helpless in his bed, Pattullo expected the worst.

However, he would write, while the planes let go of ten bombs, only three exploded, and they landed in a field adjacent to the hospital. "We lay there waiting for more, because we could hear other planes up. However, they were going after other villages . . ."

After reporting on the marines at Belleau Wood in his story "Hellwood" and writing other stories, Pattullo and his wife—who had remained in Paris while he gallivanted around France—returned to New York in the fall of 1918.

On November 12, 1918—the day after the signing of the Armistice at least suspended the killing on the Western Front—Pattullo left Hoboken, New Jersey, aboard the S.S. *Northern Pacific*, sailing with an army medical contingent. In France, he would soon learn of the amazing exploits of a semiliterate, semi-conscientiously-objecting backwoodsman from Tennessee, and produce a story that would make both Pattullo and Sgt. Alvin Cullum York famous the world over.

BY THE TIME George Pattullo landed in France in late November 1918, Alvin York's actions in that ravine west of Chatel-Chéhéry the month before were garnering notice—at least within the military.

His captain, E. C. B. Danforth, had been unaware of what York and the other sixteen men of the patrol had been up to on October 8, only learning of their actions the following day. He quickly recommended York for the Distinguished Service Cross, and Eighty-Second Division commander Gen. George Duncan approved the recommendation on October 30—while York and Company G were still in the thick of the fighting above Sommerance.

After the Eighty-Second Division was relieved the next day, York and company began a slow drift southward, staying first at an old German rest camp near Varennes and then marching and busing to a former French camp in the Argonne Forest near Ste. Menehould.

On November 5, selected men were given passes; York was among these, and he was in Aix-les-Bains when the war ended on November 11. Those in the 328th Industry Regiment who were not granted leave were on the march and passing through Neufchâteau when they got the word that the war was finished; for them, the news was anticlimactic.

"Anyone who expected wild demonstrations would have been sadly disappointed," the regiment's history notes. However, after stopping at a small village that evening, "wild enthusiasm was evidenced by the natives and Vin Blanc was everywhere."

The regiment finally stopped moving in the area around Prauthoy, south of the Champagne region. It was there that York caught up with the 328th, which, with the rest of the Eighty-Second Division, soon engaged in "maneuvers" that were aimed at correcting problems that had been encountered during the fighting that fall.

Though the Armistice had been signed, final peace terms were still being worked out, and the Eighty-Second, like most American divisions that were waiting to head home, trained for the possibility of a resumption of hostilities. That even included bivouacking in the cold and snow for several nights apiece—but when men came down with pneumonia as a result, I Corps commander Gen. Charles Summerall ended the practice.

Mostly, though, the men waited, Alvin York among them. On

Christmas, York and his mates gained a small reprieve from the on-going drudgery when they were sent with other units of the A.E.F. to be reviewed by President Woodrow Wilson and his second wife, Edith—in France for the opening of the treaty negotiations at Versailles—at nearby Chaumont.

York would recall that he enjoyed himself—despite the absence of a Christmas dinner.

In January, at the recommendation of the Eighty-Second Division's chaplain, York traveled through France speaking to the men of various American units, beginning with the Eighty-Second. "I would jes go to a place and the boys would come around and I would hold a meeting and talk to them," York recalled.

The method of travel—riding shotgun on a speeding motorcycle—scared York more than the Germans had. "It was asking too much of God, traveling like that . . . ," he would say. "There was no sense rushing like mad over those old roads on a motor cycle." He finally refused to hop on one.

It was also in January that the legend of Alvin York began to emerge from the shadows of the army and onto the national and world stages. A noted artist, Joseph Cummings Chase, had been asked by the Liberty Loan Committee to paint portraits of the A.E.F.'s commanders and "four boys who had done deeds of extraordinary heroism," Chase recalled.

Chase painted the portraits of the four unnamed heroes—and enjoyed it so much that he ended up painting fifty, those who had "performed the most extraordinary deeds of valour," he would later write in his book of portraits titled *Soldiers All*.

Chase arrived at Prauthoy to paint a portrait of the Eighty-Second's commander; while sitting for the work, George Duncan mentioned the exploits of one of his own men. The man, of course, was Alvin York—and Chase would quote Duncan as saying, "The exploit of this tall, raw-boned, Tennessee mountaineer, with a red face and red hair, is the most remarkable I have heard of in the whole war."

There were plenty of American heroes in the war, among them one who by sheer numbers eclipsed York's feat.

Sgt. Harry Adams of Company K of the 353rd Infantry, Eighty-Ninth Division had on September 12, 1918, chased a German soldier into a house in Bouillonville on the first day of the St. Mihiel offensive.

The German subsequently disappeared through a door and into a cave behind the house, which Adams found to be a German dugout. The door was closed, and Adams had just two bullets left in his .45—and he fired these through the door while calling for the German to *Raus!* Germans flooded out of the dugout, among them a lieutenant colonel.

Perhaps sick of the war, the Germans, unaware that Adams was out of ammunition, allowed themselves to be captured en masse and without a struggle. The poker-faced Adams coolly escorted three hundred of the enemy to the rear.

But York had something more to offer—the backstory of his objection to killing, of which Chase was made aware. Chase was taken with his new subject, and would write in amazement of how York had broken up "an entire battalion" almost by his lonesome.

Various sources credit Chase with tipping George Pattullo off to the story of the conscientious objector turned war hero. Pattullo would say only that he received the tip from "a traveling companion on a ride to the Argonne after the Armistice . . . That I hit on the story was an accident."

The tip was confirmed by Maj. Edward Buxton, York's initial battalion commander, who as a former correspondent knew a good story when he heard one—and would certainly have been happy to send some good PR the Second Battalion's way.

By the end of January, Pattullo, then at the Third Army's head-quarters at Coblenz, Germany, was arranging to interview York—and also to travel in early February with York, Buxton, Duncan, and a U.S. Signal Corps photographer to the site of York's feat in the Argonne Forest.

Coincidentally, and fortunately for Pattullo, York by then was being considered for a Medal of Honor, and the trip back to the environs west of Chatel-Chéhéry was part of an investigation of York's feat—as were the subsequent depositions given by Pvts. Percy Beardsley, Joseph Konotski, George Wills, Patrick Donohue, and Michael Sacina.

Bertrand Cox, who as a lieutenant with Company F, 328th Infantry Regiment, had led his men through the ravine where York did his work just hours after the battle, also gave a statement supporting York's heroism. In a subsequent interview with Pattullo, Cox estimated in both his statement and interview that he saw at "between 20 and 25" German bodies splayed on the hillside. Interestingly, he would also remember seeing a dozen dead Germans "lying along a path." Some of those might have been in the doomed squad that charged downhill toward York, following Lt. Fritz Endriss to their deaths.

Lt. Joseph Woods, the Second Battalion's adjutant, also gave a statement to the adjutant of the Eighty-Second Division. Woods recalled that those at the battalion headquarters on the western edge of Hill 223 "heard some heavy and almost-continuous fighting on the other side of our hill and in the direction taken by Sergeant Early, Corporal York and their detachment.

"Some time later I personally saw Corporal York and seven privates returning down the hillside . . . I personally counted the prisoners when Corporal York reported the detachment and prisoners. Corporal York was in entire charge of this party and was marching at the head of the column with the German officers."

Pattullo spent a week in the Argonne and at Prauthoy reporting the story.

"I questioned every soldier in the detachment with York, checked up every detail with the official reports and information, and went over every step of the ground while he told his story," Pattullo would write. "In telling it he was far more prone to leave out than to amplify; men who do big things seldom like to talk about them, and are never fluent."

In sum, Pattullo would write that his own investigation convinced him that York "had performed the most remarkable individual feat of fighting to the credit of the American Expeditionary Force."

Pattullo knew he had a big "beat"—a scoop. But he had a problem.

Because of the *Saturday Evening Post*'s printing schedule, it would be six weeks after he sent his story overseas that it would finally be printed. His daily newspaper competitors would have no such problem. "I knew my story might be given to the newspaper correspondents who could beat me six weeks by cable," he would write.

Deeply concerned that he might easily be scooped should the story of the York Patrol be discovered by other newsmen, Pattullo went to Gen. Dennis Nolan, an assistant chief of staff to John Pershing who was in charge not only of the A.E.F.'s intelligence section but the press section, which routinely censored correspondents' copy.

Pattullo pitched Nolan—"in whose integrity I had implicit faith," he would write—that he wanted to send his story to the *Post*, but worried that one or more of Nolan's censors might leak it to others—in which case it would be "water-over-the-dam for me," Pattullo wrote.

He asked Nolan if he could personally meet with Pershing to

persuade him to help keep his scoop. (Pershing, ironically, would be "sore" at Pattullo over his story about York, Pattullo wrote, because Pershing wanted to promote Sgt. Sam Woodfill as the A.E.F.'s greatest hero. Pattullo, though, found Woodfill's story to be "cold and routine.")

Nolan told Pattullo that a meeting with Pershing would not be necessary, and offered him a deal.

"If the correspondents discovered the story on their own, he would let their stuff go through—and could not suppress it for me," Pattullo wrote. "But if they didn't come up with it, he would guarantee there would be no leak through the censors.

"Well," Pattullo happily wrote in 1958, "they didn't come up with it."

16

A CLEAR CONSCIENCE

He didn't understand all the fuss, he would say, didn't know, really, why when his ship, the S.S. *Ohioan*, docked in New York at two P.M. on May 22, 1919, there was a throng of people there to meet it—to meet *him*. Among the crowd was Dr. J. J. King, president of the Tennessee Society, plus a number of other esteemed society members; there was E. A. Kellogg, chairman of the New York Welcoming Committee, a U.S. congressman from Tennessee, and newspaper reporters and photographers who made him pose for their cameras before he was hustled into a car and driven through New York City and through, as well, a blizzard of ticker tape and confetti and past crowds of ordinary people who lined the streets and cheered until he reached the Waldorf Astoria Hotel on Park Avenue where he was shown to his room—"a whole suite of rooms," he would recall—for the next several nights.

He hadn't understood what all the fuss was about until he asked someone next to him during the motorcade. "I thought that they did the same thing for 'most every soldier that came back," he would say. "I thought it was a New York habit. And a very nice habit, too."

No; all the fuss was for him, about him, he who had captured 132 German soldiers almost by his lonesome and three dozen machine guns, too. It was about Sgt. Alvin Cullum York, Company G, 328th Infantry Regiment, whose mates were rolling on to Camp

Merritt, New Jersey, while he tried to figure out which of the two beds at the Waldorf he should sleep in. "I tried them both," he said.

News of his arrival, it turned out, had preceded him by about a month.

While he and the other men of his unit rode forty-and-eights to a camp near Bordeaux, on France's southwest coast, George Pattullo had been busy writing his account of York's deed just west of Chatel-Chéhéry and then submitting it to the army's censors and then waiting; waiting and nervously pacing and hoping and praying that it would hold, hoping that it wouldn't leak, hoping that Dennis Nolan was being true to his word to keep quiet about York unless and until another correspondent stumbled on to it, as Pattullo had.

And it was perhaps remarkable that the story the *Saturday Evening Post* would title "The Second Elder Gives Battle" had not been discovered by any other prying, ink-stained wretch. Though York himself had lain low during his time at Bordeaux, where he endured "cold, stormy days with nothing to do but sit around and think of home," or took leaves to Paris to stave off the boredom, his actions were being scrutinized and investigated and finally determined to be, indeed, worthy of a Medal of Honor.

In a cable to the adjutant general of the army in Washington, D.C., A.E.F. commander John Pershing himself delivered judgment on the significance of York's deed, writing:

> It is recommended that the Medal of Honor be awarded to Corporal Alvin C York, Company G 328 Infantry (1, 910, 421) for conspicuous gallantry and intrepidity above and beyond the call of duty in action with the enemy near Chatel-Chehery, France, 8 October 1918.
>
> After his platoon had suffered heavy casualties and 3 other noncommissioned officers had become casualties, Corporal

York assumed command. Fearlessly leading seven men, he charged with great daring a machine gun nest, which was pouring deadly and incessant fire upon his platoon. In this heroic feat, the machine gun nest was taken, together with four officers and 128 men and several guns . . .

Corporal York has previously been awarded the Distinguished Service Cross for this act; and if this recommendation is approved, the Distinguished Service Cross will be recalled.

On April 18, 1919, the Tennessee backwoodsman was feted by Gen. George Duncan and the Eighty-Second Division. Duncan called York's deed a "fine example of courage and self-sacrifice" that was "evidence of that spirit and heroism which is innate in the highest type of American soldier and responds unfailingly to the call of duty wherever or whenever it may come."

Not to be outdone, Marshal Ferdinand Foch, the Allied supreme commander, in a separate ceremony on April 24 presented York with two French medals—the Medaille Militaire and the Croix de Guerre with Palm. Foch called York's feat "the greatest achievement accomplished by a common soldier in all the armies of Europe."

Heady stuff, that.

More medals followed, from Montenegro and Italy. And still George Pattullo's scoop held, until finally the *Saturday Evening Post*, circulation two million, went to press and featured it on the cover of its April 26, 1919, edition.

Even as Alvin York toiled and drilled and pined for Gracie and his mother and the Valley of the Three Forks of the Wolf River, he was becoming a national and an international star. Pattullo's story was picked up across the country. On May 8—two days before York and others from Company G sailed from Bordeaux aboard the S.S. *Ohioan*—one newspaper would sum it up under the head-line "Lone Tennessee Boy Wipes Out Battalion."

While York and his mates were still en route to New York, his family members deep in the hollers of Fentress County were being apprised of his heroics. One enterprising reporter from the *Atlanta Constitution* tracked down York's mother, Mary, who said:

"Alvin's anxious to get home. He writes that he's a-pinin' for the singin's again. Says it won't seem like home if the singin' and prayer meetin' ain't goin' on when he gets back."

As for Alvin's postwar plans, Mary York couldn't say. An offer to attend a technical school in Cookeville, Tennessee, awaited his return, but York's mother wasn't sure whether he would want to leave home.

York would go home soon enough, but first he had to endure his hero's welcome in New York City. He cut a striking figure on first sight to many of the city's newspaper reporters.

"He is a lanky Southerner, six feet tall, with a likeable grin, red hair and a ruddy face that still has freckles, though much tanned and scarred with lines placed there by a hardy life in the open," one writer would note.

"The six-footer was easily recognized as the [*Ohioan*] came to the pier," the New York *World* reported of the arrival of the con-quering hero. "Photographers and reporters rushed to him. He stayed them off while he read messages from the home folk and a wire from the pastor of the Church of Christ and Christian Union, of which he is second elder, warning him against signing contracts for vaudeville or lectures.

"One message was from his mother and another from his sweet-heart, seventeen-year-old Grace Williams, the prettiest girl in all Tennessee, take it from York, and he says he knows what he is talking about."

On the night of his arrival, the Tennessee Society threw a dinner in his honor, and the speeches and flattery made the bashful hick from the Valley of the Three Forks of the Wolf River uncomfortable.

"There were generals and statesmen all over the place," he recalled. "They asked me that many questions that I kinder got tired inside of my head and wanted to get up and light out and do some hiking . . . They seemed to having a sorter competition saying nice things about me.

"Of course, everybody was nice. But I'm a-telling you it was a tough corner for a mountain boy to be in . . . In the middle of that-there old banquet I got to kinder dreaming about home and the little log cabin and my mother and Gracie and them-there hound-dogs of mine. I knowed I was to be with them soon."

The next day, York stretched his legs, walking the city and marveling at its hustle and bustle. He tried to call his mother but couldn't get through. When he was asked if he wanted to do anything special, he said he'd like to ride in the subway; a private train was soon secured and Alvin C. York rode it from borough to borough.

On the evening of May 24, York boarded a train for Washington, D.C., and arrived there at six A.M. on May 25. He was ushered into the U.S. Capitol, where he was met by Peter Charles Harris, adjutant of the army, and members of Congress, who "enthusiastically clasped the hand of the man who had upheld the traditions of America in fighting for democracy in France," the *Washington Times* would fairly gush.

Once he was seated in the gallery of the U.S. House of Representatives, his presence was noted from the floor. "The House rose and cheered," the *Times* reported. "York, in the gallery, stood at attention and saluted."

Then it was back to New York for more whirlwind activities, including a de rigueur visit to the New York Stock Exchange. In between and along the way, York was asked again and again to talk about his brush with becoming a conscientious objector—and how he felt about killing twenty-five Germans.

"He denied he was a conscientious objector when, as second elder of the Church of Christ and Christian Union, he had been drafted into the army," the *New York Times* reported.

York once more repeated his doubts about the war.

"If you go into a thing, you ought to know what it is all about," York said. "When they took me to Camp [Gordon] and told me I was going to fight this man Kaiser, it didn't mean anything to me at all."

He blamed Pastor Rosier Pile for the misunderstanding about his objections to fighting, saying that without his knowledge Pile had "written asking for my release because I was a conscientious objector.

"I was taken to headquarters . . . I was asked if I objected to fighting. I answered, 'No, that's what I'm here for. But I wish you would tell me what this war is about.'"

He recounted his talk with Maj. Edward Buxton, "who told me the things the Germans had done to other nations and to us." When Buxton had finished his arguments, York said, "I couldn't see how anybody who wanted peace in the world could do anything but fight."

As for the Germans dead by his hand? "My conscience is clear," York said. "The blame is on the Germans for starting this war."

He told another reporter:

"Sure, I killed twenty-five Germans the day I captured 132 prisoners. If I hadn't killed them quick I wouldn't be here."

One sour note was struck when the *World*'s correspondent told York that "some of his company who arrived here two days ago accused him of grabbing all the glory and medals of the success of the attack in which they took part."

"Well," York replied, "all I can say is every man who was with me swore to an affidavit telling just where he was and what happened that day, before I got these medals. I sure am surprised that they are saying such things."

It would not be the last time York would have to answer to the unfair charge that he was a spotlight-stealing glory hound.

ON HIS LAST night in New York, the humble Tennessee sergeant was once more feted, this time at a fund-raiser for the Salvation Army at the Winter Garden. By then he was tired of all the fuss, and tired of being asked about . . . well, everything.

As the *New York Herald* reported in its June 1, 1919, issue:

> Sergeant York conquered New York with less effort and as few words as he employed in killing twenty-five Germans and capturing 132 others. "I hain't no talker," insisted the red-haired hillman from Tennessee at the Winter Garden last Monday night when he was enjoying, or rather enduring, the last hours of his five-day furlough.
>
> Half a dozen men and a couple of alluring Salvation Army girls were pleading with this combination Stonewall Jackson and St. Anthony to leave his box and appeal for dough for doughnuts from the stage. "No, I just won't," he vowed, as a member of the New York Society of Tennessee leaned over his chair, patted him on the back and explained that he could lure thousands of dollars from the pockets of the audience simply by standing up and saying that the Salvation Army had proved itself worthy of support.

"No" was all Alvin C. York would say.

He would say no to other beseechings—these of a commercial

nature. "They"—he didn't say exactly who—offered him plenty of money for his appearances onstage or even in movies—or to write stories for the newspapers or endorse products.

But his uniform, he said almost as a mantra, was not for sale. He had not gone overseas and done what he did for financial gain.

Ever the second elder of the Church of Christ and Christian Union, York would say: "I didn't take their thirty pieces of silver and betray that-there old uniform of mine . . . I jes wanted to be left alone to go back to my beginnings. The war was over."

17

THE SPOILS OF WAR

The prodigal son finally made it home, home to the Valley of the Three Forks of the Wolf River and home to that shotgun shack and Rosier Pile's general store, where he encountered the same gaggle of mountain girls and "the little church on the hill" where he had come to Jesus and home to his hounds and his maw and the dark hills and the tawny farms on which generations of isolated folk had tried to scratch a living out of the near-barren soil and were still toiling away under the hot sun of late May 1919 when Alvin York stepped from a train in Crossville, Tennessee.

Across the United States, millions of veterans were on their way to homes in cities and towns and farms, most with little or no fanfare, or were already home, home and wondering what they would do with the rest of their lives, home to think over what they'd been through and the boys they'd seen hideously wounded or gassed or blown to bits or that died at the hand of a machine gun, or a bayonet, or disappeared in the churning blast of an artillery shell—fifty-three thousand American boys killed in action or died of wounds; home, now, from a world war, a Great War, some with scars or hacking coughs from the mustard gas that had seeped into their lungs, some missing a leg or an arm or worse; home to live out their lives in relative anonymity, the vast majority of them, and home to try to forget and never talk about the things they'd seen, and the things they'd done.

Alvin York would be some of the above. He'd seen terrible things, he'd killed men—a *lot* of men—but he carried a burden borne not so much of the things he'd witnessed or done but of fame. He would become one of the twentieth century's first great celebrities, fawned over and asked to tell his amazing story of single-handedly capturing the whole damn German army, over and over and over again. His life was now part of the public domain, part of the public psyche, a flesh-and-blood embodiment of all that was good and right with America the Beautiful, the sweet land of liberty, and if he'd wanted to he could have become a very wealthy man very quickly . . . if he'd wanted to.

But he didn't.

One of the first things he did when he returned to that cabin in the hills on May 30, 1919, he would say, was go "a-hunting—not for coon, or possum or fox or squirrels. I went a-hunting for Gracie."

After those crazy days and nights in New York and Washington, D.C., York had entrained for Fort Oglethorpe, Georgia, where he received $60 and his discharge from the army and from which he left by train for northern Tennessee.

At Crossville, a delegation of Fentress County dignitaries who had been alerted to his impending arrival met York, who was still in uniform, at the station.

"Professor" B. B. Gross, the principal of Jamestown High School, headed the reception committee, and as York stepped down from the train the other passengers, headed for points yonder, gave "three cheers mixed up in a bedlam, with numerable cheers mixed in and tangled up together," a wire service story would say.

Six automobiles—"the entire flivver population of Jamestown"—awaited him, and he settled in as the cavalcade, following sure-footed mules, bumped along the narrow country lanes toward Jamestown, where it arrived at seven P.M.

There, he was met by his mother, and more admirers, and the

trip to the Valley of the Three Forks of the Wolf River was taken up again, heading into the descending nightfall, and at every scattered home along the way "neighbors ran out to greet the man who was returning," the report said.

"Hello, Al," these neighbors said. "How are you, Al?"

"Oh, fair to middlin'" was Alvin York's reply. "How's the hogs and the crops?"

At the door of the brightly lit York cabin, the entourage halted in the dark, and then other neighbors—among them the preacher, Rosier Pile—appeared out of the gloom to welcome their hero home. "For a long time they pressed him to tell his big story, the story that others have told until all the world knows it.

"But it was only a 'Yep' or 'Nope,' and that was about as far as Sergeant York would permit his tale of exploits to get away with him."

At one point, someone mentioned to him a farm that the Nashville Rotary Club had purchased for him. York said he didn't know much about it, "'cepting what I've just heard some people say."

The club's president, Edgar Foster, had brought the club the idea of raising money to buy banker W. L. Wright's four-hundred-acre farm in Fentress County. The club and Foster, who was the business manager of the *Nashville Banner*, intended to raise enough money to buy the farm and stock it with equipment so York could get right to work farming. With the help of public appeals in the *Banner*, and without York's knowledge, or endorsement, money began trickling in.

When he was finally told of the deal, York was at first skeptical. But he went along after the Rotary Club in late 1919 made a down payment of $6,250 on the farm; the Rotarians kept the title, and were required to pay the balance off in annual installments spread across four years.

Despite promises to the contrary, the farm, which had a price

tag of $25,000, was only half paid for by the club because dona-
tions dwindled. After just one payment by the Rotary Club in
1920, York was left with more than $12,000 in notes "to pay off
as the crops matured," one newspaper noted. The farm would, in
fact, become something of an albatross to York in ensuing years.

But at his homecoming, any future troubles were unknown and
unseen, and there were other issues to tend to—among them the
fact that York had, despite his earlier convictions against taking another man's life, become a renowned killer.

The subject was raised at the York cabin that night, and Alvin
and Rosier Pile huddled for a time; in reply, Pastor Pile gave no
indication that the parson harbored a grudge over his protégé's actions in that ravine west of far-off Chatel-Chéhéry, France.

"It's all in a man's own conscience what [is] right or wrong,"
Pastor Pile told York. "The hand of God was on you, Alvin."

Pile added that to his mind, York had to have been "right" to
perform as he did. "Sergeant York thought he was doing the right
thing," he told the *Knoxville Sentinel*. "There are times when a
man has to fight. Even the Bible makes reference to this fact."

Finally, Alvin C. York bolted into the night and raced half a mile
to the Williamses' cabin. He found Gracie there, and they talked.
He wouldn't reveal their conversation, but of course the next day
it pretty much came out. Alvin had popped the question, and she
had given her answer.

"I told it to him," Gracie told a reporter the next day.

The reporter would add:

"And then friends and relatives started to complete plans they had
been making for a long time for the event in the little church where
the rip-roaring mountain swain was converted and became the Second Elder of the Church of Christ and Christian Union, the strong
mountaineer who became a devout man of peace, then went to war,
and became an earnest crusader for the ideals of his country."

A few days later, the second elder laid aside his uniform and cleaned and greased his trusty muzzle-loader. "It was all over," he would say. "I was home."

He soon enough was also a married man. On June 7, 1919, he and Gracie exchanged vows at the spring near the family cabin. Pastor Pile and Tennessee governor A. H. Roberts jointly presided, and after the vows, the newlyweds and their several thousand admirers who came from all over Tennessee sat down to a feast.

"People came from miles around with loaded baskets of good things," one paper would report. Sides of beef and a whole hog were placed on spits over searing coals; those as well as one hundred turkeys, four sheep, and too many chickens to count were devoured before the guests left and York and his new bride retired to the York cabin.

The couple honeymooned, briefly, in Nashville at the behest of the governor. York spoke to six thousand people at the famed Ryman Auditorium, the future home of the Grand Ole Opry, with thousands more would-be listeners being turned away at the door. A planned visit to Salt Lake City, where the Rotary Clubs were holding their convention, was nixed by York and Gracie, both of whom quickly wearied of the spotlight.

So they returned to the York family cabin, where they waited for a home to be built on the promised plot of ground, and where York plotted his next move.

It was while wandering the same old hills around the same old valley that York realized he had changed. He had seen Paris, New York, the U.S. Capitol; he had seen men die and killed men, too, and would later say, "The whole outside world seemed to have changed. But not our valley. Everything there was kinder the same."

Where he previously had considered the Valley of the Three Forks a "shield" against the outside world and its wickedness and avarice and iniquities, he now came to realize that that shield had also made the inhabitants of the valley backward, and poor.

More worldly now, he saw that the mountains had kept out much modern progress—good roads, good schools, and "libraries, up-to-date homes, and modern farming methods," he would say. "I knowed we had to have them."

York came to believe that his time in the service—"all of my trials and tribulations in the war"—was simply the precursor to a new life. "All of my suffering in having to go and kill were to teach me to value human lives," he would say.

As well, the temptations of the outside world, and his rubbing shoulders with different kinds of men—"my buddies"—molded his character and made it stronger, and taught him to "understand and love [his] brother man."

He decided his life's work would be helping his neighbors and their children rise from ignorance and poverty and backwardness. His first act was to go to the state highway department and convince them to build an actual road through the hills that would replace the barely passable horse-and-mule track.

"And they done it," York would say happily. Today, the route from Pall Mall to Jamestown is known as the Alvin C. York Highway.

Second, he wanted to build new schools in Fentress County, including a vocational school that could evolve into a "mountain college." Putting aside his qualms about profiting from his military deed and ensuing fame, he decided that speaking for a good cause didn't violate his principles and went out on a fund-raising tour, though it was cut short when he was struck with appendicitis.

In the meantime, he and Gracie moved onto the farm that had been promised him and he began work on planting and reaping crops. Unfortunately, a prolonged drought, a postwar economic depression, and a resulting drop in produce prices cut his earnings to basically nothing, and by the summer of 1921 he was facing foreclosure.

York remained adamant that his uniform was not for sale, though, and continued to refuse a sure way out of debt—hitting the vaudeville circuit or even acting in movies for pay.

"He realizes that the managers of vaudeville and movie pictures offer him big wages to work for them, not because he is an actor or possesses stage qualifications, but because he was the big hero of the war and people would pay to see and hear him make a few remarks, telling of his exploits," one paper reported.

"This suggestion was repulsive to York. He refuses to commercialize his war record and declares he will lose his farm and starve if need be rather than resort to such a scheme to earn a living. Thus it seems York is a peace hero as well as a war hero."

But by the summer of 1921 he had an outstanding grocery bill of $250, in addition to an unpaid balance of $12,500 on the farm. He also had one more mouth to feed, Alvin York Jr., the first of eight children Alvin and Gracie would have.

To the rescue came Thomas H. Johnson, a Knoxville businessman, who initiated an Alvin York Farm Fund and, with the cooperation and aid of the *Knoxville Sentinel*, appealed to the public for help.

Johnson wrote to York via the *Sentinel* and sent along three checks in the amount of one dollar each from himself, W. P. Davis of the Knoxville Iron Company, and John S. McClure of the McClure Clothing Company in Knoxville.

Johnson, through the newspaper, asked that 12,497 other Tennesseans pitch in to help York by sending one dollar each to him. Rotarians across the country also pledged to donate fifty cents each toward bailing York out—a move that was appropriate, considering it was partly the fault of the Nashville Rotarian Club that York was in dire straits in the first place.

The ploys worked, and by November York was able to pay the mortgage installment when it came due. And so did the Hero of the Argonne stave off homelessness.

But the episode would repeat itself in the coming years. Though he was pious and charitable to a fault, the great fame that had been thrust upon him would often be more of a burden. York had grown up ill educated in what amounted to a barter society and never really learned how to manage his money.

"Alvin York was no Rhodes scholar," Dr. Michael E. Birdwell, the curator of York's papers, wrote in a 1989 analysis of York's ongoing financial troubles. "He possessed few real skills beyond marksmanship and also had a real tendency to avoid physical labor."

And York believed that if the farm the Rotary Club had presented him was indeed a gift, "why should he have to pay for it?" Birdwell wrote. "When America lauded him as a hero and gave him a house and other gifts, he began to believe that he was entitled to such preferential treatment."

Complicating matters were the tenets of the Church of Christ in the Christian Union. "Money was associated with sin, and sin had to be rooted out of one's life," Birdwell wrote. York felt a need to cast the sin aside, and to do so he acted financially irresponsible and became a "soft touch" for almost anyone with a sad story to tell.

He remained conflicted by his faith and by an adamant refusal to profit from his celebrity, but he also had no means, really, to handle all of the adoration, nor the demands that came with it. "There was no point of reference in his early life to prepare him for celebrity status or success," Birdwell writes.

"Thousands of people have achieved fame and frittered away their fortunes. York consistently made bad value judgments and received poor advice from people just as myopic."

Some of those survivors of the patrol who would complain in coming years that York had made a back-stabbing glory grab at their expense had it wrong: the fame and attention that York legitimately garnered throughout his postwar life actually led to a lot of anguish and woe, and one has to wonder if he would have been happier had he returned to Tennessee in anonymity, living out his life among the people he knew as his own.

SAMUEL K. COWAN was a Tennessean, a Nashville man, a former correspondent for the weekly paper the *American*, former associate editor for the *Southern Lumberman*, and by 1908 the vice president of the Baird-Cowan Publishing Company.

At about the same time that Alvin York was facing bankruptcy because of the Rotary Club farm, Cowan was hired to do publicity work for some Nashville do-gooders—perhaps the same ones soliciting donations for York—who wanted to help York with his dream of establishing a foundation to fund schools and other public works for his impoverished local friends.

Cowan, then forty-eight, traveled into the Tennessee hills to visit Pall Mall and York and his family, and he set up shop for a few months in the Valley of the Three Forks. While he was there, he befriended York and became smitten with his story, and over time got York to agree to help him with a book project that had begun percolating in the back of Cowan's brain.

York would have nothing to do with a book that dwelled solely on him, or on his heroic deed. Sensing his reservations, Cowan instead proposed writing a book that would paint a portrait of the valley and of its inhabitants.

York's consent was ultimately given "for the publication of the story of his people, but it was with the pronounced stipulation that 'it be told right.'" When Cowan asked what exactly that meant, York replied, "I don't want you bearing down too much on that killing part. Tell it without so much of that!"

In 1922, Funk & Wagnalls published the result—*Sergeant York and His People*. The fairly short book celebrated the proud Anglo-Saxon heritage of the locals, and left plenty of room to walk through York's time in the army and his one-man-army tale of how he captured 132 Germans, including the supposed "major"—Lt. Paul Vollmer.

But it also celebrated the difficult life of the locals, containing such story-book passages as this:

> Their life was primitive, rugged, but contented. Deer and bears were in the mountains, and wild turkeys were to be found in large flocks, while the cry of wolves added zest to the whine of a winter wind.
>
> A cook-stove was an unknown luxury, and the women prepared their meals in the open fireplace. The men cut their small grain with a reap-hook and threshed it beneath the hoofs of horses.

In characterizing York and his ancestors, Cowan added: "The mode of life made men of strong convictions and deep feelings. But those feelings were seldom expressed except under the influence of religious devotions."

The book was generally well received. "It is as gripping and interesting as a novel, and a volume which will be an inspiration to every American," the *Arkansas Democrat* proclaimed.

"To boys and girls it will prove an inspiration for bravery, true manhood and for love of home and country," gushed the *Atlanta Constitution*.

But other reviewers were more circumspect. The *Wisconsin State Journal* asked first whether a "novel-biography" that centered around York was "really worth while," and its reviewer parodied its contents, writing, "The reader will get just what the title suggests when he reads 'Sergeant York and His People,' and perhaps a bit more of the good old home life of these good old mountain folk in the good old mountains, in good old Tennessee, in good old U.S.A, etcetera . . ."

If York, or Cowan for that matter, had high hopes that the book would help York's finances, they were disappointed. Priced at $2 a copy—the equivalent of about $30 now—sales were slow, and York, the most famous doughboy in the entire A.E.F., continued to tread water financially.

Even as he did, ironically, he became the target of solicitations and "many strange requests," Cowan would write, "pathetic begging letters, as tho the Sergeant were a rich man; some came from prison cells, asking his influence to secure a pardon; some from those still desirous of securing a business partnership with him." Among those letters, too, were "matrimonial proposals, describing the writers' attractive qualities." Those he gave to Gracie.

In some ways, civilian life would prove to be more difficult for York than battling Germans had been. In February 1924 his barn burned, and he lost his machinery, two hundred bushels of corn, and some cattle and hogs. York had no insurance, and all told, the losses ran to $10,000—about half what the farmstead was worth.

Not long after, newspaper writer Roy Grove stopped by Pall Mall to check up on the famous doughboy. He found York to be disconsolate as he listed the litany of woes concerning his farm.

"It will be a long time before I can get it into shape," York said. "There is a lot of work to be done."

York complained as well of rheumatism in his right arm, "caused by exposure, I guess." But he still resolutely refused to parlay his fame into riches, and explained why he had turned down offers worth hundreds of thousands of dollars:

"You know, most people think I am crazy for not accepting all the golden offers that have been pushed my way," he told Grove. "I know, I have heard them say, 'Well, if I had the chance that York has to make a lot of money, I sure would hop to it.'

"Folks outside think I am just a religious lunatic. But I am not, though I do believe deeply in religion. Most of the people are no different than I am, and if they were in my shoes and had the fortune or misfortune, as you might call it, to have been through what I have, I know they would understand me and feel the same way I do about commercializing my life."

Despite his own troubles, York continued to work toward his dream of building a school for Fentress County, and he was not shy about asking for donations at talks he gave throughout the south and midwest.

By 1925, his Alvin C. York Foundation had garnered $15,000 toward that dream, and in the same year, the state of Tennessee and Fentress County each authorized spending $50,000 for the purchase of land and the construction of the Alvin C. York Agricultural Institute. A Board of Trust was also created to oversee the project and to control the funds.

But his bad luck persisted; before long, squabbles erupted between the Board of Trust's members and York over the site of the school. The board wanted to place it south of Jamestown, the county seat, while York insisted it should be built on a site one mile north of Jamestown.

York became bitter about the experience, and would say that the fight was a "much worser one than the one I had with the machine guns in the Argonne. The politicians and real estate people tried to use me. The small-time bankers tried to get in on it. Jealous factions wanted to get a-hold of it and handle it their way."

By March 1926, York had had enough. He turned his back on the $100,000 that the state and county had appropriated for the school and resigned from the Board of Trust. He said he would begin over with the $15,000 he had raised himself. He continued to raise funds for the school, and had help from the newspapers, with one—the *Pittsburgh Press*—asking its readers to give "One Penny, One Dollar, for Each German York Captured!"

With such help, he was able to break ground on two buildings for the school, located on the brand-new Alvin C. York Highway one mile north of Jamestown, and was hopeful that once he could show they could be self-supporting, the Board of Trust would reallocate the funds for it.

In the end, York used his fame and stature once more to get the state legislature in 1927 to remove the Board of Trust from oversight of the planned school and place it instead under the auspices of the state Board of Education. York and the other original members of the Board of Trust were named as trustees, and the original funding was restored.

A visitor to the school's site in early 1927 would write of York: "After eight years of being paraded as a hero, a circus attraction to draw people so that they may hear his plea for the boys and girls of Fentress County, he looks twenty years older. Strangers have passed before him like a kaleidoscope; he likes people but he still dreads meeting strangers. He hates to talk of his experiences to people who are interested only in the spectacular aspect of them. A man of simple means, he hates to struggle with money problems."

Speaking of money problems, York by then was open to the idea of getting some personal help with his own. A bill then in the U.S. Senate, sponsored by Tennessee senator Kenneth McKellar, sought to give York the rank and pay of a retired army captain, and pay him $180 per month.

"It would come in mighty handy and would help a heap," York said. "I could certainly use it."

18

A ONE-MAN ARMY?

Bernard Early, the actual leader of the search-and-destroy party that would become known as the York Patrol, suffered the consequences of his war for years and years; hit four times by machine-gun fire in that ravine west of Chatel-Chéhéry—once in the left arm and three more in his left side—he had spent the rest of the war in a hospital in France before being shipped out from St. Nazaire on January 20, 1919, with scores of other sick and wounded American soldiers aboard the S.S. *Mongolia*.

He arrived back in the States on January 31, to face more hospital time and physical therapy and an uncertain future. That spring, George Pattullo's story about the Second Elder appeared, and Bernard Early to his surprise found that Alvin York was suddenly an international celebrity. York, Early discovered, had become the most famous doughboy in the whole A.E.F. for what had gone down in that ravine, on that day—the same day Early had failed to hit the dirt soon enough and had come very close to being laid to rest in the French mud next to Savage and Wareing, Dymowski and Swanson, and Weiler and Wine.

And while Alvin York raced somewhat reluctantly around New York at the end of May, Bernard Early was a stone's throw away, in New Haven, grumbling to "friends"—the local newspaper would call them that—that he and the other ten survivors from the patrol that skirted the German lines on October 8, 1918, had not received their due.

Early was already home when Beardsley and Konotski and Wills and Donohue et al. were being deposed as to their accounts of the York fight, and he had no idea of either the accolades that York was garnering or the Medal of Honor they had pinned on the sergeant's chest. But he had been on the minds of the others in the patrol, and the men of Company G, even before the *Ohioan* docked in New York Harbor on May 22, 1919, and their concerns had made their way into the newspapers within days of returning to America.

While "Officers and men on the Ohioan were unanimous in praise of York," the *New York Times* reported that May, "several officers expressed regret that other members of Sergeant York's patrol squad which surprised the Germans at Hill 223 in the Argonne Forest, had not won recognition."

In fact, four privates with the patrol—Percy Beardsley, Joseph Konotski, George Wills, and Patrick Donohue—were cited for their "splendid conduct" by the 164th Brigade on May 4, 1919. Michael Sacina was also cited.

And on the same day the *Ohioan* docked, the Eighty-Second Division's commander, Gen. George Duncan, went out of his way to commend York and pooh-pooh any whispers of criticism over who should have the lion's share of glory and recognition for the actions of October 8, 1918.

"The case was thoroughly investigated after York had been recommended for the Distinguished Service Cross," Duncan told reporters, "and the result was the recommendation for the Congressional Medal, which he now possesses."

Duncan would add: "The more we investigated the exploit, the more remarkable it appeared. He is one of the bravest of men and entitled to all the honor that may be given to him."

Besides the citations awarded Wills, Beardsley, Early, Konotski, and Sacina, more recognition would eventually come to the former acting sergeant Bernie Early. He had been denied the spotlight for his role in the capture of 132 Germans, but on February 20, 1920, his former battalion commander, Edward Buxton, set the record straight in a speech Buxton gave in Norwich, Connecticut.

Toward the end of that speech and almost as an aside, Buxton brought up Alvin York, who, he reminded his listeners, was "one of a party" who took part in the patrol.

"But I think that you Connecticut men and women ought to feel an endless pride in the fact not so popularly understood," Buxton said. "The man who commanded that little expedition of seventeen; who led them by an exceedingly skillful reconnaissance around the enemy flank, who made the decision to attack irrespective of what the enemy numbers might be, and who was shot down by a machine gun in the fight that followed with three bullets in his back and one through his arm—that man was a citizen of your state, and I rejoice that Sergeant Bernard Early is nearly recovered from his terrible wounds and is now living in your city of New Haven."

Buxton would go on to talk out of both sides of his mouth, saying that he hoped to secure "full recognition from the military authorities which is his due and which will in no measure detract from the great honor justly accorded to his comrade York."

It's more than possible that Bernie Early put Buxton up to the recognition. Since learning of the fame accorded his former underling York, he'd been telling anyone who would listen that the other members of the patrol, living and dead, had had a hand in the capture of the Germans in that ravine that day. By September 20, 1920, unnamed "friends" of Early were telling his side of the story to the *Hartford Courant*.

"It appears that Early was in command of the platoon during the attack and capture of the German prisoners, and when he was wounded York assumed command and took the 132 Boche back to the American lines," the paper reported.

"It may develop that the honors are even or possibly that Early has the advantage of York. Anyway, officials of this state and Early's friends believe the matter should be thrashed out between the squirrel-hunting deacon and the New Haven sergeant."

While Early's "friends," the *Courant* added, had no intention "to deny York his place in the nation's success, they remember that York was feted on Broadway as the 'greatest hero,' while Early laid helpless with four bullet wounds.

"The war is over, they admit, still 'Honor to Whom Honor is Due,' is a phrase they are quoting."

The Legion already had its own doubts about York being worthy of the title of "greatest hero of the war." In a roundup looking at the postwar lives of five men who had earned Medals of Honor, Phillip Von Blon, writing in the *American Legion Weekly*, turned his attention to York and wrote, "Of course he would be a rash man who should seriously attempt to make the distinctions on which such a title might be claimed."

York, Von Blon wrote flat-out, "happened to ride into a fuller fame than most of his brother Medal of Honor men because an American magazine writer gave to the world the story of his deed at the moment when the public was seeking just such a war idol."

Then things quieted down until 1927, when a writer for the *American Legion Monthly*, C. E. Scoggins, caught up with York and in a whatever-became-of story in the February issue recounted York's deed, and claimed that York had "whipped" the 132 Germans "in pitched battle—single-handed! That's not applesauce. That's official."

In response, a North Dakota veteran wrote to the magazine, and rebuked it for perpetrating the myth that York acted entirely alone.

O. H. Johnson said that the names of the dead, and of the survivors, in all fairness should have been mentioned.

"In all the publicity Sergeant York has received, the only mention of these survivors has been that six members besides Sergeant York returned and most of the time this even is not mentioned . . . ," Johnson wrote. "Surely the other sixteen men in the patrol must have been of some aid in capturing these prisoners."

The magazine, in its response and after a little research, not only outed Bernie Early as the leader of the patrol, but named Percy Beardsley, Joseph Konotski, Patrick Donohue, Michael Sacina, George Wills, and even the enigmatic Private Feodor Sok.

"These heroes were not intentionally slighted in the story," the magazine solemnly assured O. H. Johnson.

Back in Connecticut, the name Percy Beardsley caught the eye of an attentive reporter for the *Waterbury Republican,* and soon enough Beardsley, like Early before him, was being outed as a member of the most famous patrol of the Great War. The Connecticut Yankee, for his part, was reticent about what had occurred on October 8, 1918, when the reporter turned up at his family's Roxbury farm—he had, in fact, never even discussed it in any detail with his father, Nate.

Beardsley described Early's wounding, and how he wrapped his own overcoat around him as Early lay bleeding. He also said, importantly, that "when Sergeant Early was shot down, York took command."

Beardsley also was adamant that he had continued to fire his Chautchaut "and accounted for several Germans" while York, in a nearby clump of bushes, worked his weapons "and several of the others were firing their rifles."

But the quiet Beardsley, it was made clear, was "very loath to say anything that would be interpreted as belittling York's achievements." However, he did say "that he thinks Sergeant Early should be given equal credit with York for the result and that all the men in the detachment did their full part in making the victory possible."

Beardsley also, in what would become a refrain, intimated that York, as senior noncom, "naturally took charge of the 132 German prisoners, delivered them to the prison pen and as the result received credit for taking them single-handed," the *Republican*'s reporter wrote.

It would be the writer, and not Beardsley, who would somewhat disdainfully pass judgment on the actuality of York's heroism. He would echo the idea that were it not for George Pattullo, York would not have become the star of the war. But he also acknowledged that conditions were ideal for York's canonization:

"The country at that time was demanding an individual hero. The war was about over. Heretofore, all the publicity had been about the mass; there had been no outstanding hero."

One more former doughboy would add to the brewing controversy over the characterization of Alvin York as a "one-man army."

After it was announced that the Army War College would be putting on a re-creation of the York Patrol fight at a benefit military fete in Washington, D.C., in the fall of 1929, Otis Merrithew, a.k.a William B. Cutting, finally went public with his true identity—and with his own version of what had occurred on October 8, 1918.

The survivors of the patrol were all invited to appear at the event, and it was only after Merrithew asked for time off from his job with the Brookline, Massachusetts, Highway Department that his role in York's exploit became known.

Merrithew, like some of the patrol's other survivors, had upon returning from the war complained only privately to friends, family members, and to each other that York didn't deserve all the honors and attention he had received. Worried, perhaps, that they'd be derided as after-the-fact, whiny glory seekers if they spoke their minds in public, they demurred and went about their lives.

Meanwhile, though, resentment festered—and in 1929 Merrithew, for one, finally couldn't hold his tongue any longer.

"It is about time it were known that York did not make a single-handed capture, but that there were others," Merrithew told the *Boston Globe*. He would go on to say that after the six patrol members were killed and he, Early, and Muzzi were wounded by the burst of German machine-gun fire, Bernard Early ordered him—and not York—to take command of the detachment.

"Early ordered me to take charge, as I was his corporal," Merrithew said. "'Get me out of here if possible,' he told me."

Merrithew's intent, it seems, was not so much to discredit York as to get some recognition—medals would be nice, too—for him and the others. He credited York for being a good shot, but added that even after being wounded, he and others in the patrol were also firing at the Germans on the hill above, and shot their share of Germans. Merrithew also claimed that it was he, and not York, to whom Lieutenant Vollmer handed his pistol upon surrendering his men.

"After the surrender, I ordered the prisoners to line up in a column of twos and march back to the American lines," Merrithew said. "I gave all the orders myself, because I was in command.

"I detailed York to cover the prisoners with his rifle," he would add, "and we lined them up in a column of twos."

One account, indeed, would quote Sgt. Harry Parsons with saying that Merrithew returned to the American line with the prisoners while "swinging a German mauser pistol by its strap, and saying, 'I got what I wanted.'"

Merrithew said years later that he sold the pistol "to an orderly at the base hospital" while still in France—which contradicts claims from some of his descendants that the famous pistol had long been a family heirloom before it one day went missing.

The possibility exists, of course, that Merrithew obtained the pistol not from Vollmer, but from another of the German lieutenants; however, one of those lieutenants, Karl Glass, stated clearly in his later testimony about the fight that he still had "a fairly clear picture of the American soldier *in charge* . . . He was a large and strong man with a red mustache, broad features and, I believe, freckle-faced" [italics added]. In other words, Acting Cpl. Alvin C. York.

Lt. Paul Vollmer, in charge of the German force at the ravine, also gave no notice to Merrithew, but testified that he was indeed "disarmed" by the same American soldier who then led the prisoners "to the American advance guard company" while keeping his—York's—"pistol in the small of my back."

Merrithew, in summing up, would add that York had been ordered to bring the gaggle of German prisoners to the back lines while his own wound was being dressed—and thus was falsely and solely credited with their capture.

As for the affidavits sworn to by the other patrol survivors in the early winter of 1919, Merrithew would several times over the years claim that the men had no idea what exactly they were signing, and that they "probably thought it was a supply slip for underwear or something."

Still in the hospital and separated from the other patrol members when they gave their affidavits about York's actions, Merrithew was never deposed himself. Just what version of events he might have given, had he been asked, will forever remain unknown.

But the real question, anyway, is why Merrithew would keep his tongue for ten years and then offer a version of events that cast him as the True Hero. The answer probably lies in his early and ongoing disregard for York as a man and a soldier, and his conviction that the conscience-conflicted Tennessean was unworthy of his respect; one can only imagine how Merrithew seethed and inwardly raged as he saw his nemesis elevated to the status of a godlike public hero.

Merrithew's best friend in the patrol, Bernard Early, had also derided York and considered him unfit to serve in the army. But Early pretty much kept his counsel and played both sides of the fence in a 1928 affidavit about the firefight, saying of Merrithew's role: "I called on Corporal Cutting [Merrithew] to take command and get the prisoners out . . . A little later Corporal Cutting was wounded and Corporal York took command."

But Early also complained that York's role was being overplayed in the press, telling a reporter: "I don't blame York for grabbing all the glory he can, but the thing that riles me up is the fact that he got credit for something that seven other men had as much of a part in."

It would, in fact, be Early—and not Merrithew or the others— who would ultimately be rewarded in the quest for recognition. At the War College exposition in Washington, D.C., where Early, Meritthew, former sergeant Harry Parsons, and former privates Percy Beardsley and Joseph Konotski—and Alvin York as well— were guests of honor, Early on October 5, 1929, was awarded a Distinguished Service Cross for his actions.

Edward Buxton had a large hand in getting the award for Early. Although the 328th Infantry Regiment's commander, Lt. Col. Richard Wetherill, had in 1919 notified the 164th Brigade that "investigation shows that men with Sgt. Alvin York do not deserve recommendation for D.S.C. or special mention," Buxton had, as already noted, publicly championed for Early to be cited as early as 1920.

The same year, Buxton wrote Gen. George Duncan and recommended Early for a D.S.C. Buxton, the author of the Eighty-Second Division's history, had never bought into the claim that York had single-handedly captured 132 Germans, and was happy to spread some glory among the men he had once led as battalion commander.

However, Buxton would also note that York "bore the chief burden of initiative and achievement in the fire fight and during the later stages of the engagement." And he would credit York for his modesty.

"York has never, to my knowledge, in any interview [or] speech failed to talk of his comrades in that day's work and the part they played. Time and ceaseless repetition have added certain mythological aspects to the story, as had probably all men whose deeds become woven with military legends."

With some hyperbole, Early's citation reads that while leading the patrol, he and his men were "suddenly confronted by about 200 of the enemy. Sergeant Early decided to attack despite the disparity of numbers. By his quick decision and excellent leadership Sergeant Early effected a successful surprise attack which he led and commanded until severely wounded by machine-gun fire.

"The conspicuous gallantry and outstanding leadership on the part of Sergeant Early so inspired the remainder of his small command that it continued the attack until the enemy battalion was either killed or taken prisoner."

Bernie Early afterward denied any hard feelings over the delay in receiving an award.

Merrithew, too, was outwardly pleased with Early's award. "Even though the recognition comes very late, it makes us all happy to know that the War Department realizes that other men were in that engagement."

With a straight face, Merrithew added:

"We have never criticized the award to Sergeant York who was a brave soldier and deserved it, but we have always felt that it was not a one-man show."

Yet the *Courant* would report that on the same day Early received his award, Merrithew and the former private Joe Konotski met with Senator David I. Walsh of Massachusetts, who "presumably did not express entire satisfaction with the way things have come out. The handling of the whole case by the war department is seen as displaying politics and an effort to quiet the insurgency that threatened to ruin its military exposition."

Walsh told the men he would ask the War Department for an investigation and also order his own "personal" investigation. If the facts warranted it, he promised, he would introduce a bill seeking to get Merrithew his medal.

Despite the maneuvering and obvious ill feelings of Merrithew et al., the papers would report that York and his former patrol mates greeted each other "warmly" at the War College event. Early and York "walked across the parade ground arm in arm and were photographed together," the *Boston Daily Globe* reported.

"We are the best of friends and always have been," Early told reporters on his return home. In a seeming betrayal of his friend Otis Merrithew, Early added:

"When I was left for dead on the field of battle and other officers were wounded, Sergeant York . . . took charge of the situation and marched the Germans into the American lines. He is a brave man and I have no wish or intent to criticize any act of his."

And York? He would say that he was "much surprised to learn of the dispute over the credit for the exploit. He declared that he could not understand it and should take no part in any controversy."

"This is a complete surprise to me," said York. "I can't imagine what their purpose is in attacking my record. My exploits during the war are all on file with the war department. I can't understand what they have against me."

It would be nice to say that the whole matter ended there, but it didn't—not by a long shot.

Merrithew continued to push for recognition, writing his former battalion commander Edward Buxton and in late 1929 even getting the supposedly satisfied Bernard Early to sign off on an affidavit that made Merrithew the hero and York little more than a footnote.

Buxton, for his part, was cordial, but in letters written in 1929 and 1930 he repeated over and over that Merrithew would need supporting testimony from three or four other patrol members as to his true role in the fight before he could make any recommendation for a citation or medal.

As the man who had overseen the affidavits signed by Beardsley, Konotski, Sacina, and Wills in early 1919, Buxton was well aware of the established facts and knew as well that any serious deviation from those facts would only harm Merrithew's chances of getting his much-wanted medal.

"The whole story as told originally, in a most careful investigation, must hang together with subsequent facts or I am not in a position to effectively do anything," Buxton wrote.

Buxton went the extra mile for Merrithew, however, writing to former privates George Wills, Michael Sacina, Thomas Johnson, and Patrick Donohue and asking them if they could support Merrithew's version of events. In return, he received only signed receipts showing his letters were delivered to Sacina and Wills; Johnson and Donohue seem either to have not received his letters or chose not to reply.

Though he shied away from becoming involved in Merrithew's quest, Wills did at least obliquely concur with Merrithew on the question of credit. When an enterprising newspaper writer in the fall of 1929 set out to track down the surviving patrol members, he located Wills in south Philadelphia, where Wills made a living driving a feed wagon.

Asked about the then-burning controversy, Wills told the reporter simply:

"It was like this, all of us fellows made the capture and should be credited alike, but Sergeant York seems to have got all the glory."

Wills's opinion was countered by former sergeant Harry Parsons, who had left the stage to begin a Brooklyn auto-accessory store and who once again rose to York's defense, saying: "Alvin York deserves every bit of the credit given him. His was the greatest achievement of the war."

THE MEMBERS OF the patrol had other concerns. They had quietly tried to pick up their civilian lives where they had left off twelve years before and, like many other former doughboys, had varying amounts of luck doing so.

Former private Mario Muzzi was working as a baker at the National Biscuit Company in New York City; Percy Beardsley, still unmarried, was back on his family's farm in Roxbury, Connecticut.

Joseph Konotski worked in a mill and had two children, and he remained miffed about an oversight connected to the Army War College's reenactment of the York Patrol fight: The army, it seems, had invited him to the fete and had promised to fly him in, but when he arrived at the local airport he found that "somebody in Washington forgot to send the plane," one newspaper would report. Konotski waited four hours, then "gave up in disgust and went home." He later made his own way to the event.

Michael Sacina had a job at a wire-spring factory in New York City, and he complained that "since his return from the army he has had very bad luck, being out of a job quite often." Alvin York could certainly have sympathized with Sacina, having endured his own financial woes despite his great fame. To help make ends meet, Sacina ran the coat check at a local barber shop.

Former private Patrick "Paddy" Donohue was back in Lawrence, Massachusetts, and was in and out of a job at a local fabric mill. He, like Beardsley, remained unmarried.

The locations of former privates Feodor Sok and Thomas Gibbs

Johnson were unknown, though it appears Sok had returned to Buffalo, New York, after the war and Johnson by 1929 had left Lynchburg, Virginia, and followed a brother to Dennison, Texas.

Though they were part of the American military's greatest coup of the Great War, their roles in it would remain largely unknown through the rest of their lives.

EARLY, MERRITHEW, BEARDSLEY, and Wills weren't the only former soldiers who were in that ravine that morning and who remained miffed over Alvin York's fame.

In late 1928, after a Swedish publication ran an article headlined "The Heroic Feat Performed by an American Soldier in the World War: Sergeant York, Armed Only with Rifle and Pistol, Defeated an Entire Company of German Soldiers," a German national living in Stockholm sent a translated version of the story to the German ministry of war, asking that it be investigated.

In the body of the story, its author said that York "defeated a German machine gun detachment practically single-handed. Armed only with rifle and pistol, he killed 25 Germans and captured 132 prisoners, including three officers."

The claim smarted those in the war ministry in Berlin. The insinuation that more than one hundred proud German soldiers, including officers, would surrender to a single American soldier who carried just a pistol and a rifle was on its face preposterous and reflected very poorly on the German army.

An investigation was, indeed, ordered, and over the coming months the former German officers who were on the scene on October 8, 1918, were asked to give their versions of the affair, as was Capt. Karl von Sick, who with his Third Battalion, 120th Landwehr Infantry Regiment was located not far away from the ravine. Their accounts can be found on the preceding pages dealing with the firefight and aftermath. Most seemed to be honest about their own limited parts in the action, but one key German witness—Lt. Paul Vollmer, who was in command—hesitated for months to offer his testimony, and then omitted most of the details surrounding the firefight and his and his men's subsequent surrender.

He would write that after the American patrol entered the ravine from the south, "There was little time to deliberate. Suddenly several American soldiers came toward me constantly firing their rifles. I returned the fire as well as I could under the circumstances, until I was surrounded and—alone. I had no choice but to surrender."

Not mentioned was the order to fire from above and the quick deaths of six members of the patrol; not mentioned was the violent stand-off between York and the Germans on the ridgeline; not mentioned was his own lame attempt to shoot York with his pistol even as York was holding his own and picking off German after German with his rifle and, then, his pistol; not mentioned was his asking York how many men he had with him.

Vollmer did, though, remember seeing the mortally wounded Lt. Fritz Endriss in the meadow following the surrender, but gave no indication that he knew how Endriss had been shot. In short, Vollmer, clearly still chagrined at having surrendered himself and his men to, as he only later discovered, a single American soldier, was guilty of the sin of omission in an attempt to whitewash his actions.

The authors of the resulting German report would themselves note:

"The fact that First Lieutenant Vollmer hesitated several months before rendering his report, may be regarded as a sign that he does not consider himself entirely without blame."

Still, the report pooh-poohed as fiction the amazing story of Alvin C. York.

York, its authors concluded, "was a brave and fearless soldier"—but no more so than thousands of other German soldiers. In regard to the "surprisingly large number of prisoners" taken, they would side with Otis Merrithew's account and conclude that York led them to the rear and then selfishly claimed them as his own.

"Apparently, he, himself, captured only a few men," the report said, adding that other prisoners taken on other parts of the battlefield accounted for the large numbers that were marched to the American rear.

"Owing to the fact that the prisoners were assembled in the meadow," the report added, "it was later impossible for the officers of the American Division Headquarters at Chatel to determine the actual captors."

As well, the best minds at the German ministry of war claimed that the "brave 2nd Wuerttemberg Division did not suffer in the least by this incident . . . we have established that the incredible accusations which the article in the Swedish newspaper raised against Lieutenant Vollmer were gross exaggerations of his conduct."

It was a conclusion that York, and even Merrithew, would have taken issue with, had either known of the existence of the report. But they did not: its authors withheld releasing it to the press with the proviso that should another newspaper print a similar story about "the alleged feat of Sergeant York" that might "have the tendency of depreciating the name of the German army and, in particular, the German officer [Vollmer], we will immediately disprove this claim with the aid of the material on hand."

A copy of the German report was sent to the U.S. Army War College, where it was translated to English. One of its handlers noted that while the report attempted to "disprove the generally accepted version of York's heroism," it actually corroborated "some important elements of York's account."

Yes, Acting Cpl. Alvin C. York took charge. Yes, York also took the surrender of Vollmer and his men. The other men in the patrol were hardly mentioned, and from the German viewpoint were of little or no import in the firefight that occurred in that ravine that morning of October 8, 1918.

They said so themselves—Konotski and Early, Beardsley and Sacina, Wills and Sok—in affidavits they signed in front of witnesses. While Early lay incapacitated in the mud, the others took cover in places where they could guard their prisoners without being shot.

Beardsley may have potted a German or two, and Merrithew would insist that he kept firing, too, though he was wounded, and for that they deserve credit. Had the surviving members of the patrol not kept their prisoners under guard, the Germans could have rushed York as he popped away at the machine gunners up the hill and then at Fritz Endriss and the men he led on a wild, doomed charge. And it's no doubt a good thing that the men kept hidden, lest the Germans be able see their paltry numbers and swarm the Americans in a ten-to-one attack.

But there is no doubt York saved the patrol's members while he was saving himself. At least twenty-five Germans were left splayed on the side of that ravine; their open, dead eyes a testament to what had occurred during that desperate battle.

Which leads to the question of *why* York would allegedly lie and make a grab for personal glory at the expense of the others. He could have had no idea at the time of how the fight in that ravine would make him an international hero and, in some ways, actually ruin his life.

He was a simple, pious, and unworldly man who was not very popular among the majority of the patrol's soldiers; would he claim credit for something he didn't do alone simply in the hope of making the rank of corporal or sergeant? To attain a fame that he would have no interest in exploiting? Would he stick his neck out and claim credit for the capture of 132 of the enemy if he knew there were other men who would quickly refute him?

Some descendants of the patrol's members believe he would, and did. But their forebears—minus Early and Merrithew—offered eyewitness affidavits to the contrary. Those men had every opportunity to change the script, but they didn't, at least not until much later.

All the patrol's members were heroes, only one was more so. His name was Alvin C. York.

19

HIS WAR DIARY

They called him the Soldier-Poet of the Anzacs, signaler, and the Blind Soldier-Poet, and Tom John Skeyhill was all of those things, at least for a while. A soldier with the Eighth Battalion of the Australian Imperial Force, Skeyhill enlisted at the age of nineteen in August 1914, and on April 25, 1915, was among the Australian and New Zealand troops that landed at Anzac Cove on the Gallipoli peninsula. There, he worked to dig the first trench, was shot at, and survived, despite suffering bayonet wounds to both hands.

He was also left blind. On May 8, 1915, an exploding shell nearly took his life—and took his eyesight. Sent back to Melbourne, he became the blind poet, and produced the smashing book *Soldier Songs from Anzac*, which sold twenty thousand copies in the first four months after its publication in December 1915. He subsequently went on tour throughout his native country to recruit and raise money for the Red Cross, and by 1918 he was crisscrossing the United States as well.

"Incapacitated for further fighting, he sought to preach the gospel of the Allied effort from the lecture platform and through the press," the *Honolulu Advertiser* reported. One of his first American lectures, in San Francisco, drew 150,000 people. "Tom Skeyhill is a wizard of matchless word pictures," one paper gushed.

By early May 1918, Skeyhill was also no longer blind. While on tour in Washington, D.C., he complained of severe and debilitating pains in his neck, and was brought to Garfield Memorial Hospital.

There, Dr. Riley Moore, an osteopathist, manipulated Skeyhill's vertebrae, and within minutes Skeyhill leaped from the operating table yelling, "I can see you, Doctor! I can see you!"

A little over a year later, Skeyhill was in New York City when the most famous doughboy in the world arrived aboard the S.S. *Ohioan*. "What a day it was! . . ." Skeyhill would write. "Mobs everywhere, with banners, bands, bells, whistles, singing, screaming, clanging, whistling, and in every other way acclaiming the big hero of the day. Everybody's hero, everywhere."

Skeyhill didn't have the chance to meet Alvin C. York during York's busy barnstorming of New York, but in the summer of 1927, after an exchange of letters, York, intrigued by Skeyhill's service with the A.I.F., invited Skeyhill to visit him in Pall Mall. It's uncertain whether York was then aware that Skeyhill wanted to write his autobiography for him. Skeyhill soon enough broached the subject, only to be turned down flatly, with York once again saying he did not want to be criticized for exploiting his "war prestige."

Skeyhill "pressed the matter with vigour again and again," but York rejected Skeyhill's entreaties over a period of days. Finally Skeyhill convinced York that the best way he could help raise funds for his institute was to draw attention to himself; York handed over his sparse war diary and some letters he had written, and sat and dictated the story of his life, and of his army service, to Skeyhill "day after day."

The result was 1928's *Sergeant York: His Own Life Story and War Diary*. Skeyhill obtained $40,000 from *Liberty* magazine for a serialization; he also sold the book to Doubleday and received a $10,000 advance, which he and York split.

Skeyhill wrote that he took "great care" to preserve York's "mountain dialect," though he acknowledged that by 1927, when he sat down with York, the hero had "read many books and has met people all over the country, all of which has made his speech more literary than the average mountaineer."

Still, one wouldn't know it from reading it today. The very first lines quote York in a hokum, quasi–Huck Finn dialect, and the "great care" that Skeyhill employed to give the flavor of York's speech is fairly laughable:

"I ain't had much of the larnin' that comes out of books," York admits in those first lines. "I'm a-trying to overcome that, but it ain't easy."

Even York took some issue with the overblown speech patterns, later saying that one feature of the book was "the use of a dialect that no one in my home region used at the time . . . Visitors who came from distant states expressed surprise in finding that we talked English like they did."

Reviews were mixed. Some felt Skeyhill's dialect to be distracting, and at least one thought it was exploitative of York. "We don't doubt for a minute that the admirable Sergeant York uttered the 275 pages attributed to him by the adroit Mr. Skeyhill, or at least something very like it," the reviewer in the *Asheville (NC) Citizen* wrote. "But . . . why this laborious attempt at the Sergeant's Own Language? The Sergeant would never have written a book this way."

The book also contained, for the third time in print (following George Patullo's story in the *Saturday Evening Post* and Cowan's book), the affidavits given by Joseph Konotski, Michael Sacina, Percy Beardsley, and the other surviving members of the patrol in the early winter of 1919. And it offered one more, as well—that of Bernard Early, whom Skeyhill tracked down in New Haven, Connecticut, in April 1928.

Early, who of course had his issues with York's account of the scene in the ravine west of Chatel-Chéhéry, offers zero detail of York's actions, probably for the obvious reason that he was incapacitated during much of the fight, and was no doubt consumed with his own plight after those machine-gun bullets smashed into his limbs and back.

Early said he was "out in front" leading the patrol when the Germans were surprised at their breakfast, and "seeing the Germans throwing up their hands, I ordered my men to cease fire and to cover and close in on them. I then ordered my men to line them up preparatory to marching them back to our P.C.

"In the act of turning around issuing this order, a burst of machine gun bullets struck me . . . I called on Corporal Cutting [Early even at that late date had no idea of Otis Merrithew's actual identity] to take command and get the prisoners out and if possible come back and get me. A little later Corporal Cutting was wounded and Corporal York took command."

It was only in the following year that Early was somewhat mollified by being awarded the Distinguished Service Cross; the omission of an affidavit from Merrithew, who would claim that York was aware of his true identity by 1928, would continue to hang over York's story like a dark cloud.

The book sold well, and Skeyhill proposed another. In 1930, the John C. Winston Company published *Sergeant York: Last of the Long Hunters*. Aimed at adolescent males, the book further mythologized York and his deed.

(York's partnership with Skeyhill ended in May 1932 when the thirty-seven-year-old writer died from injuries suffered when his touring plane, which he was flying, crashed in Massachusetts.)

His Own Life Story and War Diary reintroduced Alvin C. York to America, and it also, as he had hoped, helped drive fund-raising for his institute. In late 1928, just as the book was being released, York revisited New York City to address a local chapter of the American Legion and spread the word about the good work being done in Fentress County. He had by then built two new buildings, serving a total of seven hundred students.

The book deals brought another level of celebrity to America's most famous doughboy, but keeping the schools up and running proved to be almost a full-time job. York traveled widely to lecture—at high schools, junior high schools, gatherings of the American Legion—and raise funds, charging promoters of the events as much as $400 per speech while also soliciting donations.

He continued to downplay his famous firefight of October 8, 1918, and tried his best to stay on the topic of educating the youth of Fentress County, but he could never escape the residue of the most basic fact of his life: he was a hero who had single-handedly—so it was said over and over—killed twenty-five of the enemy and captured 132 more, plus thirty-five machine guns. It didn't matter that that last part was all myth; as the newspaper editor in the film *The Man Who Shot Liberty Valance* said, "When the legend becomes fact, print the legend."

Asked to talk about his wartime service at one event, York told his audience, "I am trying to forget the war. I occupied one space in a fifty mile front. I saw so little it hardly seems worth while discussing it. I'm trying to forget the war in the interest of the mountain boys and girls that I grew up among."

His fame, as usual, was a double-edged sword, and a bit of a conundrum. He was famous for bagging 132 prisoners almost single-handedly—in the public's mind—and not for building schools, so it was only natural that the public would want to hear more about his wartime feat. His status as the greatest American hero of the war provided the platform for him to help the youth back in Fentress County, so it seems a little disingenuous for him to have shied away from talking about the exact reason he was so famous.

But even as the former patrol members Bernard Early and Otis Merrithew—and a few more—stewed over York getting the lion's share of the glory, York often went out of his way to correct the legend of his being a one-man army.

At a talk in 1930 in Milwaukee, he was met at the train station by the local media and Fr. August Gearhard, a local priest who had served as chaplain of the 328th Infantry Regiment in Georgia and in France. Once again, reporters called out for comments on his fight in the Argonne; York, a reporter wrote, was "loath to talk about his deeds."

So Gearhard described what Alvin York was so "loath" to talk about.

"Well, you see," Gearhard told the reporters and photographers gathered around him and York, "the sergeant was just a good shot. He could hit the bull's-eye and he could hide behind a tree . . . Then he picked 'em off a couple at a time—didn't you, sergeant?"

When the good father then told the assembled that York by himself "surrounded" the prisoners, "the sergeant merely laughed and looked more bashful," one reporter would write.

"There were seventeen men with me," York had quickly added.

"Do you remember Parsons?" Father Gearhard asked York. "Got killed or wounded, didn't he?"

"No," said York, "I saw him a while back."

"And the corporals who were with you?" Gearhard persisted.

"Two of them," York replied. "One was killed—four bullets, and the other wounded—Early, remember Early?"

It's almost painful to read the accounts of such encounters between York and his adoring public, given that he had steadfastly refused to make a bundle off of his deed but, in his mind, felt a need to help the people around Pall Mall, Tennessee. Most accounts mention his shyness, many describing him as "bashful," and looking back one wonders if his many public talks and the anxiety they produced in him were payback for the extraordinary fame that he carried like an aura.

Still, as with the fund-raisers for his beloved educational institute, York used his fame to push his view on other issues—chiefly

Prohibition, which had been in place since 1920 but was by the early 1930s losing support. York, almost as famous for having given up his hell-raising as he was for killing and capturing Germans, was a vocal advocate for keeping the Eighteenth Amendment in place.

"Man cannot serve two masters, God and liquor," York said at one event in Ohio in 1930. "Either he must put his back to God, or he must relinquish the artificial enjoyment which comes from intemperance. Long experience has taught me that nothing good is to be derived from the use of alcoholic liquors as a beverage."

York even went so far as to criticize his fellow American Legionnaires, not so subtly pointing to the rampant serving of booze at its various conventions, where its members debauched and "violated the laws of the country and decency" in a "rank way."

Prohibition was, however, repealed in 1933. That didn't stop York from decrying the use of alcohol, but it did lead to his being drafted as the candidate for vice president in the Prohibition Party at its convention in Niagara Falls, New York, in May 1936. There, its presidential candidate, Dr. D. Leigh Colvin, bemoaned how the repeal of Prohibition was creating "women drinkers." York, told of his being drafted to the ticket while back home in Tennessee, said he would not accept the nomination.

The same month, York and the agricultural institute that was named after him parted ways, this time for good. York, president of the school, got involved in a power struggle with its principal in 1935, which led to York's seeking his ouster in August of that year.

The institute's board refused to fire the principal, telling York that there should only be one person in charge of day-to-day operations. "Whereupon I asked them to relieve me of responsibility as president and general manager," York said. A bitter York told reporters that one board member had told him that it was not "good diplomacy to let a man be head of a school who hasn't a college degree"—a fairly sane view of educational hierarchy, but not one York took easily.

"It's my school," York said. "I founded it and built it." He vowed to go to the state legislature and ask it to "take it out of the hands of the state board and turn it over to me, the man who founded it and fostered it without a penny of salary."

In the end, York stepped aside. He continued to fund-raise for his pet project, even mortgaging his farm to help pay for a fleet of school buses—and fell deeply into debt. But, in between bouts of arthritis that precluded physical labor for months at a time, he also focused more of his energies on his farm.

Reporters continued to beat a path to his door, especially in the fall of 1938 when the twentieth anniversary of his Argonne feat rolled around. York was aware of the date, but made no plans to commemorate it.

"Oh, no, I haven't forgotten what day it is," York told one enterprising reporter who sought him out on that anniversary. "But right now we're building a silo. We want to get it done by Monday, and, what with cutting silage, too, we're pretty busy."

Much more aware of world affairs than he had been in the spring and summer of 1917, he gladly offered his opinions, if asked, on the happenings in Europe, where Germany was invading Austria and the Sudetenland and another war seemed to be looming.

Referencing the famous "appeasement" of German dictator Adolf Hitler, York would say: "I believe if we want to stop Hitler, we must knock him off the block. He has been given what he wanted this time, but he'll ask for more."

The man who had struggled to understand what all the fuss had been about as he entered service the last time seemed to get it this time, and prophesized just what kind of war might be fought this time around.

"I think it will be fought almost entirely from the air," he said. "The infantry and cavalry will be used as clean-up squads, but certainly the major part of the next conflict will be fought above the ground."

He said he'd be "willing to go" to war again if needed, though at the age of fifty-one he recognized he was way above the age limit for military service.

Some still remembered the famous Acting Cpl. Alvin York, and twenty years on they still valued his opinion—on war, on peace, on anything. Others by then—a new generation of Americans—had to be reminded or learn for the first time about the man who, as one paper misguidedly put it in 1939, "single-handedly surrounded a trench full of Germans."

Near the twenty-year anniversary of his alleged one-man show, one paper would ask its readers, "Do You Remember Alvin York?" and note, "Never in all history has any individual war hero been more widely acclaimed than was York" for "one of the most brilliant examples of individual heroism in any war." But, the paper noted, the twenty-year anniversary that had quietly passed just three days before was also a "most vivid evidence of how fleeting is the thing called fame."

Alvin C. York had claimed for years he was trying to forget what had happened, what he had done, in the Argonne Forest on October 8, 1918. He wanted any attention aimed at himself for his bravery and military feat to be trained instead on his life in peace, and his accomplishments since the war had ended.

The fame had been a burden, his celebrity had cost him, and he had never been comfortable with his status as the Most Famous Doughboy of the World War. (Never mind that he also had, paradoxically, agreed to participate in the publication of not just one, not just two, but *three* books celebrating his life and war service.)

By 1940, he was largely out of the limelight, his skirmishes with local politicians and school boards fading as quickly from memory as was his name and heroic deed.

But fame and opportunity would come calling at his doorstep once again. And this time, it wasn't a book deal; this time, it was the star-making machinery of a place called Hollywood, California.

20

HOW A HILLBILLY GOT A FARM

Like Tom Skeyhill, Jesse L. Lasky was there that day in May 1919 when the S.S. *Ohioan* cruised into New York Harbor carrying hundreds of boisterous and relieved and saved doughboys who shouted from the decks and the lifeboats and the railings, among them Alvin York, who was met by a delirious throng at the docks and ticker-tape-paraded through the streets and avenues to the cheers of thousands and thousands of otherwise hard-nosed and cynical city dwellers.

Jesse Lasky was impressed; like Skeyhill, Jesse Lasky would never forget that day; twenty years later, Jesse Lasky would put some new *oomph!* into the then-receding legend of Sergeant York and his 132 captured Teutons and their bewildered not-major-but-lieutenant Paul Vollmer, and add a few twists while doling out some hard cash to the down-on-his-luck good sergeant, Alvin Cullum York.

Born in San Francisco in 1880, Lasky was a true pioneer, a man who began his work life in his father Isaac's modest shoe store but soon turned to the cornet, and played to the audiences at a local theater. After Isaac died in 1900, though, the responsibilities of providing for the Lasky family fell to him, and he quickly found that the meager pay he was receiving to blow his horn wouldn't allow him to support his mother, Sarah, and sisters, Blanche and Maud.

So he raised $3,000 from relatives and left San Francisco for the lure of gold in Alaska. There, his money quickly ran out, as no gold was to be found, other than the coins that trickled down to him at night as he once again put his cornet to his lips and tooted along for the dance-hall girls.

"When the miners came in they used to throw sacks of gold dust and coins at the girls," Lasky once remembered. "I was entitled to all that fell in the pit."

He soon picked up his cornet and took it to Honolulu, where he engaged once more to be a cornetist for a show. That show closed before he could collect a salary, but fate was to be kind to him: his sister Blanche had by 1902 learned to play the cornet and was booked at a music hall in San Francisco. Hearing this, Jesse sailed once more for California, and he and Blanche went on a national tour with a performer named Herrman the Great.

The sister-brother act soon grew into an act called Lasky's Military Octet, and in 1903 Jesse became the great Herrman's manager and booking agent. The pay was good, so good that by 1911 Lasky invested $110,000 in a music hall and presented the Folies-Bergère in New York. But the show bombed, and for the second time in his young life Jesse Lasky was broke.

Fate would, however, once more—and not for the last time—be kind to Jesse Lasky. His sister Blanche married a very successful glove salesman named Samuel Goldfish, who one day would become known as Samuel Goldwyn. Sam inveigled Jesse to invest in producing moving-picture shows, then a young but growing industry. Jesse Lasky, looking for new opportunities, acquiesced.

A young filmmaker named Cecil B. DeMille joined their venture, which they called the Jesse L. Lasky Feature Play Company. They decided to make their first effort in film with a western titled *The Squaw Man*, starring Dustin Farnum, Monroe Salisbury, and Winifred Kingston.

DeMille decamped for Arizona to scout locations for the cowboys-and-Indians shoot-'em-up. He soon wired Lasky to report that California, and especially southern California, might make a better locale. An area holding "fruit trees and chicken coops," as one writer put it, was selected. It was called Hollywood.

Eventually merging his company with Adolph Zukor, the Lasky company, which would evolve into Paramount Pictures, produced such films as *Wings, Beau Geste,* and *A Kiss for Cinderella* and employed such early film legends as Clara Bow, George M. Cohan, Harold Lloyd, and Pola Negri.

Despite the early successes, the Great Depression left the company in receivership, and Lasky was forced out of Paramount. He was reported to have personally lost a whopping $12 million—plus his house. Harry Warner, the head of Warner Bros. and a close friend of Lasky's, loaned him $250,000, and through the rest of the 1930s he worked as an independent film producer, and later also produced a radio talent show called *Gateway to Hollywood.*

By 1940, Lasky was hoping for a successful film venture that would bring him back to the industry he had cofounded and which had made him wealthy for a while.

Lasky had been in those New York City streets on May 22, 1919, when York returned and was paraded through downtown, and had actually sent an underling to York's suite at the Waldorf Astoria to try to sign the sergeant for a film depiction of his stirring story. Turned down, Lasky had nevertheless devoured George Pattullo's story in the *Saturday Evening Post* and followed York's ups and downs since his return to the United States.

A suggestion from another producer that York's story might make a good film now rekindled Lasky's own enthusiasm, and he set out to woo the somewhat recalcitrant York, who had turned down numerous offers for stage and film (though obviously not books) though the years. He wrote York in 1939 to seek his cooperation; not surprisingly, he received no reply.

Undeterred, Lasky continued to try to sway York, traveling to northern Tennessee four times after his initial, and unsuccessful, pitch. He appealed not to York's vanity, of which he had little, but his sense of patriotism. Previously somewhat of a disillusioned isolationist who claimed he would only fight again if America was invaded, York had also been a huge proponent for preparedness. As war broke out in Europe with the September 1, 1939, German invasion of Poland, York seemed resigned to the fact that a war involving the United States was inevitable.

York also had a new fire within, that of building a Bible school to bookend the schools he had by then lost any sway over. He said he wanted to reprise the "great revival of 1800" that had torn through the southeast—and preach the same "sound, fundamental faith" that the pioneers to the southern Appalachians had brought with them.

And fundamental it would be: York vowed that evolution would not be taught at the Alvin C. York Bible School. "Nothing is going to be taught which will hurt the fundamental Christian faith. We are going to teach the Bible, which tells us that man was created by God in his own image."

Fortuitously for Jesse Lasky, Alvin York once more needed money to achieve his dreams.

LASKY FINALLY NEGOTIATED a meeting with York at a hotel near York's Tennessee home on March 9, 1940. They talked briefly before leaving by car for a tour of Fentress County, York's schools, and the proposed site for York's new Bible school.

Five days later, they met again, and Lasky and his attorney, Walter L. Bruington, began by unveiling a "typical Hollywood contract, which, to Mr. York, appeared as a mountain thicket of non-understandable clauses," the Associated Press reported.

"What we want is a plain old Tennessee contract that simply says what you shall do and what the sergeant shall do," York's own attorney, John Hale, said.

York also insisted on downplaying his deed in the Argonne in any film Lasky might make. "My part in the war should be presented only as an incident in my life," he told reporters during a recess. "The way I've lived since then, the contributions I've made to my community, are the things I'm really proud of."

Finally, it came down to money. Lasky offered York $25,000 for the film; York declined. The offer went up quickly to $50,000, and York again declined, saying he wanted a percentage of the gross. With things at an impasse, Lasky returned to California.

By then, word had gotten around about a possible film featuring York's feat. The idea was applauded by at least one newspaper editorialist; the *Nashville Tennessean* writer hoped that York would okay such a film as a timely reminder "that the pioneer spirit still survives . . . In all the pages of fiction, there is no more amazing and thrilling story, and in this day of uncertainty in our great democracy, there is need of reassurance that the Tall Men still are a vital part of American life."

Lasky returned to Tennessee within a week. Having thought the issue over, he decided to accept York's demand for a piece of the receipts. The deal was signed in the office of the governor of Tennessee; York would get $50,000 and 2 percent of the gross, and Lasky would get his movie.

With a contract signed, Lasky brought in writers Harry Chandlee, Julien Josephson, and Abem Finkel and had them spread out through Fentress County to get a feel for York's backwoods milieu and the patois of the locals. As well, an amateur photographer from Nashville, Albert Ganier, traveled to Pall Mall to shoot landscapes and portraits of York's neighbors and their dress. By early May, Chandlee and Josephson had concocted a rough script for the movie, which was originally titled *The Amazing Story of Sergeant York*.

In a memo sent to Lasky on May 10, 1940, Chandlee and Josephson laid out their vision for the film. They wanted to be careful, they said, not to be accused of propagandizing for or against war, but present instead "the story of York, himself, and though every possible value will be given to his heroic exploit and, from the standpoint of production values this will be an outstandingly spectacular sequence, its purpose in the story will be to solve York's personal problems and the problems of his fellow mountaineers rather than aggrandize war or even heroism."

As for that other certain element that was so important to York's personal story—his being saved and his subsequent struggles with the idea of killing another human—the writers were cautious.

"It is recognized that if York's real religious attitude is included in the picture, there is great danger of his appearing to be merely a religious fanatic and thus lose heavily its audience understanding and sympathy. We feel especially, if it is even suggested that York believes he has had Divine assurance that he will not be killed, his heroism will be greatly lessened."

York did indeed feel, and often said, that he had persevered and survived on October 8, 1918, because of divine intervention; it was his strong faith that had allowed him to stand off against the German machine gunners and to shoot down Lt. Fritz Endriss and his doomed, bayonet-wielding followers. But because of the fear that more secular audience members might be offended by his piety, the story of York's conversion to Christianity would come through his mother's and Pastor Rosier Pile's appeal to York's "reason, rather than to his emotions," Chandlee and Josephson wrote.

The writers also had few qualms about further dramatizing the story, even to the point of inventing a fictitious member of the York Patrol to illustrate how the backward and ignorant future hero came to set aside his prejudices and learn to appreciate the more worldly doughboys he was thrown in among.

That fictional soldier would be "either a Brooklynite or East Sider who had never been out of the city. He and York do not understand each other at first but become pals." The tough New Yorker and the Tennessee mountain man were in the end to become great friends—until the former is cut down in the machine-gun fusillade that kills other members of the patrol.

Other dramatizations were also made, all with York's approval. Chandlee in a post-filming memo proudly mentions his idea of highlighting York's ambitions to someday own a farm, "which would be eventuated by the actual gift of the farm by the State of Tennessee at the end.

"This made the whole picture the story, not of the capture of the Germans, but of how a hillbilly got a farm," Chandlee added. "It became the story of a man and not an exploit."

Chandlee also invented a scene at a rifle range during York's training as a means of singling York out for his marksmanship and thus "getting York to the interview with his officers," where he could express his qualms about killing. That meeting became a pivotal scene in which York's battalion and company commanders— Edward Buxton and E. C. B. Danforth—change York's mind about fighting—but it also seriously condensed the reality of York's coming around.

Lastly, Chandlee admitted that he based the character of York's mother, Mary, not on herself but on someone more appealing. "I . . . invented the stark and silent characterization of Mother York," Chandlee wrote. "She was not like that in real life. She was ignorant and dictatorial but I took her from a mountain woman I knew in Virginia."

The script went through more changes, while Lasky managed to convince Warner Bros. to back the movie. More than 120 different sets were constructed on a Hollywood soundstage, including a forty-foot-high fake mountain and 121 living trees. Howard Hawks agreed to direct.

The names of different Hollywood leading men—James Cagney, Henry Fonda, Raymond Massey, and Spencer Tracy—were floated as possibilities for the title role, but Lasky had always had Gary Cooper in mind as the star. In an attempt to lure him to the project, Lasky wrote a telegram to Cooper under York's name, telling the Hollywood star that he—York—would be "honored . . . to see you on the screen as myself."

Cooper at first demurred, saying that the pious mountain man who became a war hero was "too big for me, he covered too much territory." Under unrelenting pressure from Lasky, Cooper finally told Lasky that if MGM, which held his contract, would release him from his contract temporarily and loan him to Warner, he would take the role. Lasky's brother-in-law Samuel Goldwyn, then at MGM, ultimately agreed to swap permission for Cooper to star in the York film, in return for Warner's permission for their star Bette Davis to play the lead in MGM's production of *The Little Foxes*.

Meanwhile, the movie would be based on the first two books written about York—Thomas Skeyhill's *Sergeant York: His Own Life Story and War Diary* and Sam Cowan's *Sergeant York and His People*—and permission had to be wrangled for both.

And there was still another task to perform. The film as written had numerous characters based on real people—including those in the York Patrol, of whom, one newspaper reported, York hoped to give "proper credit" for their roles in the battle that had made him wildly famous.

Each had to sign a release authorizing their portrayal, so the studio sent a veteran location manager, Bill Guthrie, on a ten-thousand-mile journey to track down each of the surviving York Patrol members, and as well Buxton, Danforth, and even John Pershing.

Pershing, Danforth, and Buxton proved to be no trouble. Next up was Percy Beardsley, who was still raising cattle outside Roxbury, Connecticut. Guthrie peeked through a farmhouse window and saw an old man—Percy's father, Nate—mending some towels. Nate, suspicious of Guthrie, summoned Percy, and soon the two were talking about the Argonne.

Before long, Nate said, "I kinda like this fellow. Fetch out the pitcher." A toast of hard cider was smashed down, and then Guthrie whipped out a release, and $50. At the sight of the bills Nate told Percy again, "Fetch out the jug!" This one contained brandy; after a few swallows, Percy Beardsley signed on the dotted line.

Guthrie found Paddy Donohue in Lawrence, Massachusetts, and bought him a new suit in return for his signature on the release. Joe Konotski wasn't far away, in Holyoke. Konotski, who had six children by then, "was pleased at the prospect of being portrayed in a movie," one newspaper reported.

Bernie Early was still in New Haven, Connecticut, the co-owner of a restaurant at which he also worked as a waiter. The former leader of the patrol, now the proud brandisher of a Distinguished Service Cross, was apparently happy to sign.

Guthrie found Mario Muzzi in New York's Little Italy. His English still poor, Muzzi had to get his sister, living across the hall, to explain Guthrie's purpose. Muzzi signed, but when Guthrie then pulled out the fifty bucks, "Muzzi jumped back as if the paper had been on fire."

His mother appeared on the scene, and things only got worse. "There's something funny here," she told Mario. "You get no money for nothing any time." It took another three hours to get Muzzi to accept the dough.

At Michael Sacina's New York apartment, Guthrie was greeted equally suspiciously by Sacina's sister. Guthrie tap-danced as best he could before she finally fetched Michael from a barber shop where he worked as a porter. He finally signed and took his money.

George Wills was still in South Philly, living in a shotgun shack near the city dump. He was happy to agree to a release in return for fifty bucks, telling Guthrie he made a living selling scrap from the trash yard. "Sometimes I make four, five dollars a week," he said.

Feodor Sok, ever the enigma, was back in Buffalo, New York, working at a Civilian Conservation Corps camp. Times were as hard for him as for most of the others after a dozen years of the Depression, and he gladly accepted his $50.

Thomas Gibb Johnson had relocated to Denison, Texas. His small, one-room house was divided by a rope holding dishcloths, and their conversation took place with Guthrie on one side, and Johnson on the other. The release, and the money, were transferred over the line—and Guthrie left without even having caught a glimpse of Johnson's face.

21

AN IMITATION OF WAR

Former corporal Otis Merrithew also signed a release, but not before a little haggling with Guthrie delivered $250—two hundred more dollars than his peers—into his pockets. Working as a truck driver, Merrithew was also struggling to make ends meet as the Depression wound down, and he gladly took the money from Guthrie in October 1940.

His oldest daughter, seventeen-year-old Anna, was just as happy. "Now I can go to school," she exulted, to which Otis told Guthrie: "It's true. I wasn't going to be able to send her to college next year, but now I can."

But things were in fact not as rosy as they appeared with Merrithew. He had learned of the pending film months prior to Guthrie's visit, and in June 1940 he had fired off a threatening letter to Jesse Lasky in which he warned him that the film had better present the facts of what occurred on October 8, 1918, as Merrithew saw them.

"I presume . . . that the scenes will deal with facts based in the United States Congressional Records and on information and affidavits which form a part of the record of the U.S. Army and which were signed by former 'buddies' of Sg't. York's," Merrithew wrote.

Merrithew told Lasky he had been in touch with "all of York's and my former 'buddies' and they claim that they did not sign any affidavits." Merrithew then trotted out once more the bogus claim that if some of the patrol members had in fact signed affidavits supporting York for a medal, "they thought that they were signing a 'supply slip' for a suit of underwear or some such thing. These same men today will sign an affidavit and forward it to the United Press, if you proceed to go through with any battle scenes, without consulting us."

Merrithew, still bitter over what he felt was a glory-grab by York at his and the others' expense, also wrote:

"It is time that the good Sergeant thought more of the . . . eye-witnesses than he does and we think that we should have prominent parts in the picture also. There is glory enough to go all the way around."

Merrithew closed by promising to provide "bad publicity" should the film depiction of the York Patrol's actions omit the role played by himself and the other ten survivors, and signed off by saying: "I think we should get together and talk this over."

It was the same-old, same-old, but Merrithew was nothing if not persistent. In a letter to Guthrie in March 1941 he continued to make threats, telling him that he would sue Warner Bros. if the film did not portray "the German Major"—Lt. Paul Vollmer—surrendering to anyone but himself. "In handing me that pistol," Merrithew wrote, "the Major knew that *I* was in command and *not* York."

The Warner Bros. attorney, Walter Bruington, forwarded Merrithew's first letter to York's attorney, John Hale, asking for his comments, and Hale dismissed Merrithew's assertions.

He told Bruington: "No where in the Congressional Record, in any of the books about Sergeant, nor in any of the reports of the battle, in so far as I know, has there ever been one word which casts any reflection on the parts played by the other survivors. Every man has been given credit for doing his duty, but Sergeant [York] was given credit for doing something above and beyond the call of duty. I think there is nothing whatever to Corporal Cutting's letter . . . His letter is merely a demand for a little 'hush' money which should receive no consideration whatever."

Sergeant York had its premiere at the Astor Theater in New York on July 2, 1941; on July 14, 1941, there appeared a notice in the *Boston Globe*. It was anonymously written in the names of seven members of the York Patrol but was no doubt the work of Otis Merrithew.

Once again, the survivors claimed they had not signed any affidavits in France in early 1919, and once again asserted that if they had signed anything they thought it was a "supply slip." None of the survivors, the notice said, "are in agreement with Warner Brothers or with Sergeant York's version of what really happened 'over there.'"

There is, in fact, no way the patrol members who gave affidavits could have upon reflection thought that they were merely signing "supply slips." Their former battalion commander, Edward Buxton, served as the Eighty-Second Division's inspector after the war, and he personally took the affidavits of Percy Beardsley, Michael Sacina, George Wills, and Paddy Donohue. The Twenty-Eighth Regiment's Second Battalion adjutant, Lt. Edwin Burkhalter, took the affidavits of Joseph Konotski and, for a second time, Beardsley. Feodor Sok "subscribed" to Konotski's affidavit "word for word."

Each of the soldiers swore to his affidavit's veracity, and though they are in places similar, they are not simply boilerplates of each other. Buxton also noted that each of the four affidavits he took was read back to each soldier "to which he made an oath before me."

If there were language problems among any of the immigrant affiants that might have led them to not understand what they were signing, they are not noted among the affidavits as presented in either Tom Skeyhill's or Sam Cowan's books; Konotski signed his affidavit with an "X" instead of his name, indicating he could not write English. But he certainly knew enough English to have understood Bernie Early's orders to stay close to the patrol's German prisoners as they prepared to leave the ravine on the day in question.

The ad also contained an anecdote that seems, given all of the evidence, to be farcically false on its face. The men said they "always had figured Sergeant York out to be 'yellow' and not a conscientious objector; we recall one morning as we were to go over the top, York went stark mad with fear. He jumped up on top of the parapet and started to holler, 'I want to go home, for God's sake why isn't the war over?'

"Sergeant Early rushed up to him and pushed his automatic pistol to his head and said 'If you don't shut up I'll blow your brains out.'"

Despite all of Bill Guthrie's hard work and travels, the only members of the York Patrol to make the final cut on-screen were William B. Cutting (Merrithew), Murray Savage, and Bernie Early.

Their battalion commander, Edward Buxton; company commander, E. C. B. Danforth; and former sergeant Harry Parsons also appeared—as did the fictional patrol member "Pusher" Ross, the tough-talking New Yawker who turned from York's nemesis to his best friend before being killed by a grenade hurled by one of the captured Germans.

It was perhaps unfortunate for Alvin C. York that art did not imitate real life as it pertained to his former "buddies" in the York Patrol; in the end, though, the survivors' specious claims and threats failed to tarnish either the record of Sergeant Alvin York or the film *Sergeant York*.

The film would make Gary Cooper a star; it also brought the real Sergeant York back to prominence and into the black. Jesse Lasky had given York $25,000 after he signed on to the movie, the first installment in the $50,000 plus 2 percent of the gross that they had agreed upon. *Sergeant York* would prove to be a cash cow for Alvin York, grossing $4 million before the year was out, making it the highest-grossing film of 1941.

Cooper would earn an Academy Award for Best Actor for the role, which would remain his favorite. The two men had met while York paid a brief visit to the California set during filming in the spring of 1941, and Cooper, originally from Montana, and York found common ground in their upbringing.

Jesse Lasky and Cooper invited York to Cooper's home, where at first the two men found little to talk about. "Cooper is a man of few words," one newspaper writer would note. "York is one of fewer."

Lasky finally broke the ice by saying, "Gary, I think you have a gun Alvin might like to see."

"That started them talking," Lasky said later. While Lasky retreated to a corner of the room, Alvin and "the Coop" talked shooting, hunting, "and everything else," Lasky said. "You never heard two fellows talk so much."

Cooper noted that he had been raised in the mountains, too, and said he had ridden horses and hunted "as a natural part of growing up." He said he had finally given in to the idea of playing York "because of the background of the picture, and because I was portraying a good, sound American character."

Despite the efforts by Harry Chandlee and the other writers (including a large amount of input from the actor/writer/director John Huston) to straddle the line between isolationism and being prowar, some viewers and reviewers found *Sergeant York* to be jingoistic.

But by the time it was released, war clouds were not only on the horizon but drifting toward the American naval base at Pearl Harbor in Hawaii, which would be attacked by the Japanese just five months after the film's release. Like Alvin York, many Americans had reconciled themselves to the probability that another world war was unavoidable, and there were reports of young male viewers leaving the theaters and heading straight to the enlistment stations after watching it.

Most reviews of *Sergeant York* were positive, with *Newsweek* magazine saying that while it could have been a "jingoistic cross between *Billy the Kid* and *The Fighting 69th*"—another Great War film—it was instead "an engrossing and humorous record of the American way of life in a backwoods community, as well as a timely drama of the inner struggle of a deeply religious man who weighs the horrors of killing against what he feels is the greater necessity to stop all killing."

The film, and York's story, were indeed timely, with the world ablaze, with Germany invading Russia, France under Nazi domination, and the Japanese up to who-knew-what in Asia. As early as September 1940, President Franklin Roosevelt authorized a peacetime draft; isolationism and pacifism were not likely to keep danger from the shores of America. The story of a simple man who wrestled with ideals before agreeing to fight for a higher principle struck a chord amid the growing chaos.

Bosley Crowther said as much in his review of Sergeant York in the *New York Times*.

"At this time, when a great many people are thinking deep and sober thoughts about the possible involvement of our country in another deadly world war, Warner Brothers and a bewildering multiplicity of collaborative producers and writers . . . have brought forth a simple and dignified screen biography of that famous Tennessee mountaineer who put aside his religious scruples against killing for what he felt was the better good of his country and the lasting benefit of mankind."

The *Los Angeles Times* echoed that refrain, saying *Sergeant York* was "today's American story, a relentlessly intimate, agonizing sympathetic portrait of the struggle which is now taking place everywhere in the land where men love peace and are faced by the necessity to fight for it."

The *Brooklyn Daily Eagle* focused its attention on York, its reviewer writing: "No man could want a finer tribute to his character or his courage . . . 'Sergeant York' is a stunning motion picture."

The film *Sergeant York* indeed hit all the high notes, including York's wild days back in Tennessee, his coming to Jesus, and his struggle with his conscience. And the film accurately portrays some of what happened west of Chatel-Chéhéry that day, including the death of Murray Savage and the wounding of Bernard Early—indeed in command of the patrol—and "Cutting" (Early at one point says, "York—take over," which York understands as an order to set out as a one-man army).

The Germans indeed surrender when confronted by the patrol on a ridgeline above them; several German machine gunners turn their weapons around and fire on the Americans after one sees the surrender below and the German commander shouts the order to get down; York subsequently moves forward and soon guns down six Germans charging with fixed bayonets.

But there was some hokum, as well. Unable to hit two machine gunners, York resorts to gobbling like a turkey—an act that was supposed to reflect how he'd caught the attention of the reclusive birds back in Fentress County—and when they pop out, he kills them. He sneaks up on a line of Germans firing from a well-established trench and shoots them down, one by one, while the rest remain unaware. "Just like a flock of turkeys," our mountain-man hero says to himself.

The ground over which the doughboys advance is war-torn and shell-pocked, nothing like the verdant, mostly untouched condition of the western slope of Hill 223 at the time.

As well, the patrol after being sent on its mission by Sgt. Harry

Parsons soon enters a duck-boarded, sandbagged, fortified trench system—nothing like the shallow property boundary it followed behind the German lines in real life. But Americans had become well accustomed to photos and descriptions of the horrible conditions of the Western Front, and it can be assumed that the film's producers worried that the film would seem inauthentic if it, too, did not portray the mud and trenches and shell-pocked terrain of a Great War battlefield.

As for York's mates? They huddle behind him, keeping low. When "Pusher" says they should move up to support York, another tells him no—they need to stay and guard their prisoners. Meanwhile, the rest of the Germans finally succumb one by one to the lone American, and surrender. Then all march back, being shunted from one American headquarters to the next as Alvin York walks into history.

It is all very stirring, but for the other ten survivors of the York Patrol, watching the battle sequence must have been doubly infuriating. According to a possibly apocryphal story, as far back as the 1920s former private Joseph Konotski and several other still-angry members of the patrol while well-inebriated came up with a plan to drive down to Tennessee and kill York; fortunately for all, the plot was never carried out.

And in 1935, the Connecticut branch of the American Legion, either with or without Bernard Early's blessing, adopted a resolution asking that Early be awarded the Congressional Medal of Honor. His physician, a Dr. Frank Mongillo, indicated that Early was not behind the resolution and was in fact "very modest, extremely cheerful and very reluctant about discussing the war." But, the doctor added, "it is a known fact among the boys in his outfit that Sergeant Early accomplished the feat for which Sergeant York has been credited."

York continued to suffer the niggling doubts of others about the film and the reality of his feat. When the movie opened, Otis Merrithew popped up again and made a point of visiting theaters where *Sergeant York* was playing "and talking to audiences about what really happened—even if they didn't like it," a modern newspaper story says.

Merrithew had threatened legal action and bad publicity if the film didn't portray him taking the surrender of Paul Vollmer and his men; no such suit was apparently ever filed, but Otis did what he could to spoil York's party. The others remained largely quiet, though Bernard Early told a granddaughter later in life, "It didn't happen that way."

Perhaps not by coincidence, York—as he had many times—went out of his way in a 1941 radio speech to spread some glory to the others in the York Patrol.

"Although I was credited with wiping out the whole battalion of 35 machine guns, I was only one of the 17 who did the job," he said in his address. "Anyone of the other boys could have done the same thing I did if fate had put them in my place. If any of my buddies are listening tonight I want the whole world to know that without their cool courage none of us would be alive today."

It was inevitable, perhaps, that others would claim to have been part of the famous York Patrol, or at the least claim some part in York's coup. One, Saul Odess, made his claim, conveniently, after Skeyhill's book about York was published and the exact details of the fight made known, and his local congressman in Massachusetts went so far as to introduce a bill seeking to have Odess awarded the Distinguished Service Cross.

There was but one problem: Odess was indeed a member of Company G, 328th Infantry Regiment, but there was no evidence he'd been with York and the others that day. His account of what occurred was published in the *Boston Globe* in May 1931; it closely parrots the narratives found in George Pattullo's story and Skeyhill's book, with the exception that he gave himself an integral and heroic part in the action. No other accounts, from those of Bernard Early or York or any of those who gave affidavits, even mention Odess.

With less drama and fanfare, another member of Company G who was interviewed after the film *Sergeant York* came out said that he had been among those who helped get the captured Germans to the American lines. George H. Bosley didn't claim to be a part of the patrol, and fully credited York with the capture of the enemy; however, he disputed one detail—that of the grenade that was flung toward York by one of the surrendered Germans.

For what it's worth, Bosley said the German did throw the grenade, only it was while the Germans were being herded from the ravine. He said he was near enough to be slightly wounded on his nose and cheek by the blast, and recalled that another soldier, and not York, shot the offending German and killed him.

Also for what it's worth, the former York Patrol private George Wills was said to have claimed credit for York's feat through his adulthood, which he spent at that scrap heap in South Philly.

One resident who knew him in the 1950s, a former union leader named Joe Sullivan, in 2008 remembered Wills—who died in 1966—saying, "York was nothing!"

"He told me that he himself was really the one who killed and captured all of those Germans. He said that he hadn't wanted any of the glory, so he let York take credit for all of it."

This, from the man who in his affidavit after the war expressly said, "I heard Corporal York several times shouting to the machine gunners on the hill to come down and surrender, but from where I stood, I could not see Corporal York. I saw him, however, when the firing stopped and he told us to get along the sides of the column."

If only . . .

If only the army had seen fit to quickly award D.S.C.s to every man who came out of that ravine alive, the York Patrol, minus its six dead, might have remained a cohesive unit, bonded by the significant impact it had made on October 8, 1918; the lingering bitterness and jealousy that marked some of their lives might not have existed, and all could have pointed proudly to Alvin York and said, *Do you see that man? I was there with him that day . . .*

Instead, the patrol's survivors returned from their war to find that Alvin York had become a national hero—no, *the* national hero. There were already whispered disputations about what really went down in that ravine before the S.S. *Ohioan* docked; those whispers would fester and turn into recriminations over the coming years, even as York shunned the offers thrown his way and tried his best to do some good for his people back home.

The York Patrol, seventeen brave men, walked into that ravine as "buddies," as York would say, bonded by training and a specific mission to perform. After one of them walked out a hero, the York Patrol became a collection of individuals.

That is the sad coda to the story of the York Patrol, but not yet the end.

22

OLD SOLDIERS

The creek still barely gurgles turgidly underneath sticking, broad-leaf plants that now cover the forest floor. The canopy overhead is dense, and little sunlight gets through. Above and just east, the ground still rises, and from various spots, including a scratched-out depression that no doubt one time held a machine gun, the approach from Hill 223 can still be seen, the long green slope drifting downward and west toward the tree line.

Look there, just to the north and close your eyes. Imagine what that day was like, imagine the line of German soldiers loading and firing and firing and reloading as the Americans came on in rushes before going to ground in bunches, trying like hell to avoid the fire from the front, left, and right. Imagine Karl Glass and Max Thoma directing that fire; imagine the trees spotted with the red and yellow hues of autumn; imagine the mist that lolled and blanketed the field; imagine the *pup-pup-pup* of the Maxims; imagine the shouts, some in German, others English; imagine Paul Vollmer standing just behind the line in that ravine below; imagine seventeen nervous American soldiers making their way from the south and along that turgid creek, its banks crowded and choked with brush.

Imagine the yells of the Americans, and the ensuing shots, and the quick surrender of the large group of Germans resting on the eastern slope of the ravine while Lieutenant Vollmer harangues them and urges them to rise and take the field; imagine the surprise on both sides, and the mass surrender; imagine the shouted order, in German, to get down; imagine the bursts of machine-gun fire and the instant destruction of six young American lives; imagine Alvin York, acting corporal, holding his ground and firing up that hill, first with his rifle, then his pistol, as Fritz Endriss and his five men attack with their bayonets; imagine six prone Germans, five dead, the other mortally wounded with a bullet in his belly.

A short walk from Chatel-Chéhéry will take you to that spot; just follow the country lane down Hill 223 for less than a kilometer and to the tree line, to the spot where the languid creek gently curdles at the road bed, to the now almost-anonymous place where the members of the York Patrol entered the lives of their German counterparts, to the place where men died and men were wounded and men surrendered, to the place where a Tennessee backwoodsman performed a military deed that colored his life, and those of the others, for good or ill.

It's the place that surely remained ingrained in the minds of all of the survivors of the patrol, and the place to which Alvin York, though trying to forget, must have visited in his mind's eye for the rest of his life as he reflected on his deed and sought justification for the taking of lives only to arrive at the conclusion each time that he had to do it, had to kill or be killed.

Most of the survivors of the York Patrol dutifully registered anew for the second war, though each was too old to serve by late 1941, when the United States mobilized for a two-front war against Japan and Germany. York filled out his registration form at Pastor Rosier Pile's country store, the same place he had filled out his card for the Great War. But it was a "graying, heavier Alvin C. York who offered his services, gladly," one paper would report.

By then, he had already volunteered his famed marksmanship to the U.S. Army. As the soldiers under Gen. Douglas MacArthur were being besieged by Japanese forces on the Bataan Peninsula in the Philippines, a correspondent relayed a perhaps tongue-in-cheek request to "Alvin York and his mountain neighbors" to help reduce the "rattlesnakes of Bataan"—Japanese snipers.

"I'd be mighty proud to start for there tomorrow," York said in February 1942. "Why, there's enough old-time squirrel hunters scattered around the hills of Tennessee and Kentucky to pick out the eyes of every Jap in the Philippines without wasting a shot. I'm a little older than I was in the last war, but I can still shoot just as straight."

Instead, York lent his name to a daily syndicated column called "Sergeant York Says," which was written by his personal secretary, Arthur Bushing, with help from a columnist from the Nashville *Tennessean*. In the folksy, plain-spoken style that had graced his autobiography, his messages were the same: he was all-in for the United States' effort and you should be as well.

"I had to be persuaded to fight last time," Sergeant York said just a week after Japan bombed Pearl Harbor. "Nobody needs that today. At one blow the Japs have welded every last American into one solid chunk of steel. They have forged the sledgehammer that will smash them."

York had quickly apprised the threat of Japanese aggression, but it had taken him longer to size up Germany's intentions. His association with *Sergeant York* producer Jesse Lasky, a Jew, brought him around to the threat posed by Adolf Hitler, and York served as a spokesperson for the Fight for Freedom Committee, which advocated intervention in the European war.

That stance soon pitted York against another American hero: Charles "Lucky" Lindbergh, who in 1927 had become the first person to fly across the Atlantic Ocean. Using his own platform with the America First Committee, Lindbergh, who had on a visit to Germany received a medal from Luftwaffe head Hermann Goering, saw Winston Churchill, and not Hitler, as the real threat to the world.

In a speech given in New York on the day after the film *Sergeant York* opened, York blasted Lindbergh as an isolationist and appeaser. Pointing to the nonaggression pact between Russia and Germany that had been cast aside just weeks before when Hitler invaded Russia, York concluded:

"Can ex-colonel Lindbergh now say that appeasement hasn't been given every conceivable chance to prove itself?" And he added one little dig, mentioning that "of all the medals I was fortunate enough to get, none of them came with the blessing of Adolf Hitler."

The most famous doughboy in World War 1 in turn found himself the target not of adoration and worship, for once, but of savage criticism from some of Lindbergh's supporters. One, a J. R. Doran, addressed his letter to "Skunk York" and let him know that there was more "Americanism" in Lindbergh's little fingers than in "your whole rotten carcass you pro-British un-American Wall Street warmonger. They should take cowards like you and put [them] against a brick wall and shoot you."

Another nonadmirer, a retired U.S. Army colonel named J. V. Kuznik, took pains to mention that "little band of fearless buddies" who were with him in that ravine and who, he intimated, had not gotten their due.

"In this now glamorous exploit," Kuznik wrote, "you must admit that the real danger of your mission was in the approach under a withering fire and not in the act of making prisoners the remnants of an isolated detachment of the enemy that was trapped in a dugout and who were in mortal fear of being blown to bits in their rathole by your hand grenades."

Just for good measure, the good colonel accused York of acting as a dupe for an "internationally-minded minority"—the Jews—and becoming "for big pay, their No. 1 smear artist in the moving picture industry . . ."

Thus did the former almost conscientious objector become, in some American minds, a warmonger and tool for Zion.

But before 1941 was out, York was being proven correct. His various offers of military service turned down, he used his renewed celebrity status for the U.S. Signal Corps, signing on as morale officer and also serving as a "roving ambassador" for the War Department, pushing war bonds and urging his listeners to contribute to the various drives—paper, tin, rubber—to help win the war.

He also hosted a weekly variety-news radio program called *Tennessee Americans*, which aired on Sunday evenings. And in 1943, York along with John Pershing's favorite doughboy, Sam Woodfill, became consultants to the army on training infantry.

Even as he toured the country making patriotic speeches, York's aforementioned problems with money continued. He earned $134,338 from the film *Sergeant York* in 1942 and another $15,949 in 1943—the equivalent of about $2.5 million in today's money. But, possibly following the advice and lead of Jesse Lasky—who had his own tax troubles—York paid his taxes in both years claiming the income as capital gains, which carried a much lower tax rate than ordinary income would have entailed.

By 1951, the Internal Revenue Service was on his case. The director of the IRS's Audit Division told one of York's handlers that York "cannot receive special or different treatment in their tax cases unless that authority comes from an act of Congress."

The agency said York owed more than $85,000 in back taxes and accrued interest—money which York had largely already spent on his Bible school.

York would be defiant over his calculations. "I paid 'em the tax I owed 'em and I don't owe 'em no more," he said of the IRS. "When I got that money I paid them half and told 'em the other half was mine."

His attitude contradicted his earlier behavior when he had told all suitors that his uniform was not for sale. However, since then he had nearly been wiped out financially, and since then he had undertaken the building of the Alvin C. York Institute and, now, a Bible school.

He was a hero; he had done good deeds after returning as such; truly flush for the first time on the proceeds from *Sergeant York*, he saw no good reason for a good portion of those proceeds to be handed over to the government when he could put them to what he figured was better use.

Eventually, the intervention of two sympathetic politicians— Speaker of the House Sam Rayburn and Joe Evins, a congressman from Tennessee—resulted in a compromise between the IRS and York, who by 1959 owed more than $172,000 in back taxes and interest. York paid $25,000 to the agency, and the case was closed.

As that amount was about equal to York's net worth at the time, Rayburn and Evins formed the Help Sergeant York Committee, and over a six-week period thousands of Americans sent money to Alvin and Gracie York, once more lifting them from near bankruptcy and into the black.

Another benefactor also came to York's rescue. S. Hallock du Pont, a Delaware financier, created a trust fund that paid York $300 a month for the rest of his life. Besides the pledges from total strangers, the most famous doughboy of the Great War received a whopping ten bucks a month as a retired earner of the Medal of Honor.

In the meantime, York's health had begun to fade. He had had surgery on his gallbladder far back in the mid-1920s, and he suffered from what he in 1937 said was "rheumatic fever and arthritis" that he traced back to "those days of mud and water in the trenches. I think that dampness, days and nights in wet uniforms—mud and more mud—all helped bring this about."

In 1942, he battled pneumonia, and as he approached his sixtieth year his weight had ballooned to 250 pounds and he developed high blood pressure. In 1948 and 1949, he suffered strokes, one of which left the right side of his face temporarily paralyzed. In 1954, a devastating stroke left him bedridden, after which circulatory problems left him nearly blind.

Old soldiers, goes the old barracks ballad, never die; they just fade away. By the age of seventy, the old soldier Alvin Cullum York had made his last public appearance, accepting the gift of a car with a wheelchair from the Eighty-Second Airborne Association. In 1960, the American Legion presented York—by then semiparalyzed—with a pushbutton bed that allowed him to move around the home he shared with Gracie.

"Seems like everything is push-button these days, including me," York joked.

As the United States entered into yet another war—this one in Vietnam—the former acting corporal remained in the national conscience, and he continued to be sought out for his opinion on world affairs, and for causes. Though he rued the demise of the ordinary grunt in the nuclear age, he supported the use of nuclear weapons against Russia, saying: "If they can't find anyone else to push the button, I will."

And in the early 1960s, he also allowed his name to be used in a campaign to halt any reduction to the National Guard, saying nothing would please Soviet premier Nikita Khrushchev more.

But he continued to fade away, and suffered a series of heart attacks until, finally, a urinary-tract infection put him into a coma—and into a Veterans Administration hospital in Nashville. On September 2, 1964, York, seventy-six years old, slipped away.

He was gone, but not forgotten. Among the tributes to him was one from President Lyndon Johnson, who said York "epitomized the gallantry of American fighting men and their sacrifices in behalf of freedom."

He was eulogized at York Church in Jamestown, Tennessee, and paratroopers from the Eighty-Second Airborne Division—the descendant of the old Eighty-Second Division—served as pall bearers. Gen. Matthew Ridgway attended the ceremony on behalf of Johnson. York was laid to rest in the nearby Wolf Creek Cemetery not far from where he'd been raised, and raised hell, and courted his future wife, and struggled with his conscience before picking up a rifle and heading to France.

The born-again Christian bumpkin former acting corporal turned hero walked through the valley of the shadow of death on October 8, 1918, and came out as one of America's greatest and most enduring heroes; he would live out his life, sometimes for good, sometimes for not, under the burden and glow of what happened in that ravine just west of Chatel-Chéhéry during what they used to innocently call the Great War.

MEANWHILE, OTIS MERRITHEW finally got his due.

Having written every U.S. president since Herbert Hoover to plead his case for recognition of his part in the York Patrol's fight, he in 1965 wrote President Johnson, attaching newspaper clippings to support his argument and telling LBJ he was his "last resort." In September of that year, Merrithew, then sixty-nine years old, was notified that he would be awarded a Silver Star.

The ceremony took place in Fort Devens, Massachusetts, on October 21, 1965—almost exactly forty-seven years from the day that he was wounded. Merrithew, like York before him, used the occasion to pass on his opinion on an issue of the day: men who were burning their draft cards in protest of a then-escalating war in Vietnam.

"The fellows who are protesting the Vietnam War should have their heads examined," Merrithew said. "What if, during WW1, we decided not to help out the French?"

Perhaps mollified, finally, by getting some measure of official recognition of his war service, Otis appeared to bury the hatchet with the late Alvin C. York, telling those at his ceremony:

"There was a fellow in our outfit who was a conscientious objector, but once he was in the thick of battle he knew why he was there. He fought like a tiger and almost captured the whole damned German army single-handed . . . His name was Sergeant York . . . He was a hero."

And so forty-seven years following the firefight in that ravine, Otis Merrithew finally got his shiny star, and Alvin York finally got his due from his cantankerous fellow corporal. If only he had been around to hear it.

Otis, too, would not be around to bask in the glow of one more honor. After he died at the age of eighty-one in April 1977, the city of Brookline, Massachusetts, dedicated a square in his honor. The Corporal Otis B. Merrithew Square is still there today at the intersection of Whitney Street and Meadowbrook Road.

OTIS WAS THE second-to-last surviving soldier of the York Patrol to pass, according to all available sources.

The first to die was Joseph Konotski, who earned a citation for his work on October 8, 1918. He returned home to Holyoke, Massachusetts, sired seven children, and worked as a shift supervisor for a paper company. He died at the age of sixty-four in 1959.

Konotski was quickly followed in death by Feodor Sok. Following the war, he had returned to Buffalo, New York, and by 1941 was working for the Work Projects Administration. Outside of a statement to army investigators looking into the patrol's firefight, he said nothing that was recorded about his service and lived out his life in quiet obscurity. He died in Black Rock, New York, on January 27, 1960.

The next to pass was Bernard Early. After receiving his D.S.C. in 1929, Early maintained a relatively low profile, running a New Haven restaurant with a partner and marrying and having five sons and a daughter. Plagued through the years by the wounds the German machine gunners had caused him, he retired in 1956 and died on April 11, 1961, at a Veterans Administration hospital in West Haven, Connecticut.

Five months later, Thomas Gibbs Johnson passed away. He had returned to Lynchburg, Virginia, following his mustering out of the service, and worked as a clerk in a shoe store. By 1930, he had gone to Texas with his mother, his brother John, and two nieces and a nephew.

There, he worked as a clerk at the Denison Overall Factory, which had been founded by his brother and his brother's business partner, A. C. Barrow. By 1933, the overall business had been superseded by another company, and while Thomas remained in Denison, his brother moved to Kansas City, where he died in a hotel room in February 1939. Thomas dutifully retrieved his brother's body for burial in Denison's Fairview Cemetery.

By 1941, Bill Guthrie of Warner Bros. found him living alone in a one-room house; newspaper reports say his nerves had been shattered by the war and that he spent most of his postwar life going in and out of Veterans Administration hospitals. When well, he quietly managed a secondhand magazine shop.

Only once did he comment on his service, telling a reporter in 1941, "York did most of the work with a rifle, capturing an officer and forcing the rest to surrender." Johnson suffered a fatal heart attack on September 23, 1961. He was sixty-six years old.

Johnson was followed into death by Paddy Donohue, on February 8, 1962. Donohue had returned to Lawrence, Massachusetts, following the war and once more worked in the mills, though by 1940 the U.S. Census listed his occupation as a laborer for the

Works Progress Administration. A grandniece, Pat Waters, said he spoke little of the war.

"He'd come visit us, but most of the time, he spent by himself," Waters said. "He'd smoke his pipe and he'd meet people."

For a while, Donohue had a girlfriend named Lillian—but gradually he became a recluse, and he died alone in a boardinghouse. After his death, a nephew retrieved his Purple Heart and Silver Star with the intention of sending them to a surviving sister in Ireland; instead, the Silver Star with Donohue's name on it was found inside a dresser drawer that had been anonymously left at a Lawrence thrift store in 2006. The Purple Heart was never located.

With the medal in its leather case was a faded newspaper article about the York Patrol. A little digging brought a call to Pat Waters, who was handed the precious heirloom connected to a great-uncle she hardly knew.

Inscribed on the medal were the words "For Gallantry in Action"—a reminder, if anyone needed one, that it was a patrol, and not just one individual, that had caused chaos on the German left flank in that ravine just west of Chatel-Chéhéry.

George Wills lived out his postwar years in obscurity, working odd jobs and scavenging dumps for scrap metals and later being employed in a coal-handling facility in the Philadelphia Navy Yard. In 1938, shortly after his youngest son, Jimmy, burned to death in a tragic fire, his wife took their older son, George Jr., and moved out of their South Philadelphia home.

The man who had survived gas attacks and machine-gun strafing on the Western Front finally died at the age of sixty-nine of a respiratory ailment caused by coal dust on March 15, 1966.

Michael Angelo Sacina, who had been promoted from private to corporal in March 1919, followed Wills into death just six weeks later, dying on April 27, 1966, at the age of seventy-seven in New York City. He, too, had lived a quiet postwar life, and outside of a few newspaper stories timed to the ten-year anniversary of the York Patrol's fight and, in 1941, the pending production of the film *Sergeant York*, little is known of him other than he was married and worked as a porter in a shoe store and by the 1940s had opened his own barbershop on West Fifty-Seventh Street in New York.

Percy Beardsley, who was also cited for his actions in that ravine, returned to the family cattle farm and its famous cider cellar after the war, where he lived with his father, Nate, and a housekeeper until Nate sent her away because he felt she was being too "covetous" of Perce.

He picked up the yoke again—regularly wearing bright red shirts while tending a one-ton bull—and lived a quietly bucolic life, which at one point included visits from a couple of famous neighbors—Arthur Miller and Marilyn Monroe, for whom he carved a large letter *M* onto a cask of cider in her honor.

He remained a bachelor for much of his adult life before finally marrying Louise Lingsch in 1949, when he was fifty-six years old. They lived amicably—except for on one occasion when Percy grew concerned that a new furnace was upsetting the necessary cool temperature in the cider cellar.

"For a moment we thought that either the furnace or the cider had to go," Louise told a reporter in 1966. "And if the furnace went, I went." Percy managed in the end to balance his cider, the furnace, and the wife—"in that order," Louise said.

Shortly after York died in 1964, Beardsley told a reporter he was "content" to let Alvin York keep the lion's share of glory for the capture of all of those Germans. Beardsley died on September 17, 1968.

Mario Muzzi, who was slightly wounded in that ravine on his thirtieth birthday, was the last of the York Patrol's members to die. He had returned to New York after the war and picked up his job as a baker, and married his wife, Concetta, in 1923. Though he was naturalized as a U.S. citizen the same year, it appears he moved back to Italy at some point, and died there in April 1978 at the ripe old age of eighty-nine.

Early. Beardsley. Merrithew. Muzzi. Sacina. Wills. Donohue. Sok. Johnson. Konotski.

York.

Thrown together in Company G, 328th Infantry Regiment, they endured the clingy mud and blistering gas and unceasing fire of the Western Front, and were there to witness and participate in, to varying degrees, the penultimate American military feat of World War 1. Six of their comrades—Savage, Wine, Dymowski, Wareing, Swanson, and Weiler—were there as well on that day of days, but weren't lucky enough to get out alive.

Both the quick and the dead should be remembered and honored when talk turns to Acting Cpl. Alvin C. York; each did their duty and plowed into the deep woods on the left flank of their regiment's advance into the Argonne Forest, some paying the ultimate price.

Remember their names, and their sacrifice; but remember Alvin York as well, the man who performed his duty with steely determination and skill—and paid for it in one way or another for the rest of his life.

ACKNOWLEDGMENTS

I would like to thank Deborah York, Alvin York's great-granddaughter and executive of the Sergeant York Patriotic Foundation (www.sgtyork.org), for her help in creating this book; Luis Blandon of Blandon Research for retrieving documents from the National Archives; Michael Kelly, author of *Hero on the Western Front*, for reviewing portions of the manuscript and offering helpful comments; and the staff at the Tennessee State Library and Archives for copying and providing me the Alvin C. York Papers.

I would also like to acknowledge the aid of Courtney Cashman, Otis Merrithew's great-granddaughter, for supplying various documents; and Carol Schulthies, Maryan Dymowski's grandniece, who was kind enough to provide photos. Also many thanks to Frederic Castier, a very able, amiable, and knowledgeable guide who took me to the scene of the York Patrol's fight.

Thanks as well to Peter Hubbard and Nick Amphlett of Harper-Collins, Peter for seeing the promise in a book about the York Patrol and Nick for bringing it home. And thanks, as always, to my literary agent, James D. Hornfischer, who inspired the idea for the book and was key in making it happen.

James Carl Nelson
April 2020

SOURCES

Adams, Harry. Account of his capture of three hundred Germans from *History of the 89th Division, U.S.A.* (see bibliography).

Beardsley, Percy. Statement on York's actions from *Sergeant York: His Own Life Story and War Diary* (see bibliography, hereafter *Sergeant York*). Background information from *Hartford Courant*, June 22, 1947. More on York fight found in *Hartford Courant*, May 29, 1927. Account of signing a release for the film *Sergeant York* from the story "Man Hun" in the New York *Daily News*, July 6, 1941. Information on his postwar life from *Roxbury Remembered* (see bibliography).

Bosley, George H. Account of helping with German prisoners from "Concerning an Unsung Hero—One of Sergeant York's Buddies," *Pittsburgh Press*, October 12, 1941.

Bruington, Walter. His correspondence regarding Otis Merrithew found in the Warner Bros. file, Alvin C. York Papers.

Buxton, G. Edward. Information on his background from his obituary in *New York Times*, March 16, 1949. Statement on York's actions found in *Sergeant York*. His praise of Bernard Early from "Col. Buxton on the New America," *Norwich (CT) Bulletin*, February 21, 1920. His comments on the investigation into York's actions from *Providence Journal*, September 13, 1931. Correspondence between Buxton and Otis Merrithew in the 1920s and 1930s provided to the author by Courtney Cashman, Merrithew's great-granddaughter.

Chandlee, Harry. His correspondence with Jesse Lasky found in the Warner Bros. file, Alvin C. York Papers.

Cowan, Samuel K. Biographical information from www.ancestry.com. Account of his writing *Sergeant York and His People* from the book (see bibliography) and *Atlanta Constitution*, May 22, 1922.

Danforth, E. C. B. Danforth's account of the activities of Company G, 328th Infantry Regiment from ABMC, Box 250. Also see *Sergeant York*.

Day, Charles M. Account of the 328th Infantry Regiment's assault on Hill 223 from ABMC, Box 250.

Donohue, Patrick. Biographical information from Newburyport *Daily News*, April 18, 2016, and www.lawrencehistory.org/node/235. Account of patrol's actions on October 8, 1918, from *Sergeant York*. Account of signing release for the film *Sergeant York* from the article "Man Hunt" in New York *Daily News*, July 6, 1941. Affidavit regarding the York Patrol's actions from *Sergeant York and His People* (see bibliography).

Dymowski, Maryan. Biographical material from www.ancestry.com. Account of October 8, 1918, death from ROQC.

Early, Bernard. Account of receiving Distinguished Service Cross from "Sergt. Early Is Awarded Hero's Medal," *Hartford Courant*, October 6, 1929. His account of capturing German prisoners from "Says Former Resident Should Share in Glory," *North Adams (MA) Evening Transcript*, October 7, 1929. Additional Early account of action from "New Haven Sergeant May Share Honors of 'Greatest War Hero' with Alvin York," *Hartford Courant*, September 26, 1920. Edward Buxton's praise of from *Norwich (CT) Bulletin*, February 21, 1920. Additional account of the York Patrol in action from *Hartford Courant*, September 26, 1920. His affidavit regarding the patrol from *Sergeant York*. Account of Connecticut American Legion seeking to have Early awarded the Medal of Honor from *Hartford Courant*, August 11, 1935.

Ely, Frank D. His recollections about the Eighty-Second Division's battle in the Argonne Forest from ABMC, Box 348.

Glass, Karl. His account of the action on October 8, 1918, from "Testimony of German Officers and Men Anent Sergeant York" (see bibliography). Hereafter referred to as GR (German Report).

Guthrie, Bill. Account of his getting York Patrol members to sign waivers for the film *Sergeant York* from New York *Daily News*, July 6, 1941.

Johnson, Thomas Gibbs. Background information from Denison (TX) *Herald Democrat*, November 10, 2015, and Lynchburg (VA) *News & Advance*, July 5, 2008. Account of receiving check for the film *Sergeant York* from "Man Hunt," New York *Daily News*, July 6, 1941.

Konotski, Joseph. Affidavit regarding the patrol's actions west of Chatel-Chéhéry from *Sergeant York*. Biographical information from the story

"There's More to the Story of Sgt. Alvin York" posted on www.masslive. com, June 26, 2009. Account of aborted plot to kill Alvin York from *Hamden (CT) Daily News*, March 7, 2008. Account of signing release for the film *Sergeant York* from the story "Man Hunt" in New York *Daily News*, July 6, 1941. Affidavit regarding York's actions from *Sergeant York*.

Kübler, Karl. His version of the events on October 8, 1918, from GR.

Lasky, Jesse L. Biographical information from his obituary in *New York Times*, January 14, 1958. See also *Celluloid Soldiers* in the bibliography.

Merrithew, Otis B. (a.k.a. William B. Cutting). Account of mother's arrest from *Fitchburg (MA) Sentinel*, July 30 and August 17, 1912. His accounts of the York Patrol's actions from "Brookline Man Is Revealed as Hero who Aided Sergt York," *Boston Globe*, September 21, 1929; "Merrithew Says He Was Leader," *Boston Globe*, October 3, 1929; and "Legend of Sgt York Born 40 Years Ago," *Boston Sunday Globe*, October 5, 1958. Account of receiving payment for the film *Sergeant York* from the article "Man Hunt" in New York *Daily News*, July 6, 1941. Another account of the York Patrol and Merrithew's comments when receiving the Silver Star from the story "Alvin York and Frank Lucas," *American Legion Magazine*, vol. 5 no. 5, November 1968. His December 1, 1929, affidavit regarding York and the patrol found in the Alvin C. York Papers, Tennessee State Library and Archives, Nashville, Tennessee. Account of receiving his Silver Star from *Boston Globe*, September 17, 1965. His correspondence with Jesse Lasky and Bill Guthrie regarding the film *Sergeant York* from the Alvin C. York Papers.

Odess, Saul. His discredited account of the York Patrol's actions from *Boston Globe*, May 3, 1931. Additional information on his failed attempt to receive a Distinguished Service Cross from *Boston Globe*, October 3, 1929, and December 7, 1929.

Parsons, Harry M. Statement on York's actions from *Sergeant York*. Account of Company G's actions on October 8, 1918, and in subsequent battles from *Brooklyn Daily Eagle*, June 5, 1919.

Pattullo, George R. His account of uncovering the York story found in the Alvin C. York Papers, Tennessee State Library and Archives (the account originally from the Westbrook Pegler Papers, Herbert Hoover Presidential Library, West Branch, Iowa). Background information from Bonham (TX) *Daily Favorite*, January 15, 1924. Account of his hospitalization in France from the *Chicago Tribune*, February 18, 1918. Account of injury from *El*

Paso Times, October 16, 1917. Account of his leaving to cover the war from *Victoria (BC) Daily Times*, July 6, 1917. September 18, 1917. His letters of September 18, 1917, February 1918, and November 1, 1918, accessed on-line from "Pattullo Family Correspondence and Other Papers," MS-1188, sub-series MS-1188.B, "Letters from George Robson Pattullo, Jr. [GP] to George Robson Pattullo, Sr. and others," Box 1, File 4, the archives of the Royal British Columbia Museum, Victoria, British Columbia. His account of reporting the York story "The Second Elder Gives Battle" from *Saturday Evening Post*, vol. 191 no. 45, April 26, 1919.

Pile, Pastor Rosier. Background and relationship with Alvin York from the book *Sergeant York*. His comments on York's actions in the war from *Knoxville (TN) Sentinel*, June 2, 1919.

Sacina, Michael Angelo. Biographical information from "The Men Who Went Through Hell with Sergeant York," Jefferson City (MO) *Post Tribune*, November 11, 1929. Affidavit regarding patrol's fight on October 8, 1918, from *Sergeant York*. Account of signing release for the film *Sergeant York* from the article "Man Hunt" in New York *Daily News*, July 6, 1941. Affidavit regarding the York Patrol from *Sergeant York and His People* (see bibliography).

Savage, Murray. Biographical information from www.ancestry.com and *Ontario County (NY) Journal*, January 8, 1915. Account of friendship with Alvin York from the book *Sergeant York*. Account of his October 8, 1918, death from ROQC.

Skeyhill, Tom. Account of his military service and blinding from *Sydney (Australia) Herald*, July 22, 1916. His own account of the treatment that restored his eyesight from *Washington Times*, May 5, 1918; *Honolulu (HI) Advertiser*, May 24, 1918; and *Western Carolina Times*, February 14, 1919. Skeyhill's account of convincing Alvin York to cooperate with a biography from *Sergeant York*. Account of his death from *Wilmington (DE) Morning News*, May 23, 1932.

Sok, Feodor. See the book *Sergeant York* for a brief mention of Sok. Account of signing a release for the film *Sergeant York* from the article "Man Hunt" in New York *Daily News*, July 6, 1941.

Stewart, Kirby P. Account of early patrol from the book *War Memories* (see bibliography). Account of death on October 8, 1918, from ROQC.

Swanson, Carl F. Biographical information from *Sergeant York of the Argonne Tour Guide* (see bibliography). Account of October 8, 1918, death from ROQC.

Thoma, Max. His version of the battle on October 9, 1918, from GR.

Tomasello, Adone. Account of the Eighty-Second Division's advance from Varennes from *Official History of the 82nd Division* (see bibliography). His account of York's arrival with his German prisoners from the article "'Dice of Destiny' to Pick War Hero—York's Officer" in *Medford (OR) Mail Tribune*, November 26, 1942. Account of march into the Argonne from *Official History of the 82nd Division* (see bibliography).

Vollmer, Paul. His version of the events of October 8, 1918, from GR.

Wareing, Fred. Biographical information from www.ancestry.com. Account of October 8, 1918, death from ROQC.

Weiler, Ralph E. Biographical information from "Hanover Tribe Has Record for Service," Hanover (PA) *Evening Sun*, November 23, 1918, and *New Oxford (PA) Item*, November 28, 1918. Account of his October 8, 1918, death from ROQC.

Wills, George W. Biographical information from *Philadelphia Daily News*: "Sgt. York Got Glory—with Help, They Say," October 8, 2018; "Was S. Philly Man 'Real Sgt. York?,'" October 27, 2008; and "Tied to History," December 5, 2008. Affidavit regarding patrol's actions on October 8, 1918, from *Sergeant York*. Further accountin "Shares War Glory of Fighting Elder," Philadelphia (PA) *Evening Ledger*, May 24, 1919. Also see "The Men Who Went Through Hell with Sergeant York," *Jefferson City (MO) Post-Tribune*, November 11, 1929.

Wine, William E. Biographical information from www.ancestry.com. Account of death on October 8, 1918, from ROQC.

York, Alvin. Biographical information and account of conflicts about fighting and wartime service from the book *Sergeant York* and *Sergeant York and His People* (see bibliography). Other York comments regarding his prewar and postwar life and his training, service in France, and account of the firefight of October 8, 1918, from the book *Sergeant York* (used with permission). His letters to his fiancée, Gracie Williams, from the Alvin C. York Papers.

Account of his return to the Unites States from *Laurens (SC) Advertiser*, May 28, 1918; *New York Tribune*, June 1, 1918; *Washington Times*, May 24, 1918, and *New York Herald*, June 1, 1918. Account of his return to Pall Mall from Cedar Rapids (IA) *Gazette*, June 7, 1919. Account of York's wedding from *Crossville (TN) Chronicle*, June 11, 1918. Accounts of his financial struggles and salvation in the early 1920s from the following: *Washington Times*, July 27, 1921; *Staunton (VA) News-Leader*, July 28, 1921; *Richmond (VA) Times-Dispatch*, August 4, 1921; *Knoxville (TN) Sentinel*, August 5, 1921; *Bristol (TN) Herald Courier*, August 8, 1921; *Staunton News-Leader*, October 5, 1921. Account of mortgage being paid off from *Knoxville Sentinel*, November 30, 1921, and December 25, 1921, and *Waterloo (IA) Evening Courier and Reporter*, December 15, 1921. Account of barn burning and subsequent financial troubles from *Vineland (NJ) Evening Journal*, February 18, 1924; *Owensboro (KY) Messenger-Inquirer*, May 29, 1924; and *Pittsburgh Press*, November 9, 1926. Account of early disagreement with local school trust from *Chattanooga Daily Times*, March 17, 1926. His comments on trying to forget the war from "Sergeant York Winces," *New York Times*, January 19, 1927. His discussing the patrol from "Sergeant York, Schoolmaster," *Baltimore Sun*, May 3, 1930. His disparaging the use of alcohol from "Sergeant York Attacks Liquor in Speech Here," *Mansfield (OH) News,* May 4, 1932. His criticism of the American Legion from "Sergeant York Makes Criticism of Legion" in *Dothan (AL) Eagle*, May 30, 1930. Account of York's attending a reunion of the Eighty-Second Division from "Buddies of 82nd Keep York Busy Signing Autographs," *Atlanta Constitution*, September 28, 1930. Account of being drafted to the Prohibition Party presidential ticket and subsequent refusal to run from "Prohibition Party Names First Ticket" and "Sergeant York Says He Will Not Accept" in York (PA) *Daily Record*, May 8, 1936. Account of his resignation from the Alvin C. York Agricultural Institute from "Hero Quits His School in Fight with Board," *Atlanta Constitution*, May 9, 1936. His praise for members of the York Patrol in radio address from "A Tale of Two Sergeants" in *Jewish Magazine*, June 2008. His views on teaching evolution from *Knoxville (TN) News-Sentinel*, August 7, 1939. His comments regarding the coming of the Second World War from *Chattanooga Daily Times*, October 9, 1938. Details on his agreeing to cooperate with the making of *Sergeant York*, and the production of the film, from *Celluloid Soldiers* (see bibliography). Additional account of his negotiations with Jesse Lasky from *New York Times*, March 16, 1940. His meeting with Gary Cooper from *Dayton (OH) Sunday Journal-Herald*, July 27, 1941. His initial refusal of a contract for the film *Sergeant York* from "Sergeant Balks at Lasky Film Offer; Like Trading for a Mule, Says War Hero," *New York Times*, March 16, 1940. Account of York's activities during World War 2 from "Sergeant York and World War

II" by Michael E. Birdwell (found online at sgtyork.org/sites/default/files /DrBirdwellYorkWWII.pdf). York's comments on helping Gen. Douglas MacArthur in the Philippines from "Alvin York Is Ready," *Greenville (SC) News*, February 19, 1942. Further information on York's postwar life from his obituary in *New York Times*, September 3, 1964.

York, Gracie (Williams). Background and account of courting Alvin York from the book *Sergeant York*. Account of Alvin York's return home to Pall Mall and proposal of marriage from *New York Times*, June 1, 1919, and Cedar Rapids (IA) *Gazette*, June 7, 1919.

York, Mary. Her comments about Alvin York being anxious to return home from France from *Atlanta Constitution*, May 18, 1919.

BIBLIOGRAPHY

BOOKS

American Armies and Battlefields in Europe. Washington, D.C.: United States Government Printing Office, 1938.

Birdwell, Michael E. *Celluloid Soldiers: Warner Bros.'s Campaign Against Nazism*. New York and London: New York University Press, 1999.

Cahill, Robert Ellis. *New England's Little Known War Wonders*. Salem, Mass: Chandler-Smith Publishing House, Inc. Second Edition, 1980.

Chase, Joseph Cummings. *Soldiers All: Portraits and Sketches of the Men of the A.E.F.* New York: George H. Doran, 1920.

Coffman, Edward M. *The War to End All Wars: The American Military Experience in World War 1*. Madison, Wis: The University of Wisconsin Press, 1968.

Cooke, James J. *The All-Americans at War: The 82nd Division in the Great War, 1917–1918*. Westport, Conn., and London: Praeger, 1999.

Cowan, Sam K. *Sergeant York and His People*. CreateSpace Independent Publishing, 2016.

English, George H., Jr. *History of the 89th Division, U.S.A.: From Its Organization in 1917, Through Its Operations in the World War, the Occupation of Germany and Until Demobilization in 1919*. Kansas City, Mo.: The War Society of the 89th Division, 1920.

Garey, E. B., O. O. Ellis, and R. V. D. Magoffin. *American Guide Book to France and Its Battlefields*. New York: MacMillan, 1920.

Gilbert, Martin. *The First World War: A Complete History*. New York: Henry Holt, 1994.

History of the Three Hundred and Twenty-Eighth Regiment of Infantry, Eighty-Second Division, American Expeditionary Forces, United States Army. Accessed online, http://www.rareflags.com/references/History_of _the_328th_Infantry_Regiment.pdf.

Holden, Frank A. *War Memories*. Athens, Ga.: Athens Book, 1922.

Kelly, Michael. *Sergeant York of the Argonne Tour Guide*. N.p.: Ennogra Forest Publications, 2008.

Kelly, Michael, Thomas J. Nolan, Brad Posey, and James B. Legg. *Hero on the Western Front: Discovering Alvin York's WWI Battlefield.* Yorkshire, Eng., and Philadelphia: Frontline Books, 2018.

Lee, David D. *Sergeant York: An American Hero.* Lexington, Ky.: University Press of Kentucky, 1985.

Lengel, Edward G. *To Conquer Hell: The Meuse-Argonne, 1918.* New York: Henry Holt, 2008.

Lengel, Edward G., ed. *A Companion to the Meuse-Argonne Campaign.* Malden, Mass.: Wiley Blackwell, 2014.

Mastriano, Douglas V. *Alvin York: A New Biography of the Hero of the Argonne.* Lexington: University Press of Kentucky, 2014.

Official History of 82nd Division, American Expeditionary Forces: "All American" Division, 1917–1919. Indianapolis: Bobbs-Merrill, 1920.

Skeyhill, Tom. *Sergeant York: Last of the Long Hunters.* Philadelphia: John C. Winston, 1930.

Sparks, George McIntosh, ed. *The 327th Under Fire: History of the 327th Infantry, 82nd Division in the Great World War.* N.p., 1920.

Ungeheuer, Frederick, with Lewis Hurlbut and Ethel Hurlbut. *Roxbury Remembered.* New York, Lincoln, Neb., and Shanghai: Authors Choice Press, 2004.

York, Alvin Cullum. *Sergeant York: His Own Life Story and War Diary.* Edited by Tom Skeyhill. 1928. Reprint, New York: Racehorse Publishing, 2018 .

PERIODICALS

Beattie, Taylor V., and Ronald Bowman. "In Search of York: Man, Myth & Legend." *Army History,* Summer–Fall 2000.

Company Clerk, The. "Then and Now." *American Legion Monthly,* vol. 2 no. 5, May 1927.

Legg, James B. "Finding Sergeant York." *Legacy,* vol. 14 no. 1, 2010, pp. 18–21.

Mahoney, Tom. "Alvin York and Frank Luke: Legendary WWI Heroes." *American Legion Magazine,* vol. 85 no. 5, November 1968.

Pattullo, George. "The Second Elder Gives Battle." *Saturday Evening Post,* vol. 191 no. 43, April 26, 1919.

Scoggins, C. E. "What's Become of Sergeant York?" *American Legion Monthly*, vol. 2 no. 2, February 1927.

Von Blon, Phillip. "Heroes Incognito." *American Legion Weekly*, vol. 2 no. 32, September 3, 1920.

ARCHIVAL SOURCES

Alvin C. York Papers, Alvin C. York Project, Tennessee Historical Commission, RG 269, Tennessee State Library and Archives, Nashville, Tenn., Rolls One and Two.

Record Group 92, Entry 2061. *Office of the Quartermaster General Army Transport Service.*

Record Group 92, *Records of the Office of the Quartermaster General, Cemeterial Division, 1915–1939.* National Personnel Records Center, St. Louis, Mo. (cited in notes as ROQC).

Record Group 117, Entry 31. *Records of the American Battle Monuments Commission, Correspondence with Former (82nd Division) Officers*, U.S. National Archives, College Park, Md. (ABMC in notes).

Record Group 391, Entry 2133. *Records of Regular Army Mobile Units, Company G, 328th Infantry Regiment.*

"Testimony of German Officers and Men Anent Sergeant York." Record Group 165, "Thomas File"; National Archives, Washington, D.C. Copy also found in the Alvin C. York Papers, Tennessee State Library and Archives.

DISSERTATIONS

Nolan, Thomas Justus. "Battlefield Landscapes: Geographic Information Science as a Method of Integrating History and Archaeology for Battlefield Interpretation." Texas State University at San Marcos, Department of Geography, 2007.

INDEX

*Note: Members of the York Patrol are identified with
an asterisk (e.g., *Beardsley, Percy Peck)*

Adams, Harry, 156
African Americans. *See* Slaves/slave ownership; U.S. Ninety-Second ("Buffalo Soldiers") Division
African Transvaal, 29
Aircraft/air support, 7, 46, 57, 88–89, 153, 209
Alvin C. York Agricultural Institute, 180, 207–208
Alvin C. York Bible School, 214
Alvin C. York Foundation, 177, 180
Alvin C. York Highway, 174, 181
Alvin York Farm Fund, 175
The Amazing Story of Sergeant York (proposed movie title), 216
America First Committee, 235
American Expeditionary Force (A.E.F.). *See also individual U.S. divisions*
    about the immigrant makeup, 25–26, 30
    arrival of the First Division, 32
    committing U.S. soldiers to the line, 38–39
    fighting at Kriemhilde Stellung, 131
    fighting at Meuse-Argonne, 77–81
    identifying its greatest soldier, 3, 159, 237
    killed and wounded, 43, 46, 49–50, 70, 77, 85, 88, 95, 146–147
    manpower requirements, 32
    presidential review of the troops, 155
    York legend, emergence of, 155–159
American First Army, 55, 57, 63–65, 67, 70, 73, 77, 79
American Legion, 204–205, 207, 228, 239
American Legion Monthly, 186
American Legion Weekly, 186
American (newspaper), 177

Anderson, Johannes S., 2–3
Anti-Semitism, 236–237
Armistice/peace treaty negotiations, 145, 147, 153–155
Army War College, 188, 191
Atlanta Constitution, 178
Australian Imperial Force, 136, 201

Baird-Cowan Publishing Company, 177
Baker, Harry, 93
Barrow, A. C., 242
Battle of Belleau Wood (June 1918), 43, 146
Battle of Cantigny (May 1918), 42–44
Battle of Château Thierry (May 1918), 43
Battle of Loos (1915), 16
Battle of Montfaucon (1918), 68–69
Battle of Passchendale (1917, aka Third Battle of Ypres), 16, 38
Battle of Reims (1918), 51–52
Battle of Seicheprey (June 1918), 45–50
Battle of Soissons (July 1918), 51–52
Battle of St. Mihiel (Sep 1918), 52–62
Battle of St. Quentin (March 1918), 38
Battle of the Meuse-Argonne, Phase 1 (Sep–Oct 1918), 55–63, 64–73
Battle of the Meuse-Argonne, Phase 2 (Oct 1918), 1–5, 73–92
Battle of the Meuse-Argonne, Phase 3 (Nov 1918), 73–92
Battle of the Somme (1916), 16
Battle of Ypres (1914), 16
Beardsley, Nathan, Sr. ("Captain"), 28
Beardsley, Nathan, Jr. ("Nate"), 28, 39, 219, 244
*Beardsley, Percy Peck ("Perse")
    actions on Oct. 8th, 4–5, 97–110, 145, 199, 245
    background before the war, 28–29

*Beardsley, Percy Peck ("Perse") (*cont.*)
   Battle of St. Mihiel, 52
   death of, 244
   movie release, 218–219
   postwar civilian life, 195
   recognition for Oct. 8th, 184, 191
   shipping out for Europe, 39
   witnessing York's actions, 114–117
   York's award, criticism of, 187–188
   York's award, support of, 157, 194,
     203, 223
Beardsley, Louise Lingsch, 244
Beardsley, Thomas, 28
Birdwell, Michael E., 176
"Blackie: A Texas Night Horse" (Pat-
   tullo), 150
"Blind tiger," 11
Bois de Belleau. *See* Battle of Belleau Wood
Boston Daily Globe, 193
Boston Globe, 189, 223, 229
Bow, Clara, 213
British Expeditionary Force, 55
Brooklyn Daily Eagle, 227
Brooks, Nancy Pile, 9
Brooks, William, 9
Brown, Charles, 130
Brunington, Walter L., 214–215, 222
Bullard, Robert Lee, 66
Burkhalter, Edwin, 223
Burnham, William, 80
Bushing, Arthur, 235
Buxton, Gonzalo Edward ("Ned"),
   21–24, 49, 53, 115, 156–157, 166,
   185, 191–194, 217–219, 223–224

Camp Gordon, 20–24, 32–35
Camp Grant, 34
Camp MacArthur, 34
Camp McPherson, 95
Camp Merritt, 161–162
Camp Upton, 37, 39
Canadian Army, 152
Central Powers, 16, 38
Chandlee, Harry, 215–216, 225
Chase, Joseph Cummings, 155–156
Chemical warfare, 17, 47, 60, 71, 126,
   130, 140, 144, 169
Chlorine gas. *See* Chemical warfare
Churchill, Winston, 235
Church of Christ in the Christian Union,

   13, 20, 164, 166, 168, 172, 176
Civil War, 9–10, 19
Cohan, George M., 213
Collier's (magazine), 151
Colvin, D. Leigh, 207
Cooper, Gary, 4, 218, 224–225
"Cooties" (lice), 17, 53
Costin, Henry G., 1, 3
Cowan, Samuel K., 177–179, 203, 218, 223
Cox, Bertrand, 157
Craig, Malin, 80
Crockett, David ("Davy"), 8
Crowther, Bosley, 226
*Cutting, William B. *See* Merrithew, Otis
   Bernard, Jr.

Dacus, Herman, 74
Danforth, Edward Courtney Bullock, Jr.,
   21–24, 60, 90, 97, 123–127, 132, 143,
   153, 217–219, 224
Davis, Bette, 218
Davis, W. P., 175
Day, Charles M., 85–88, 139–141
DeMille, Cecil B., 212–213
Distinguished Service Cross
   about: forgotten patrol members,
     230–231
   *Early, Bernard, 191, 204, 219, 242
   *York, Alvin Cullum, 154, 163, 184,
     191
   Odess, Saul, 229
*Donohue, Patrick ("Paddy")
   actions on Oct. 8th, 4–5, 97–107, 245
   background before being drafted, 29
   death of, 242–243
   movie release, 218–219
   postwar civilian life, 195
   recognition for Oct. 8th, 184, 187
   recollections of York, 32
   relationship with York, 72
   Silver Star and Purple Heat, 243
   witnessing York's actions, 115
   wounded on Oct. 8th, 123
   York's award, support of, 157, 194, 223
Doran, J. R., 236
Doubleday (publisher), 202
Dozier, James C., 3
Drum, Hugh, 79–80
Duncan, George, 80, 142–143, 154–155,
   157, 163, 184, 191

Du Pont, S. Hallock, 238
Dupuis, Adelard, 95
*Dymowski, Maryan
    actions on Oct. 8th, 4–5, 97–110
    background before being drafted, 30
    killed in Oct. 8th, 183
    killed on Oct. 8th, 112, 114, 120, 123,
        132–133, 144–145, 245
    recovery of the body and burial, 132n

Early, Beatrice, 39
*Early, Bernard ("Bernie")
    actions on Oct. 8th, 4–5, 90, 97–110,
        145, 157, 203–206, 245
    background before being drafted, 26
    Battle of St. Mihiel, 52
    command of Oct. 8th patrol, 112
    death of, 242
    Distinguished Service Cross, 191–192
    fighting in cafe brawls, 44
    Medals of Honor, 228
    movie release/appearance, 218–219,
        224, 227
    relationship with York, 31, 72
    shipping out for Europe, 39–40
    uninjured during the war, 60
    wounded on Oct. 8th, 117, 119, 123,
        132, 183, 185–186, 189, 199–200
    York's award, criticism of, 183–194,
        205, 229
Eighty-Second Airborne Association, 239
Ellis, Michael B. ("Mad Dog"), 76
Ely, Frank, 84–85, 91, 128–129
Endriss, Fritz, 102, 115–117, 121–122,
    157, 197, 199, 216, 234
Enright, Thomas, 37
Evins, Joe, 238

Farnam, Dustin, 212
Fentress County, TN, 25, 71, 180–181,
    214–215. *See also* Pall Mall, TN;
    Valley of the Three Forks of the Wolf
    River
Fight for Freedom Committee, 235
The Fighting 69th (film), 226
Finkel, Abem, 215
First Moroccan Division, 51–52
Fitchburg Sentinel, 27
Foch, Ferdinand, 39, 51, 55, 163
Fort Devens, 240

Fort Lewis, 34
Foster, Edgar, 171
Foster, Gary Evans, 3
Fowler, Joseph, 60
Fox, Walter L., 95
Frasier, Lyman, 76
French Sixty-Ninth Division, 63
French Tenth Army, 51–52
Funk & Wagnalls (publisher), 178

Ganier, Albert, 215–216
Gearhard, August, 206
George V (king of England), 41
German war ministry, 196–199
German 2nd Wuerttemberg Division, 198
German Forty-First Division, 129–130
German Forty-Fifth Reserve Infantry
    Division, 103
German 210th Prussian Reserve Infantry,
    103–104, 108–109
German 225th Division, 58
German 120th Landwehr Infantry
    Regiment, 93, 101, 103, 108, 113,
    115, 127, 196
German 122th Landwehr Infantry
    Regiment, 93
German 125th Landwehr Infantry
    Regiment, 93, 101–103, 123
Glass, Karl, 103–104, 108–109, 119,
    121–122, 190, 233
Goering, Hermann, 235–236
Goldwyn, Samuel (aka Samuel Goldfish),
    212, 218
Graham, Joseph, 93
Great Depression, 213, 221
The Great War. *See* World War I
Gregory, Earl D., 3
Gresham, James, 37
Gross, B. B., 170
Gumpertz, Sydney, 67–68
Guthrie, Bill, 218–221, 224, 242

Haig, Sir Douglas, 41–42, 55
Hale, John, 215, 222
Hall, Thomas Lee, 3
Hamilton, Lewis, 60
Harris, Charles, 165
Hartford Courant, 185–186, 192
Harvard University, 21–22
Hay, Merle, 37

Help Sergeant York Committee, 238, 244
Herman the Great (performer), 212
Hill 223. *See also* October 8, 1918
    about: planned assault on, 84–88
    advance toward, 90
    beginning attack on, 93–95
    Early's patrol actions, 97–104
    Early's patrol encounter with German
        force, 105–112
    German attack on Early patrol, 112
    York taking over the action, 112–123
Hindenburg Line, 65, 135–136
Hindenburg's Traveling Circus, 53
Hink, John G., 93
Hitler, Adolf, 208, 235–236
H.M.S. *Scandinavian*, 39–40
H.M.S. *Viper*, 41
Ho Chi Minh (aka Nguyen That Thanh), 73
Holden, Frank, 47, 49, 58, 59–60
Holderman, Nelson, 78
Hollywood, California, 213
Holt, John D., 49
Honolulu Advertiser, 201
Hoover, Herbert, 240
Hornke, Emil, 1
Howard, Everett, 95
Huff, Pres, 9
Hughes, Comer J., 93
Huston, John, 225

Jackson, Thomas ("Stonewall"), 30
Jesse L. Lasky Feature Play Company,
    212–213
John C. Winston Company, 204
Johnson, Gordon, 81
Johnson, John, 242
*Johnson, Thomas Gibbs
    actions on Oct. 8th, 4–5, 97–110, 145, 245
    background before being drafted, 30
    death of, 242
    movie release, 218–220
    postwar civilian life, 195–196
    York's award, support of, 194
Johnson, Lyndon B., 239–240
Johnson, O. H., 187
Johnson, Thomas H., 175
Josephson, Julien, 215–216

Karners, James E., 3
Keating, Earl W., 49

Kellogg, E. A., 161
King, J. J., 161
Kingston, Winifred, 212
Knoxville Sentinel, 175
*Konotski, Joseph Stanley
    actions on Oct. 8th, 4–5, 97–110, 145,
        199, 245
    background before enlisting, 29
    death of, 241
    movie release/appearance, 219
    postwar civilian life, 195
    recognition for Oct. 8th, 184, 187
    witnessing York's actions, 114–115
    York's award, criticism of, 192–193, 228
    York's award, support of, 157, 203,
        223–224
Kriemhilde Stellung, 65–66, 69, 131,
    135–136, 139–140
Krushchev, Nikita, 239
Kübler, Karl, 101–102, 108, 120–121
Kuznik, J. V., 236

Lasky, Blanche, 211–212
Lasky, Isaac, 211
Lasky, Jesse L., 211–216, 218, 221,
    224–225, 235, 237
Lasky, Maud, 211
Lasky, Sarah, 211
Le Havre, France, 40–41
Liberty Loan Committee, 155
Liberty (magazine), 202
Liedtke, John, 93
Liggett, Hunter, 66, 79–80
Lindbergh, Charles ("Lucky"), 235–236
Lindsey, Julian, 80–81, 85, 91, 124, 143
The Little Foxes (film), 218
Lloyd, Harold, 213
Lorimer, George Horace, 149, 152
Los Angeles Times, 226–227
The Lost Battalion, 77–81, 89, 128

MacArthur, Douglas, 234
Majestic Motion Picture Company, 150
Mallon, George H., 67–68
Marshall, George C., 56, 64
Maverick, Maury, 74
McAndrew, James, 79–80
McCall, Howard, 130
McClure, John S., 175
McHugh, Nellie, 27

McKellar, Kenneth, 181
McPherson, Hollis, 29
Medal of Honor (MOH)
  actions in Meuse-Argonne on Oct. 8th, 3
  *Early, Bernard, 228
  Ellis, Michael B. ("Mad Dog"), 76
  Gumpertz, Sydney, 67–68
  Mallon, George H., 67–68
  Morelock, Sterling, 74–75
  Pike, Emory, 61
  Sandlin, Willie, 68
  Skinker, Alexander Rives, 69
  *York, Alvin Cullum, 3–4, 157,
    162–163, 184, 238, 243
  *York, criticism/discrediting,
    166–167, 186–187, 189, 192–194,
    221–222, 236
Merrithew, Anna, 221
Merrithew, Julia Riley, 27
Merrithew, Nellie B., 27–28
*Merrithew, Otis Bernard, Jr. (aka
  William B. Cutting)
  actions on Oct. 8th, 4–5, 90–92,
    97–110, 191, 204, 227, 245
  background before enlisting, 26–28
  death of, 241
  movie release/appearance, 221, 224
  recollections of York, 31–32, 131–132
  Silver Star award, 240–241
  wounded on Oct. 8th, 115, 117, 123
  York's award, criticism of, 188–189,
    205, 221–223
Merrithew, Otis Bernard, Sr., 26–27
Metro-Goldwyn-Mayer Studios, 218
Meuse-Argonne American Cemetery, 133n
Meuse-Argonne Offensive, Phase 1
  (Sep–Oct 1918), 55–73
Meuse-Argonne Offensive, Phase 2
  (Oct 1918), 73–144
Meuse-Argonne Offensive, Phase 3
  (Nov 1918), 144–147
Mexican-American War (1846–48), 9
Mexican Expedition (1916–17), 151
Miller, Arthur, 244
Miricki, Stephen, 95
Mongillo, Frank, 228
Monroe, Marilyn, 244
Moonshine whiskey, 12–13
Moore, Riley, 202
Morelock, Sterling, 74–75

Mustard gas. *See* Chemical warfare
Muzzi, Concetta, 244
*Muzzi, Mario
  actions on Oct. 8th, 4–5, 97–110,
    145, 245
  background before being drafted, 30
  death of, 244
  movie release, 218–219
  postwar civilian life, 195
  relationship with York, 72
  wounded on Oct. 8th, 112–119, 189

Nashville Banner, 171
Nashville Tennessean, 215, 235
Natalie Graves (movie), 150
National Guard, 22, 95, 239
Negri, Pola, 213
Nelson, John, ix
Newsweek (magazine), 226
New York Herald, 167
New York Times, 166, 184, 226
New Zealand Expeditionary Force, 201
Nolan, Dennis, 158–159, 162
Nuclear warfare, 239

October 8, 1919. *See also* Hill 223
  about: Oct. 6–7th prelude to, 83–90
  account of York's actions, 112–124
  assault toward Hill 223, 90–97
  continuing the assault, 125–131
  Early patrol behind German lines, 97–104
  Early patrol capture of prisoners, 105–106
  German attack on Early patrol, 106–112
  German war ministry account, 196–199
  recognition for Oct. 8th actions, 1–3
  recognizing York actions, 3–4, 153–154
  recognizing York's patrol members, 4–5
  rescue of the Lost Battalion, 128
  20th anniversary recognition, 209
Odess, Saul, 229–230
O'Farrelly, John, 133n
"Over There" (going to/serving in
  Europe), ix, 32, 35

Pall Mall, TN, 3, 7–8, 18–21, 24, 35, 174,
  204–206. *See also* Fentress County,
  TN; Valley of the Three Forks of the
  Wolf River
Palmer, Frederick, 65
Palombi, Ettore, 60

Paramount Pictures, 213
Paris Peace Conference (1919), 155
Parker, Frank, 81
Parsons, Harry M., 125, 142, 189, 191,
    195, 206, 224, 227–228
    actions on Oct. 8th, 95–98
    background before being drafted, 30–31
Pattullo, Andrew, 152
Pattullo, George Robson, 149–153,
    156–159, 162–163, 183, 188, 213, 229
Pattullo, J. H., 152
Pattullo, Lucille Wilson, 150–151
Pershing, John J. ("Black Jack")
    battlefield strategy, 32–34, 62
    launch of Meuse-Argonne Offensive, 64
    naming A.E.F.'s greatest soldier, 3–4,
        159, 237
    search for Pancho Villa, 151
    York recommendation for Medal of
        Honor, 161–162
Phosgene gas. *See* Chemical warfare
Pike, Emory, 61
Pile, Conrad ("Coonrod"), 8, 10
Pile, Jeff, 8–9
Pile, Mary Catherine Rich, 8
Pile, Rosier, 13, 19–22, 166, 171–173, 216
Pile's General Store, 169, 234
Pittsburgh Press, 181
Poppy (film), 29
Prohibition, York support of, 207
Providence Journal, 22
Purple Heart, 243

Rayburn, Sam, 238
Regan, Patrick, 2
Rhodes, Charles, 80
Ridgeway, Matthew, 240
Roosevelt, Franklin D., 226
Rotary Club, 171–173, 174–176
Russell, H. H., 12
Russian Revolution of 1917, 38

*Sacina, Michael Angelo
    actions on Oct. 8th, 4–5, 97–110, 145,
        199, 245
    background before being drafted, 30
    death of, 243–244
    movie release/appearance, 218–220
    postwar civilian life, 195

recognition for Oct. 8th actions,
    184–185, 187
relationship with York, 72
witnessing York's actions, 115
York's award, support of, 157, 194,
    203, 223
Salisbury, Monroe, 212
Salvation Army, 167
Sampler, Samuel M., 1–2
Sandlin, Willie, 68
Saturday Evening Post, 149–150, 152,
    158, 162–163, 203, 213
Savage, John, 44–45
Savage, Leona, 45
*Savage, Murray L., 93, 227
    actions on Oct. 8th, 4–5, 97–110
    background before being drafted, 29
    friendship with York, 31, 44–45, 133
    killed in Oct. 8th, 183
    killed on Oct. 8th, 112, 120, 123,
        132–133, 144–145, 245
    movie release/appearance, 224
    recovery of the body and burial, 132n
Scoggins, C. E., 186
Sergeant York and His People (Cowan),
    178–179, 218
*Sergeant York: His Own Life Story and
    War Diary* (Skeyhill), 202–204, 218
Sergeant York: Last of the Long Hunters
    (Skeyhill), 204, 218
Sergeant York (movie), 4, 214–230,
    236–237
Sergeant York Patriotic Foundation, 247
"Sergeant York Says" (newspaper col-
    umn), 235
Sick, Karl von, 102–103, 127, 196
Silver Star Medal (SSM), 240
Skeyhill, Tom John, 201–204, 218, 223,
    229–230
Skinker, Alexander Rives, 69
Slack, Clayton K., 3
Slaves/slave ownership, 8
Smith, Erwin E. ("Tex"), 149–150
*Sok, Feodor
    actions on Oct. 8th, 4–5, 97–107, 145,
        199, 245
    background before being drafted, 30
    death of, 241
    movie release, 218–220

postwar civilian life, 195–196
recognition for Oct. 8th, 187
witnessing York's actions, 115
York's award, support of, 223
Soldiers All (Chase), 155
Soldier Songs from Anzac (Skeyhill), 201
Southern Lumberman (journal), 177
The Squaw Man (film), 212
S.S. *City of Brisbane*, 40
S.S. *Ohioan*, 84, 161, 164, 202, 211
S.S. *San Diego*, 40
S.S. *Thermistocles*, 40
Stewart, Kirby Pelot, 24, 48–49, 59, 93, 95, 97, 238
St. Mihiel Offensive (Sep 1918), 52–62
Submarine warfare, 17, 40
Sullivan, Joe, 230
Summerall, Charles, 81, 143, 154
Swanson, Amandus, 30
Swanson, Carrie, 39
*Swanson, Carl F., 83
    actions on Oct. 8th, 4–5, 97–110
    background before being drafted, 30
    killed in Oct. 8th, 183
    killed on Oct. 8th, 112, 120, 123, 132–133, 144–145, 245
    recovery of the body and burial, 132n
    shipping out for Europe, 39–40
    uninjured during the war, 60

Talmadge, Norma, 29
Tank warfare, 56–57, 66, 71
Tennessee Americans (radio program), 237
Thoma, Max, 118–121, 233
Tomasello, Adone, 84, 122–123
Tornsello, Michael, 96
Treaty of Versailles (1919), 155
Trench warfare, 17, 32–34, 37–38, 42–43, 45–49, 53–56, 62, 67, 71, 139, 149, 152, 228, 238
Turner, Harold L., 1–2

The Untamed (movie), 150
U.S. First ("Big Red One") Division
    arrival and training in France, 32–33
    assigned to the trenches, winter 1918, 46
    attributed with first U.S. combat deaths, 37–38, 149

author's note, ix
battle at Cantigny, 42–44
battle at Soissons, 51–52
battle at St. Mihiel, 55–62, 64
Meuse-Argonne, Phase 1, 69–70, 73
Meuse-Argonne, Phase 2, 75–81, 84, 128, 130, 135, 138, 149
U.S. Second ("Indianhead") Division
    battle at Soissons, 51–54, 73
    battle at St. Mihiel, 58
    battle in Meuse-Argonne, Phase 3, 146
    Meuse-Argonne, Phase 1, 1
U.S. Third ("Rock of the Marne") Division, 38, 43–44, 64, 69–70
U.S. Fourth ("Ivy") Division, 52, 66, 70
U.S. Fifth ("Red Diamond") Division, 3, 56, 145
U.S. Twenty-Sixth ("Yankee") Division, 38, 45–46, 52, 56, 58
U.S. Twenty-Eighth ("Keystone") Division, 52, 66, 68, 77, 80, 83–89, 94, 102
U.S. Twenty-Ninth ("Blue and Grey") Division, 1, 2, 64
U.S. Thirty-Second ("Red Arrow") Division, 52, 64, 69–70
U.S. Thirty-Third ("Golden Cross") Division, 2, 66–67, 70
U.S. Thirty-Fifth ("Santa Fe") Division, 66, 68–69, 73–74
U.S. Thirty-Seventh ("Buckeye") Division, 66
U.S. Forty-Second ("Rainbow") Division, 52, 56, 135, 138, 141–142, 144
U.S. Seventy-Seventh ("Statue of Liberty") Division, 66, 135, 145–146
U.S. Seventy-Eighth ("Lightning") Division, 143–145
U.S. Seventy-Ninth ("Cross of Lorraine") Division, 66
U.S. Eightieth ("Blue Ridge") Division, 145–146
U.S. Eighty-Second Airborne Division, 240
U.S. Eighty-Second ("All-American") Division
    arrival and training in France, 33, 40–41, 44–45
    assigned to the trenches and first combat, 42, 45–50

U.S. Eighty-Second ("All-American") (*cont.*)
  assignment of York to, 21–24
  background and training of the
    enlisted men, 25–33
  battle at St. Mihiel, 52–54, 64
  casualties, 49–50, 61, 64, 126, 130,
    144, 146
  Medals of Honor, 61
  men and heroic actions on Oct. 8th,
    1–5, 30–31, 90–110
  Meuse-Argonne, Phase 1, 55–64, 72–73
  Meuse-Argonne, Phase 2, 1–5, 80–89,
    130, 135–145
  Meuse-Argonne, Phase 3, 145–146, 154
  recognizing the actions of York, 3–5,
    154–157, 163, 184, 191–192, 223
  tributes at the death of York, 239–240
  waiting to return home, 154
U.S. Eighty-Ninth ("Rolling W") Divi-
  sion, 52–53, 56, 145, 156
U.S. Ninety-First ("Wild West") Divi-
  sion, 66
U.S. Ninety-Second ("Buffalo Soldiers")
  Division, 64
U.S. Marine Corps, battle of Belleau
  Wood (Fifth and Sixth Regiments),
  43, 146

Valley of the Three Forks of the Wolf
  River, 7–8, 91, 163–164, 169–173. *See
  also* Pall Mall, TN
Veterans Administration, 239, 242
Vietnam War, 239, 240
Villa, Francisco ("Pancho"), 151
Voiles, William, 60
Vollmer, Paul, 100, 102–104, 108–110,
  113, 116–122, 178, 189–190,
  197–199, 211, 222, 229, 233
Von Blom, Phillip, 186

Walsh, David I., 192–193
Ward, Calvin John, 3
Ward, Ralph, 79
*Wareing, Fred
  actions on Oct. 8th, 4–5, 97–110
  background before being drafted, 29
  killed in Oct. 8th, 183
  killed on Oct. 8th, 112, 114, 120, 123,
    132–133, 144–145, 245

recovery of the body and burial, 132n
Warner Brothers, 213, 218, 222–223,
  226, 242
Warner, Harry, 213
Waters, Pat, 243
*Weiler, Ralph E.
  actions on Oct. 8th, 4–5, 97–107
  background before being drafted, 30
  killed in Oct. 8th, 183
  killed on Oct. 8th, 112, 120, 123,
    132–133, 144–145, 245
  recovery of the body and burial, 132n
Wetherill, Richard, 84, 86, 138–139, 191
Whitman, Walter, 131, 136–137
Whittlesey, Charles, 77–81, 89, 128
*Wills, George W.
  actions on Oct. 8th, 4–5, 97–107, 145,
    199, 245
  background before being drafted, 30
  death of, 243
  movie release, 218–220
  recognition for Oct. 8th, 184, 187
  witnessing York's actions, 115, 230
  York's award, support of, 157,
    194–195, 223
Wills, George W., Jr., 243
Wills, Jimmy, 243
Wilson, Edith, 155
Wilson, Lucille, 150
Wilson, Woodrow, 18, 19, 22, 155
*Wine, William E.
  actions on Oct. 8th, 4–5, 97–110
  background before being drafted, 30
  killed in Oct. 8th, 183
  killed on Oct. 8th, 112, 120, 123,
    132–133, 144–145, 245
  recovery of the body and burial, 132n
Winters, Nellie, 27
Wisconsin State Journal, 178
Wold, Nels, 68–69
Women, 12, 151, 178, 207
Women's Stories, 150
Woodfill, Sam, 3, 159, 237
Woods, Joseph, 122, 157
World War I. *See also* Chemical warfare;
  Trench warfare
  about: author's grandfather in, ix
  assassination of Archduke Ferdinand, 15
  casualties, 169

declarations of war and mobilization, 16
entry of U.S. into, 18–19
questioning the reason for, 18, 24
submarine warfare, 17
terminated on Nov. 11, 146–147, 154
York legend, emergence of, 155–159
York legend, promoting, 161–168
World War II
about: events leading to, 208–209, 225–226
German invasion of Poland, 214
German invasion of Russia, 226, 236
Japanese bombing of Pearl Harbor, 235
U.S. mobilization for, 234
York registration/support of, 234–237
Wright, W. L., 171

*York, Alvin Cullum, family and growing up
arrival in Tennessee, 7–9
birth and childhood, 10–11
death of father, 11
drinking and wild times growing up, 11–12, 207
finding religion and being saved, 12–13
meeting and courtship of Gracie, 18–19
objection to the war and killing, 19–24, 31, 131–132, 166
*York, Alvin Cullum, going into the Army
draft registration, 19–20, 166
induction/training at Camp Gordon, 20–21, 32–35
recognized as conscientous objector, 70, 156, 166, 224, 237, 241
shipping out for Europe, 35, 37, 39
*York, Alvin Cullum, going "Over There"
about: author's note, ix–x
actions of others on the patrol, 4–5
actions on Oct. 8th, 3–4, 90–92, 97–124
Battle of St. Mihiel, 52
Distinguished Service Cross, recommended for, 154
the legend, creating, 155–159
making friends in the platoon, 31, 72
Medal of Honor award, 3–4, 157–158, 162–163, 184, 238, 243
Medal of Honor, discrediting/criticism, 166–167, 176–177, 183–194,

221–223, 231, 236
medals from the French, 163
praised for actions, 142
promotions, 58, 146
recovery of the patrol dead, 132–133
uninjured during the war, 60
*York, Alvin Cullum, return from "Over There"
celebration in New York, 161–165
marriage to Gracie, 172–173
recognized in Washington, D.C., 165–168
returning home, 169–172
taking off his uniform, 173
*York, Alvin Cullum, time after the Army
about: broadened visions of the world, 173–174
agreeing to book projects, 178–179, 202–205
children, 175
coping with the burden of fame, 176–177, 179, 205–206, 209–210
declining health and death, 179, 208, 238–240
flashbacks to Army combat, 7
gift of the farm, 171–172, 174–176, 217
movie project, 213–231
preserving the legacy of, 215
refusal to "sell the uniform," 175, 179–180, 237–238
registration for WWII, 234–235
school projects, 180–181, 202, 204–205, 207–208, 214, 237–238
support of Prohibition, 207
tax problems, 237–238
York, Alvin Cullum, Jr., 175
York, Gracie Williams
as prettiest girl in Tennessee, 164–165
courtship and engagement, 18–20, 31, 35, 37, 170
marriage and children, 172–175
surviving bankruptcy, 238
York Henry, 10
York, Joseph, 10
York, Mary Brooks, 9–10, 11, 12, 164, 217
York, Uriah, 9–10
York, William, 11

Zimmerman telegram, 17–18
Zukor, Adolph, 213